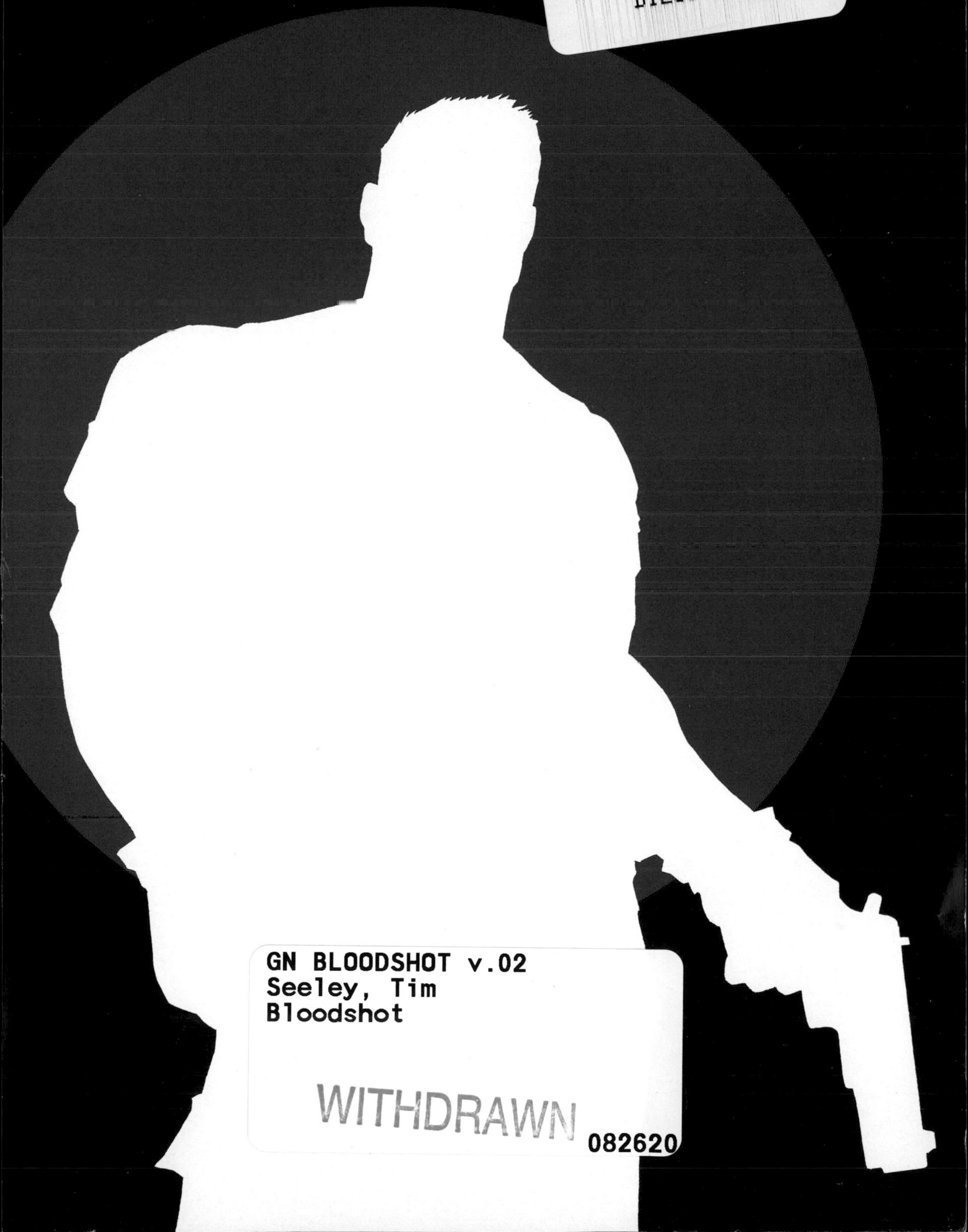

BLOODSHOT®

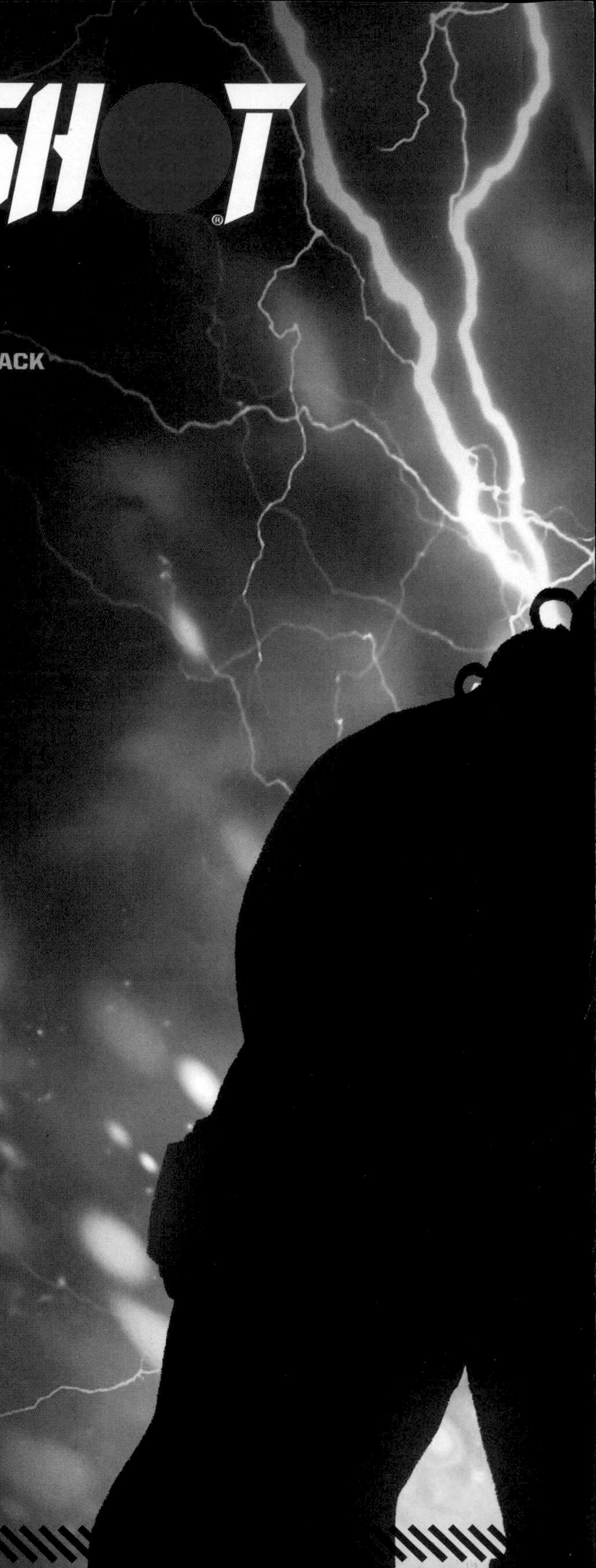

WRITERS
TIM SEELEY
ELIOT RAHAL

ARTISTS
BRETT BOOTH
ADELSO CORONA
KHARI EVANS

COLORISTS
ANDREW DALHOUSE

LETTERERS
DAVE SHARPE
DAVE LANPHEAR

COVERS BY
DECLAN SHALVEY
KANO

ASSISTANT EDITOR
DREW BAUMGARTNER

EDITOR
LYSA HAWKINS
CHARLOTTE GREENBAUM

GALLERY
SIMON BISLEY
BRETT BOOTH
FRITZ CASAS
LEO COLAPIETRO
ADELSO CORONA
ANDREW DALHOUSE
GABE ELTAEB
KHARI EVANS
CANDICE HAN
WES HARTMAN
DAVE JOHNSON
MIKE MCKONE
TIM SEELEY
BILLY TUCCI

COLLECTION COVER ART
DECLAN SHALVEY

COLLECTION BACK COVER ART
MARC LAMING

COLLECTION FRONT ART
BEN TIESMA with
BRIAN REBER
DECLAN SHALVEY

COLLECTION EDITOR
IVAN COHEN

COLLECTION DESIGNER
STEVE BLACKWELL

VALIANT®

DAN MINTZ Chairman **FRED PIERCE** Publisher **WALTER BLACK** VP Operations **MATTHEW KLEIN** VP Sales & Marketing **ROBERT MEYERS** Senior Editorial Director
TRAVIS ESCARFULLERY Director of Design & Production **PETER STERN** Director of International Publishing & Merchandising **LYSA HAWKINS** & **HEATHER ANTOS** Editors
DAVID MENCHEL Associate Editor **DREW BAUMGARTNER** Assistant Editor **JEFF WALKER** Production & Design Manager **KAT O'NEILL** Sales & Live Events Manager
CONNOR HILL Sales Operations Coordinator **DANIELLE WARD** Sales Manager **GREGG KATZMAN** Marketing Manager **EMILY HECHT** Digital Marketing Manager

ED CASEY Licensing **OLIVER TAYLOR** International Licensing Coordinator

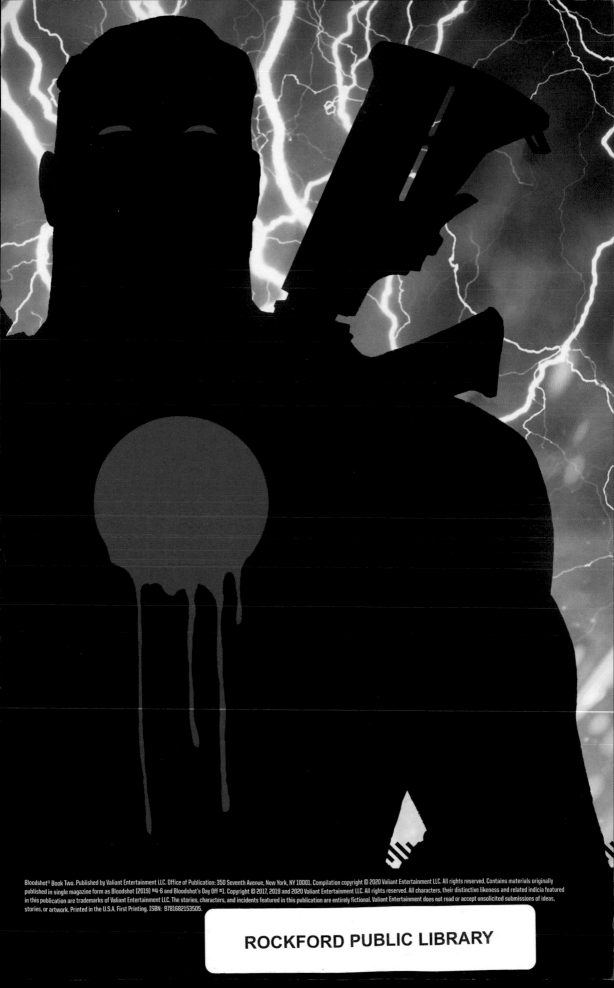

Bloodshot® Book Two. Published by Valiant Entertainment LLC. Office of Publication: 350 Seventh Avenue, New York, NY 10001. Compilation copyright © 2020 Valiant Entertainment LLC. All rights reserved. Contains materials originally published in single magazine form as Bloodshot (2019) #4-6 and Bloodshot's Day Off #1. Copyright © 2017, 2019 and 2020 Valiant Entertainment LLC. All rights reserved. All characters, their distinctive likeness and related indicia featured in this publication are trademarks of Valiant Entertainment LLC. The stories, characters, and incidents featured in this publication are entirely fictional. Valiant Entertainment does not read or accept unsolicited submissions of ideas, stories, or artwork. Printed in the U.S.A. First Printing. ISBN: 9781682153505.

ROCKFORD PUBLIC LIBRARY

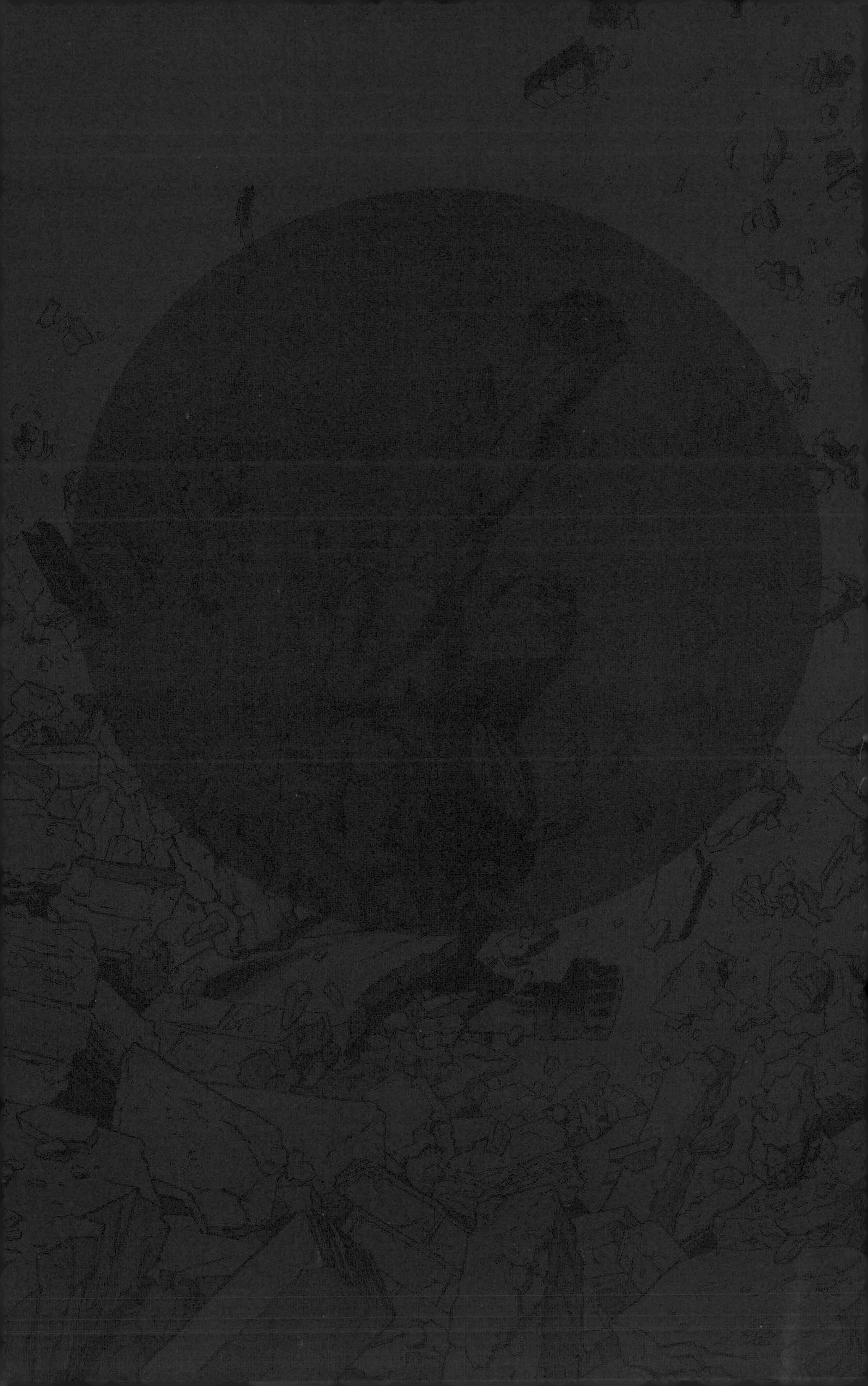

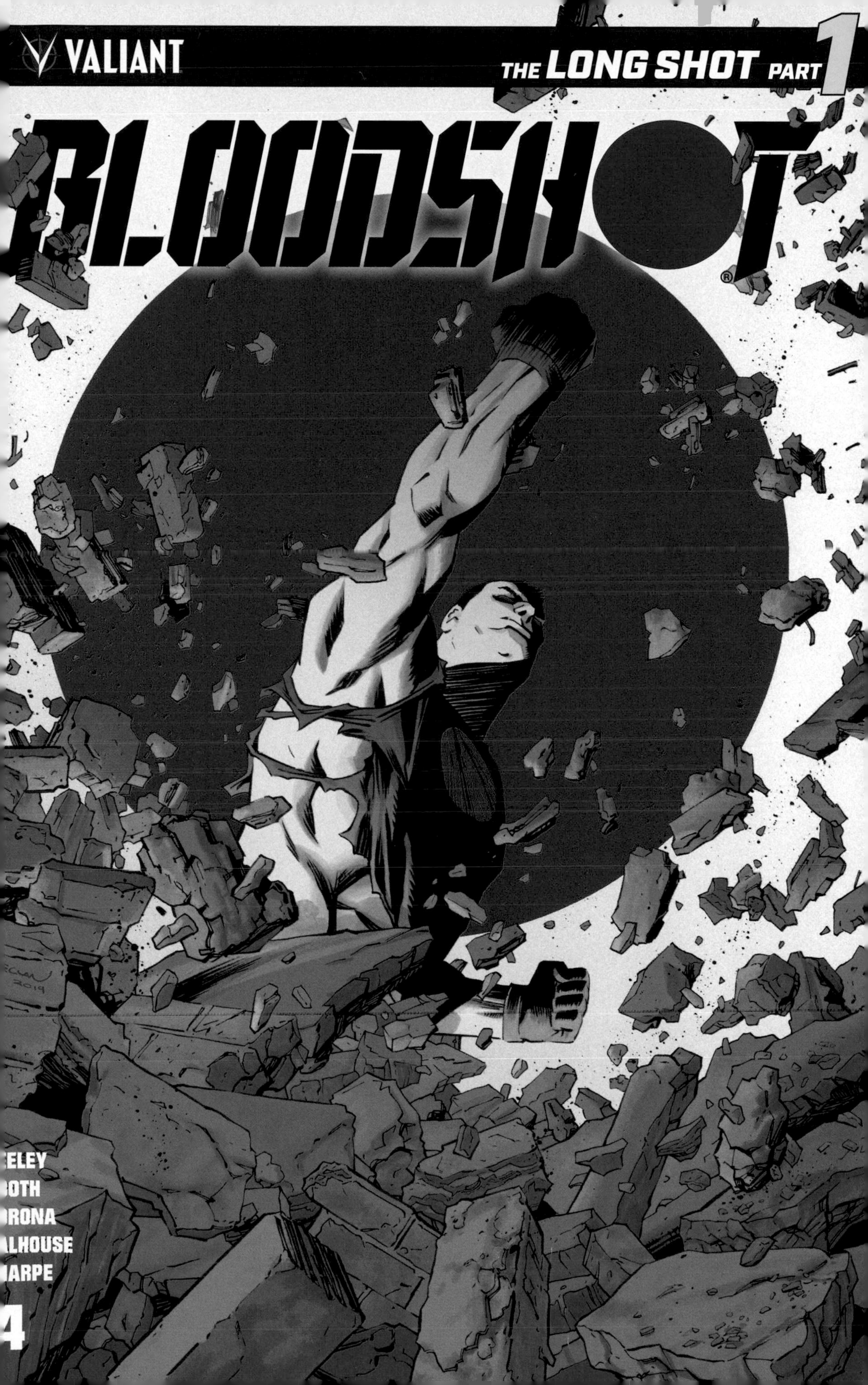
VALIANT
THE LONG SHOT PART 1
BLOODSHOT
ELEY
OTH
RONA
LHOUSE
ARPE
4

THE LONG SHOT, PART 1

BLOODSHOT #4
WRITER: Tim Seeley
ARTIST: Brett Booth
INKER: Adelso Corona
COLORIST: Andrew Dalhouse
LETTERS: Dave Sharpe
COVER ARTIST: Declan Shalvey
ASSISTANT EDITOR:
Drew Baumgartner
EDITOR: Lysa Hawkins

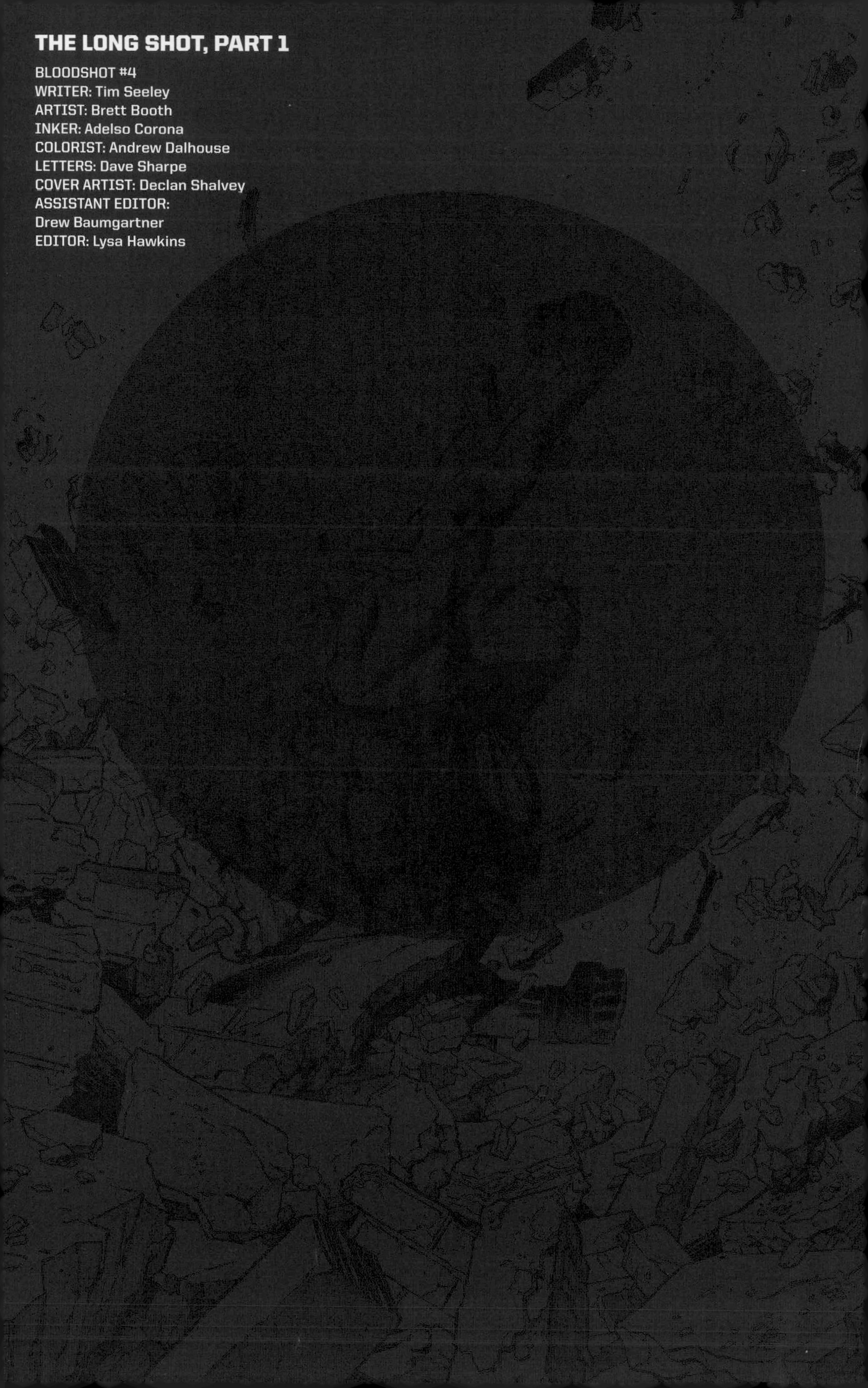

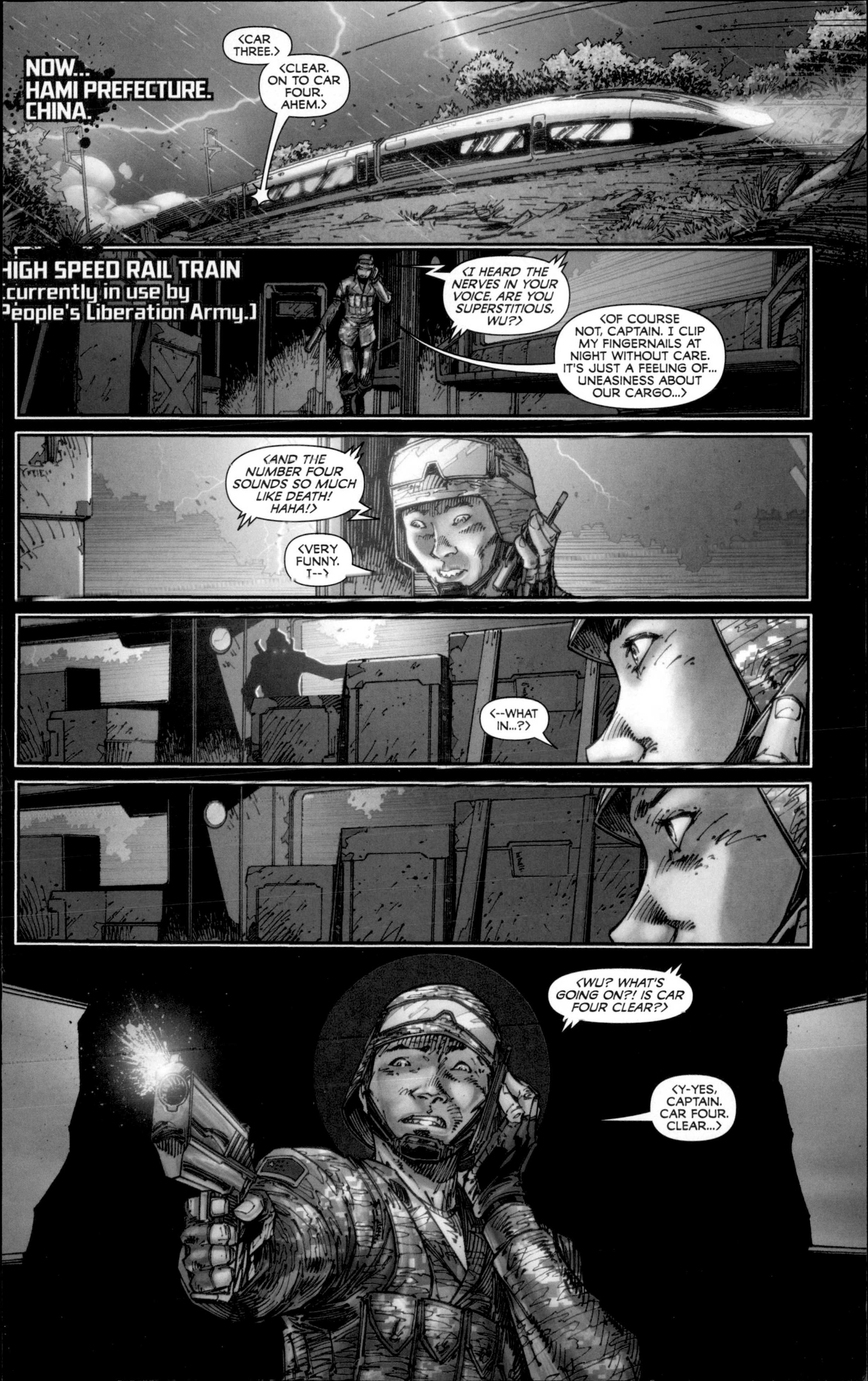
NOW... HAMI PREFECTURE. CHINA.
<CAR THREE.>
<CLEAR. ON TO CAR FOUR. AHEM.>
HIGH SPEED RAIL TRAIN
[currently in use by People's Liberation Army.]
<I HEARD THE NERVES IN YOUR VOICE. ARE YOU SUPERSTITIOUS, WU?>
<OF COURSE NOT, CAPTAIN. I CLIP MY FINGERNAILS AT NIGHT WITHOUT CARE. IT'S JUST A FEELING OF... UNEASINESS ABOUT OUR CARGO...>
<AND THE NUMBER FOUR SOUNDS SO MUCH LIKE DEATH! HAHA!>
<VERY FUNNY. I-->
<--WHAT IN...?>
<WU? WHAT'S GOING ON?! IS CAR FOUR CLEAR?>
<Y-YES, CAPTAIN. CAR FOUR. CLEAR...>

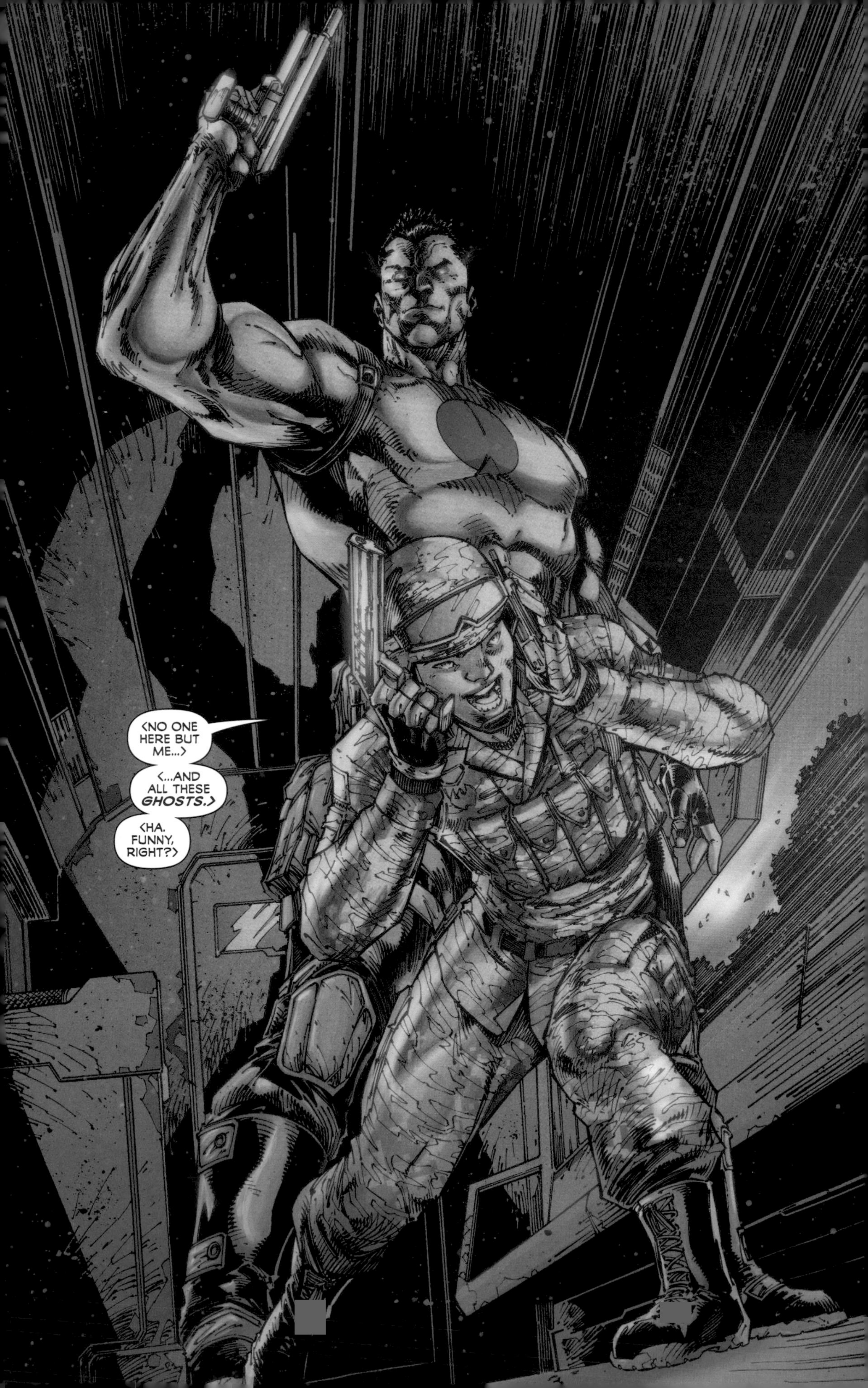
<NO ONE HERE BUT ME...>
<...AND ALL THESE GHOSTS.>
<HA. FUNNY, RIGHT?>

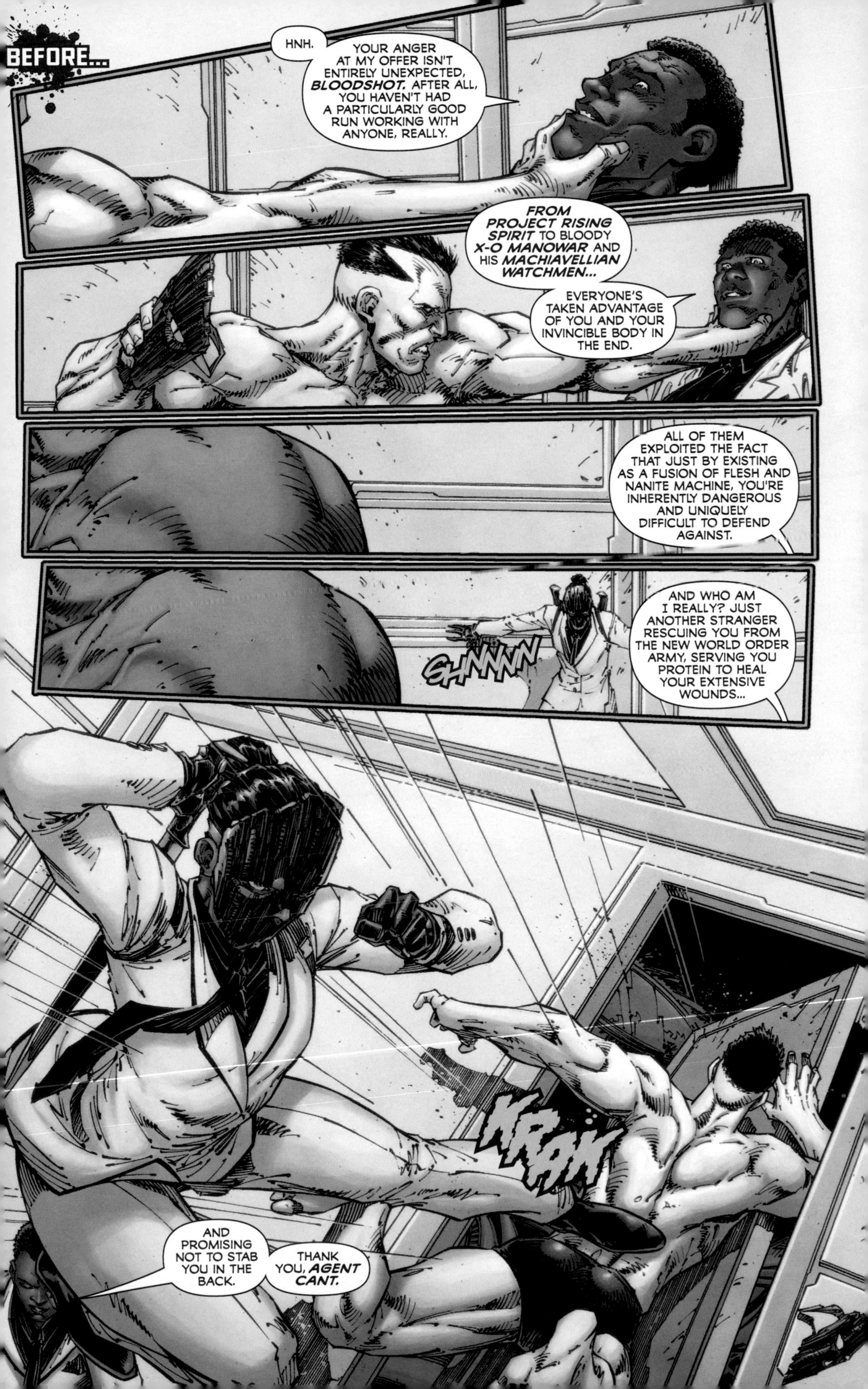
BEFORE...
HNH.
YOUR ANGER AT MY OFFER ISN'T ENTIRELY UNEXPECTED, BLOODSHOT. AFTER ALL, YOU HAVEN'T HAD A PARTICULARLY GOOD RUN WORKING WITH ANYONE, REALLY.
FROM PROJECT RISING SPIRIT TO BLOODY X-O MANOWAR AND HIS MACHIAVELLIAN WATCHMEN...
EVERYONE'S TAKEN ADVANTAGE OF YOU AND YOUR INVINCIBLE BODY IN THE END.
ALL OF THEM EXPLOITED THE FACT THAT JUST BY EXISTING AS A FUSION OF FLESH AND NANITE MACHINE, YOU'RE INHERENTLY DANGEROUS AND UNIQUELY DIFFICULT TO DEFEND AGAINST.
SHNNNN
AND WHO AM I REALLY? JUST ANOTHER STRANGER RESCUING YOU FROM THE NEW WORLD ORDER ARMY, SERVING YOU PROTEIN TO HEAL YOUR EXTENSIVE WOUNDS...
KRAK
AND PROMISING NOT TO STAB YOU IN THE BACK.
THANK YOU, AGENT CANT.

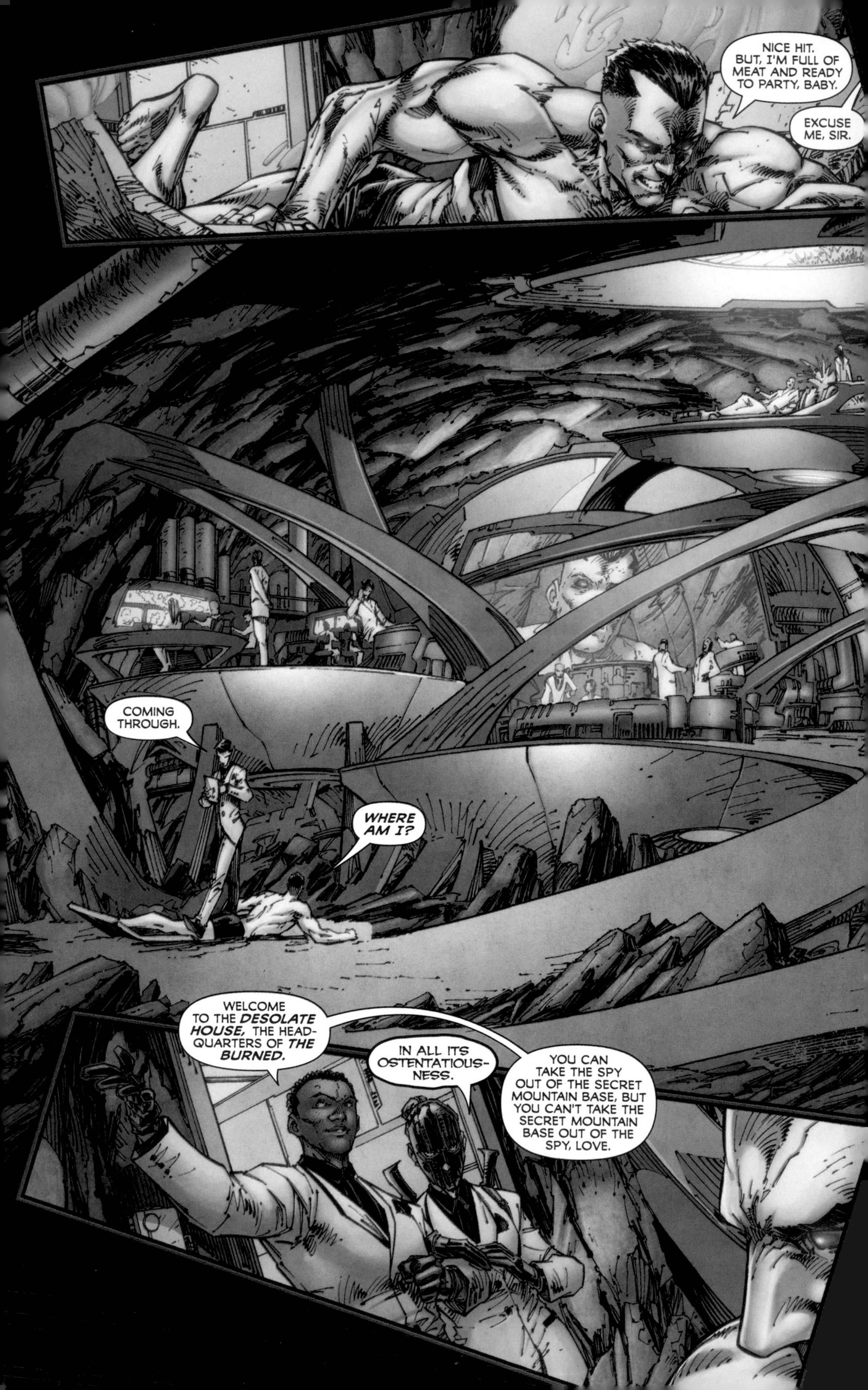
NICE HIT. BUT, I'M FULL OF MEAT AND READY TO PARTY, BABY.
EXCUSE ME, SIR.
COMING THROUGH.
WHERE AM I?
WELCOME TO THE DESOLATE HOUSE, THE HEAD-QUARTERS OF THE BURNED.
IN ALL ITS OSTENTATIOUS-NESS.
YOU CAN TAKE THE SPY OUT OF THE SECRET MOUNTAIN BASE, BUT YOU CAN'T TAKE THE SECRET MOUNTAIN BASE OUT OF THE SPY, LOVE.

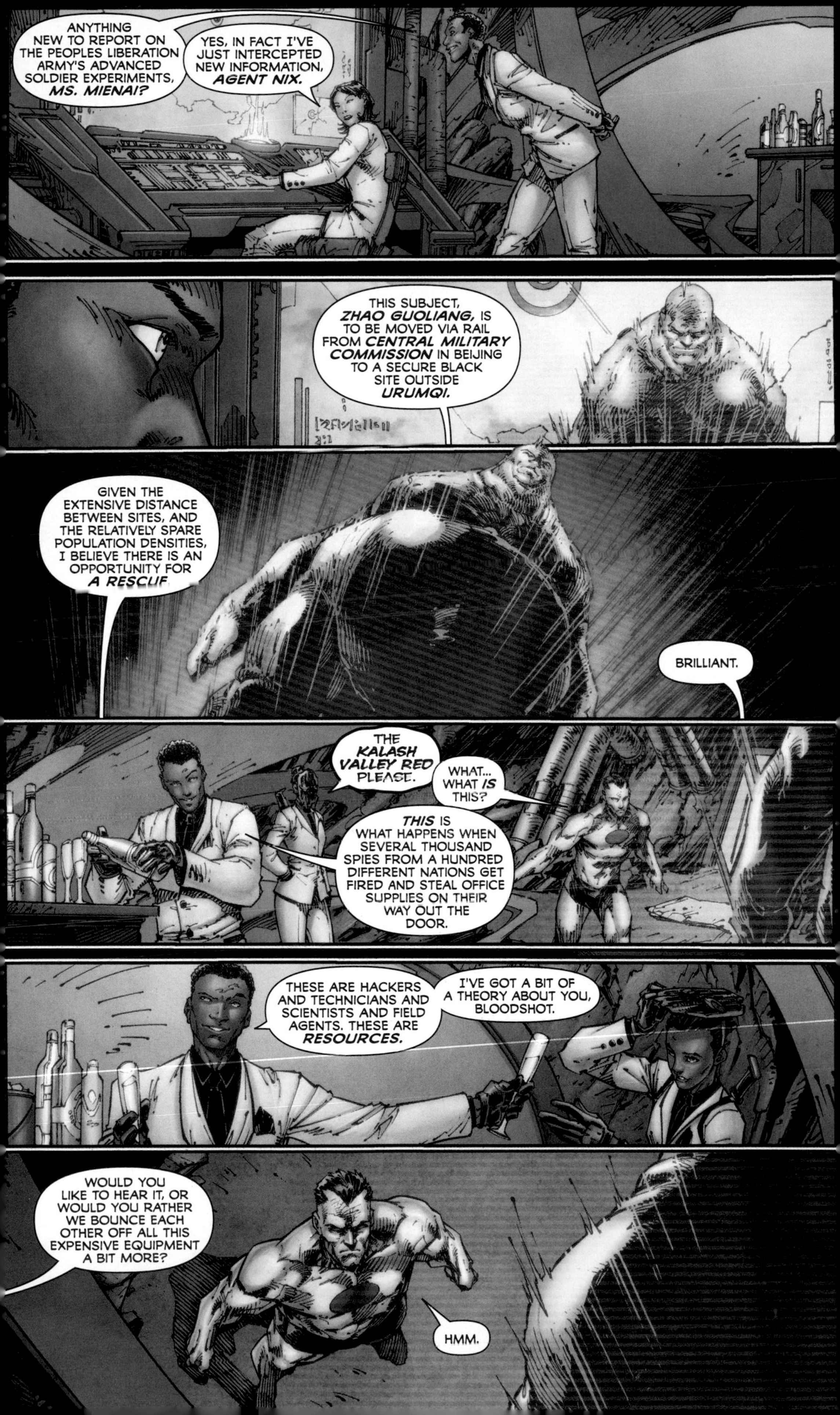
ANYTHING NEW TO REPORT ON THE PEOPLES LIBERATION ARMY'S ADVANCED SOLDIER EXPERIMENTS, MS. MIENAI?
YES, IN FACT I'VE JUST INTERCEPTED NEW INFORMATION, AGENT NIX.
THIS SUBJECT, ZHAO GUOLIANG, IS TO BE MOVED VIA RAIL FROM CENTRAL MILITARY COMMISSION IN BEIJING TO A SECURE BLACK SITE OUTSIDE URUMQI.
GIVEN THE EXTENSIVE DISTANCE BETWEEN SITES, AND THE RELATIVELY SPARE POPULATION DENSITIES, I BELIEVE THERE IS AN OPPORTUNITY FOR A RESCUE.
BRILLIANT.
THE KALASH VALLEY RED PLEASE.
WHAT... WHAT IS THIS?
THIS IS WHAT HAPPENS WHEN SEVERAL THOUSAND SPIES FROM A HUNDRED DIFFERENT NATIONS GET FIRED AND STEAL OFFICE SUPPLIES ON THEIR WAY OUT THE DOOR.
THESE ARE HACKERS AND TECHNICIANS AND SCIENTISTS AND FIELD AGENTS. THESE ARE RESOURCES.
I'VE GOT A BIT OF A THEORY ABOUT YOU, BLOODSHOT.
WOULD YOU LIKE TO HEAR IT, OR WOULD YOU RATHER WE BOUNCE EACH OTHER OFF ALL THIS EXPENSIVE EQUIPMENT A BIT MORE?
HMM.

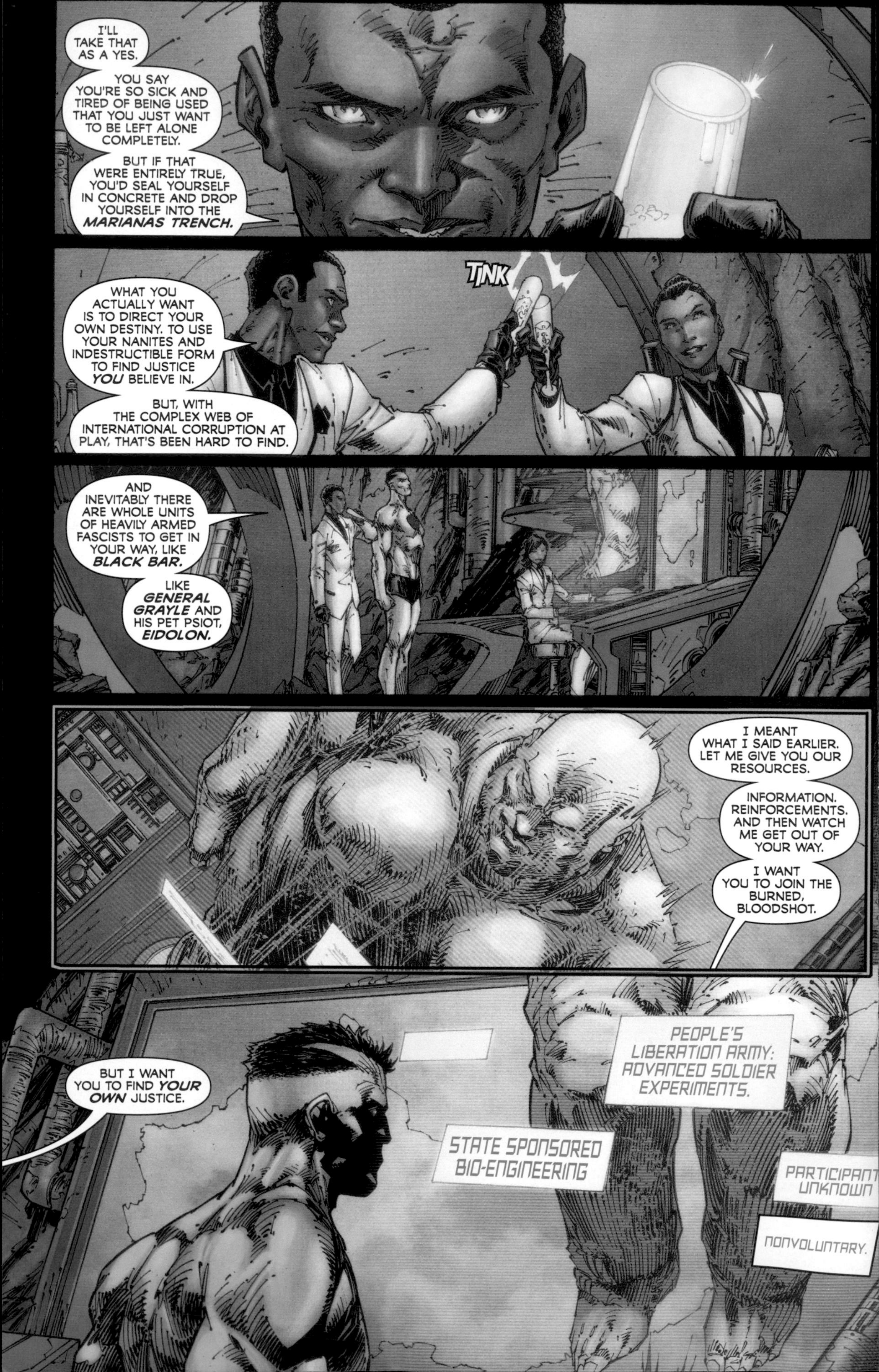
I'LL TAKE THAT AS A YES.
YOU SAY YOU'RE SO SICK AND TIRED OF BEING USED THAT YOU JUST WANT TO BE LEFT ALONE COMPLETELY.
BUT IF THAT WERE ENTIRELY TRUE, YOU'D SEAL YOURSELF IN CONCRETE AND DROP YOURSELF INTO THE MARIANAS TRENCH.
TINK
WHAT YOU ACTUALLY WANT IS TO DIRECT YOUR OWN DESTINY. TO USE YOUR NANITES AND INDESTRUCTIBLE FORM TO FIND JUSTICE YOU BELIEVE IN.
BUT, WITH THE COMPLEX WEB OF INTERNATIONAL CORRUPTION AT PLAY, THAT'S BEEN HARD TO FIND.
AND INEVITABLY THERE ARE WHOLE UNITS OF HEAVILY ARMED FASCISTS TO GET IN YOUR WAY, LIKE BLACK BAR.
LIKE GENERAL GRAYLE AND HIS PET PSIOT, EIDOLON.
I MEANT WHAT I SAID EARLIER. LET ME GIVE YOU OUR RESOURCES.
INFORMATION. REINFORCEMENTS. AND THEN WATCH ME GET OUT OF YOUR WAY.
I WANT YOU TO JOIN THE BURNED, BLOODSHOT.
BUT I WANT YOU TO FIND YOUR OWN JUSTICE.
PEOPLE'S LIBERATION ARMY: ADVANCED SOLDIER EXPERIMENTS.
STATE SPONSORED BIO-ENGINEERING
PARTICIPANT UNKNOWN
NONVOLUNTARY.

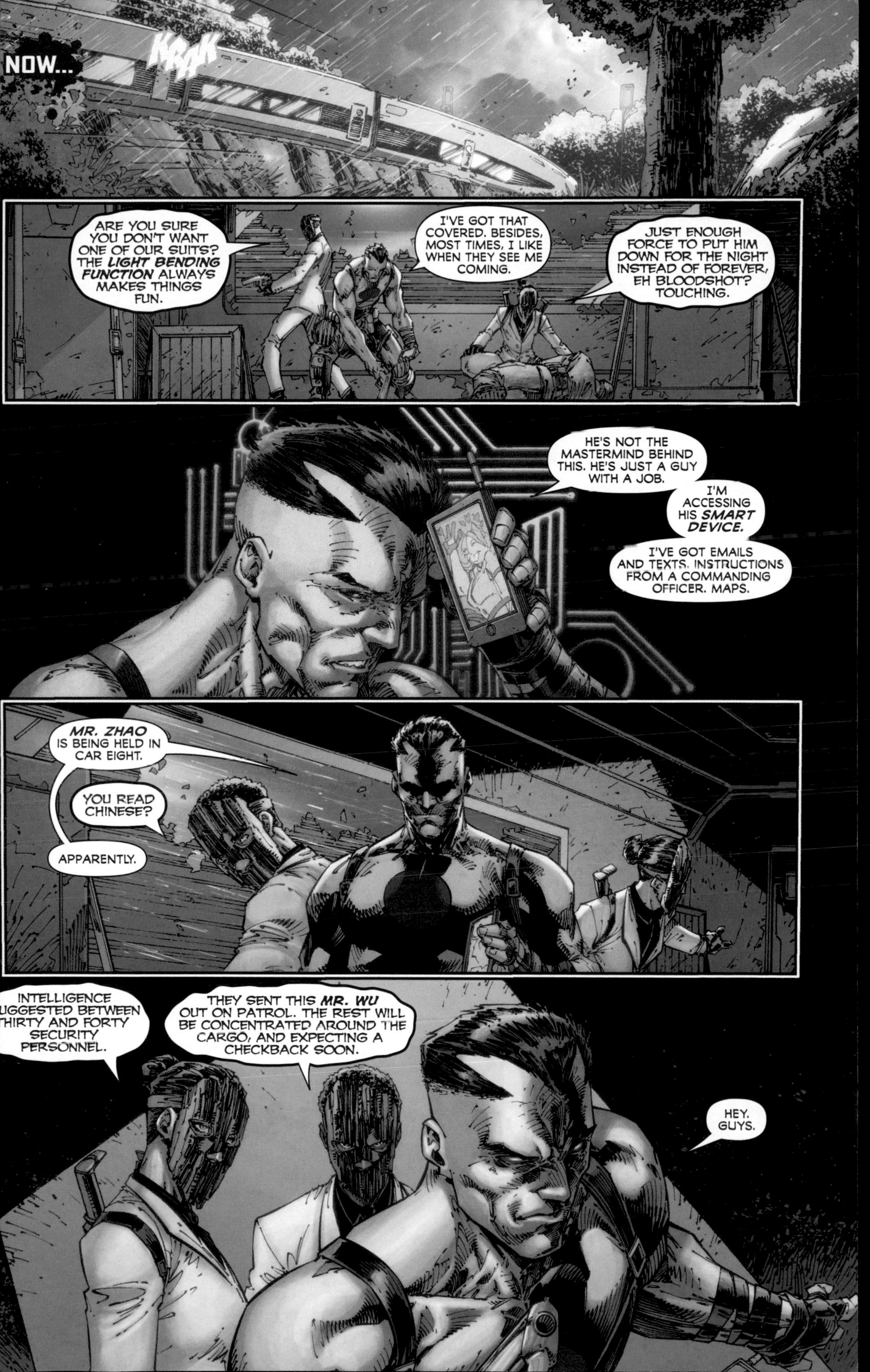
NOW...
KRAK
ARE YOU SURE YOU DON'T WANT ONE OF OUR SUITS? THE LIGHT BENDING FUNCTION ALWAYS MAKES THINGS FUN.
I'VE GOT THAT COVERED. BESIDES, MOST TIMES, I LIKE WHEN THEY SEE ME COMING.
JUST ENOUGH FORCE TO PUT HIM DOWN FOR THE NIGHT INSTEAD OF FOREVER, EH BLOODSHOT? TOUCHING.
HE'S NOT THE MASTERMIND BEHIND THIS. HE'S JUST A GUY WITH A JOB.
I'M ACCESSING HIS SMART DEVICE.
I'VE GOT EMAILS AND TEXTS. INSTRUCTIONS FROM A COMMANDING OFFICER. MAPS.
MR. ZHAO IS BEING HELD IN CAR EIGHT.
YOU READ CHINESE?
APPARENTLY.
INTELLIGENCE UGGESTED BETWEEN THIRTY AND FORTY SECURITY PERSONNEL.
THEY SENT THIS MR. WU OUT ON PATROL. THE REST WILL BE CONCENTRATED AROUND THE CARGO, AND EXPECTING A CHECKBACK SOON.
HEY. GUYS.

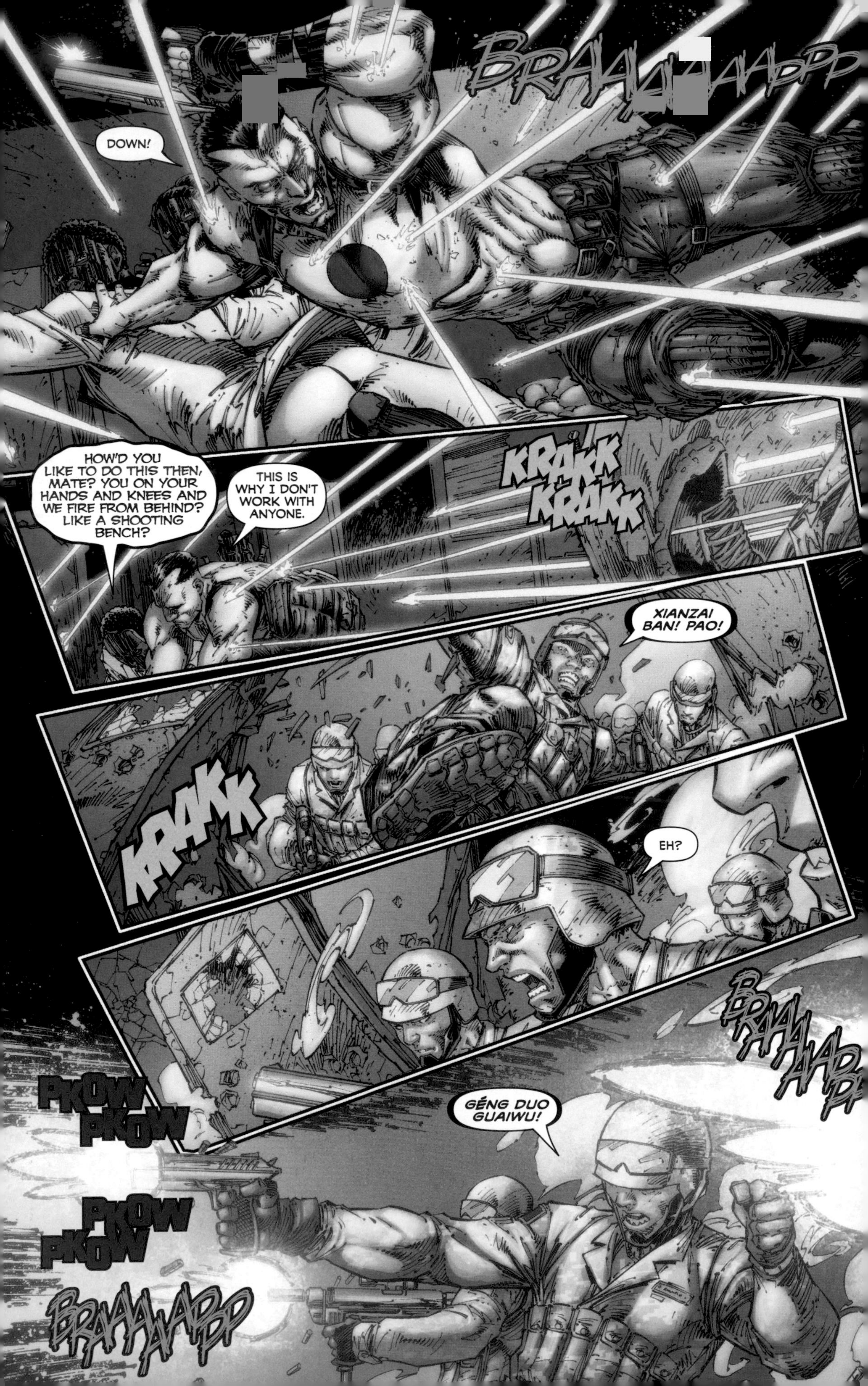
DOWN!
HOW'D YOU LIKE TO DO THIS THEN, MATE? YOU ON YOUR HANDS AND KNEES AND WE FIRE FROM BEHIND? LIKE A SHOOTING BENCH?
THIS IS WHY I DON'T WORK WITH ANYONE.
KRAKK KRAKK
XIANZAI BAN! PAO!
KRAKK
EH?
GÉNG DUO GUAIWU!
PKOW PKOW
PKOW PKOW

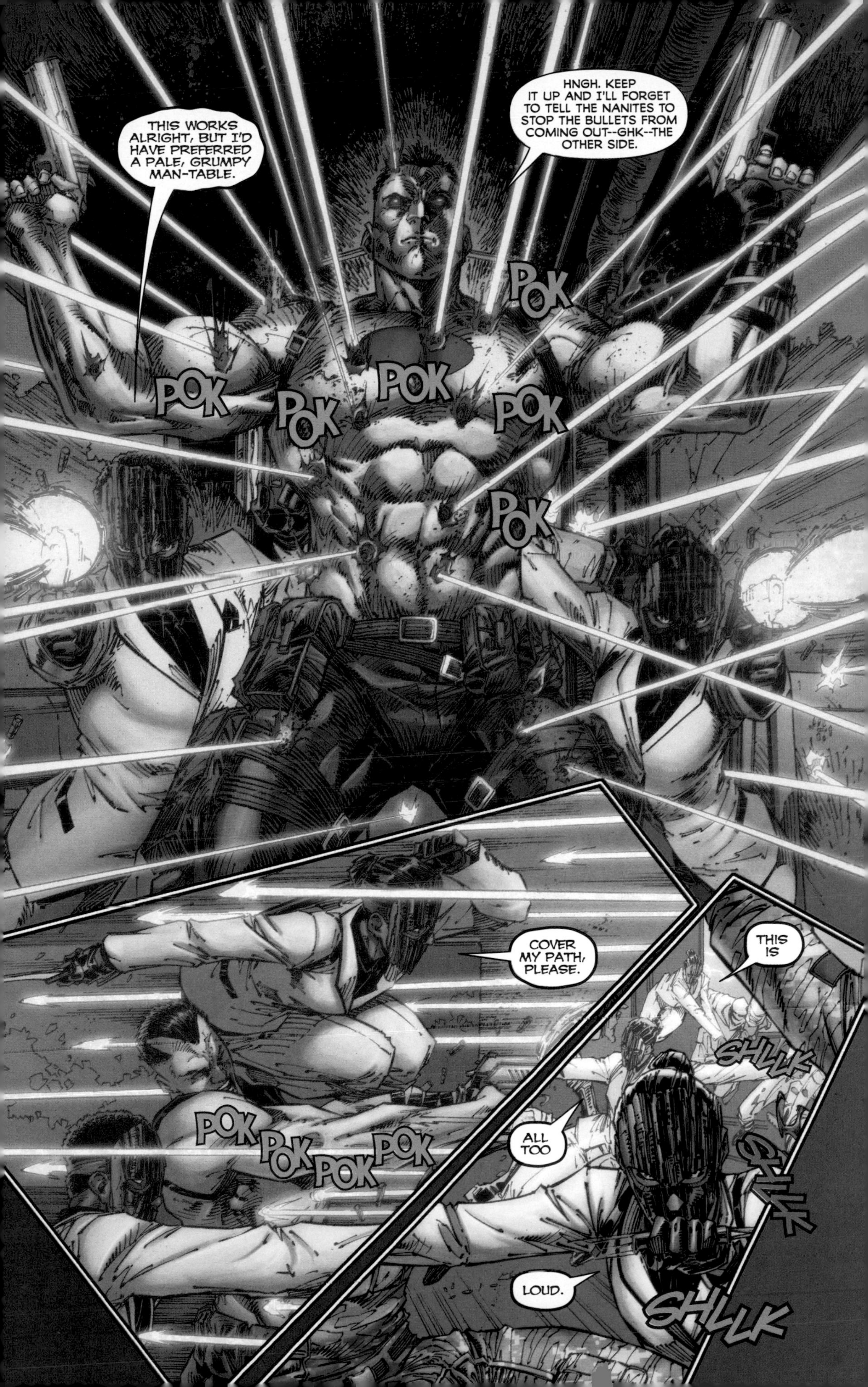
THIS WORKS ALRIGHT, BUT I'D HAVE PREFERRED A PALE, GRUMPY MAN-TABLE.
HNGH. KEEP IT UP AND I'LL FORGET TO TELL THE NANITES TO STOP THE BULLETS FROM COMING OUT--GHK--THE OTHER SIDE.
POK
POK
POK
POK
POK
POK
COVER MY PATH, PLEASE.
POK POK POK POK
THIS IS
ALL TOO
LOUD.
SHLLK
SHLLK
SHLLK

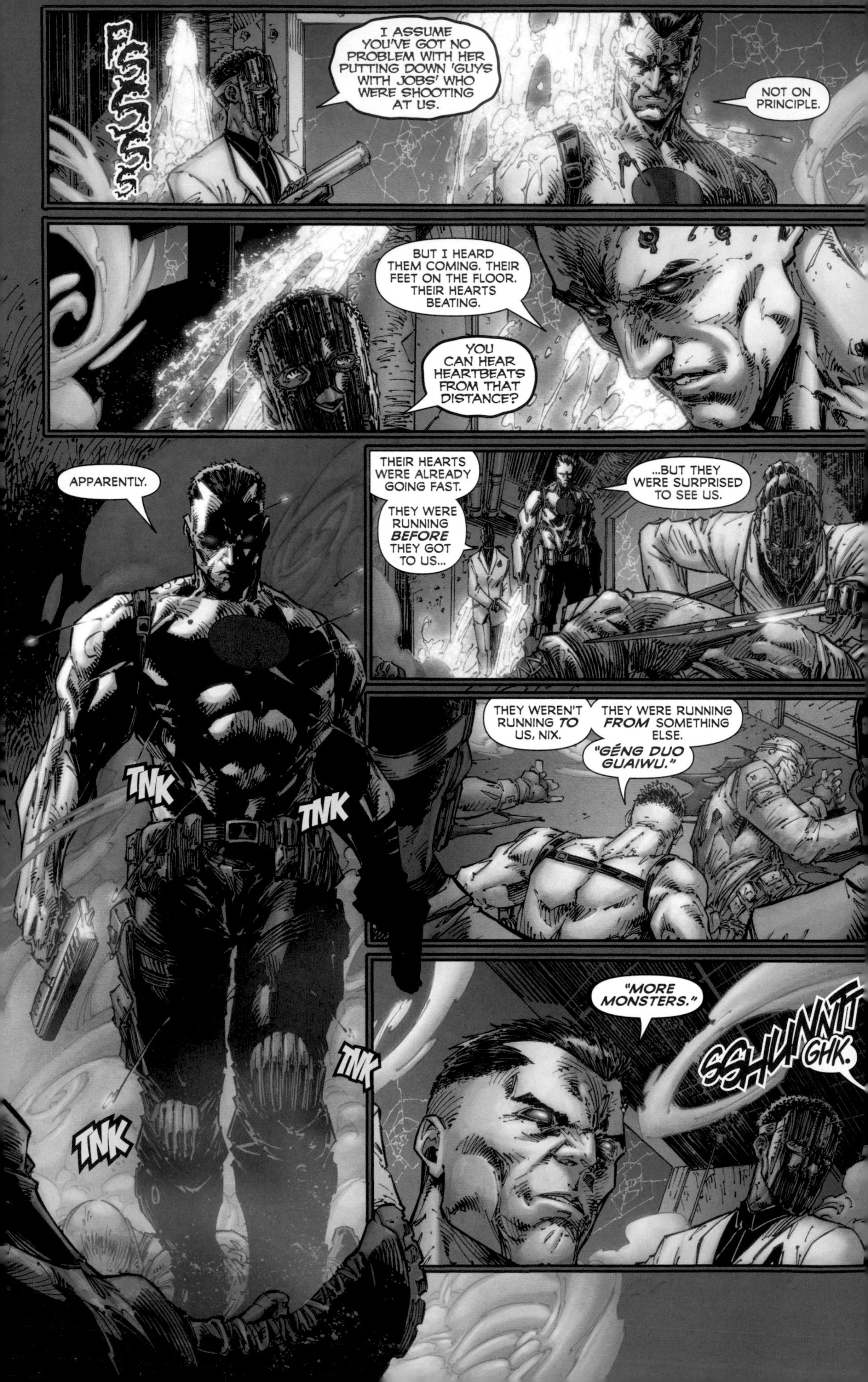
PSSSSS
I ASSUME YOU'VE GOT NO PROBLEM WITH HER PUTTING DOWN 'GUYS WITH JOBS' WHO WERE SHOOTING AT US.
NOT ON PRINCIPLE.
BUT I HEARD THEM COMING. THEIR FEET ON THE FLOOR. THEIR HEARTS BEATING.
YOU CAN HEAR HEARTBEATS FROM THAT DISTANCE?
APPARENTLY.
THEIR HEARTS WERE ALREADY GOING FAST.
THEY WERE RUNNING *BEFORE* THEY GOT TO US...
...BUT THEY WERE SURPRISED TO SEE US.
THEY WEREN'T RUNNING *TO* US, NIX.
THEY WERE RUNNING *FROM* SOMETHING ELSE.
"GÉNG DUO GUAIWU."
"MORE MONSTERS."
SSHUNNT
GHK.
TNK
TNK
TNK
TNK

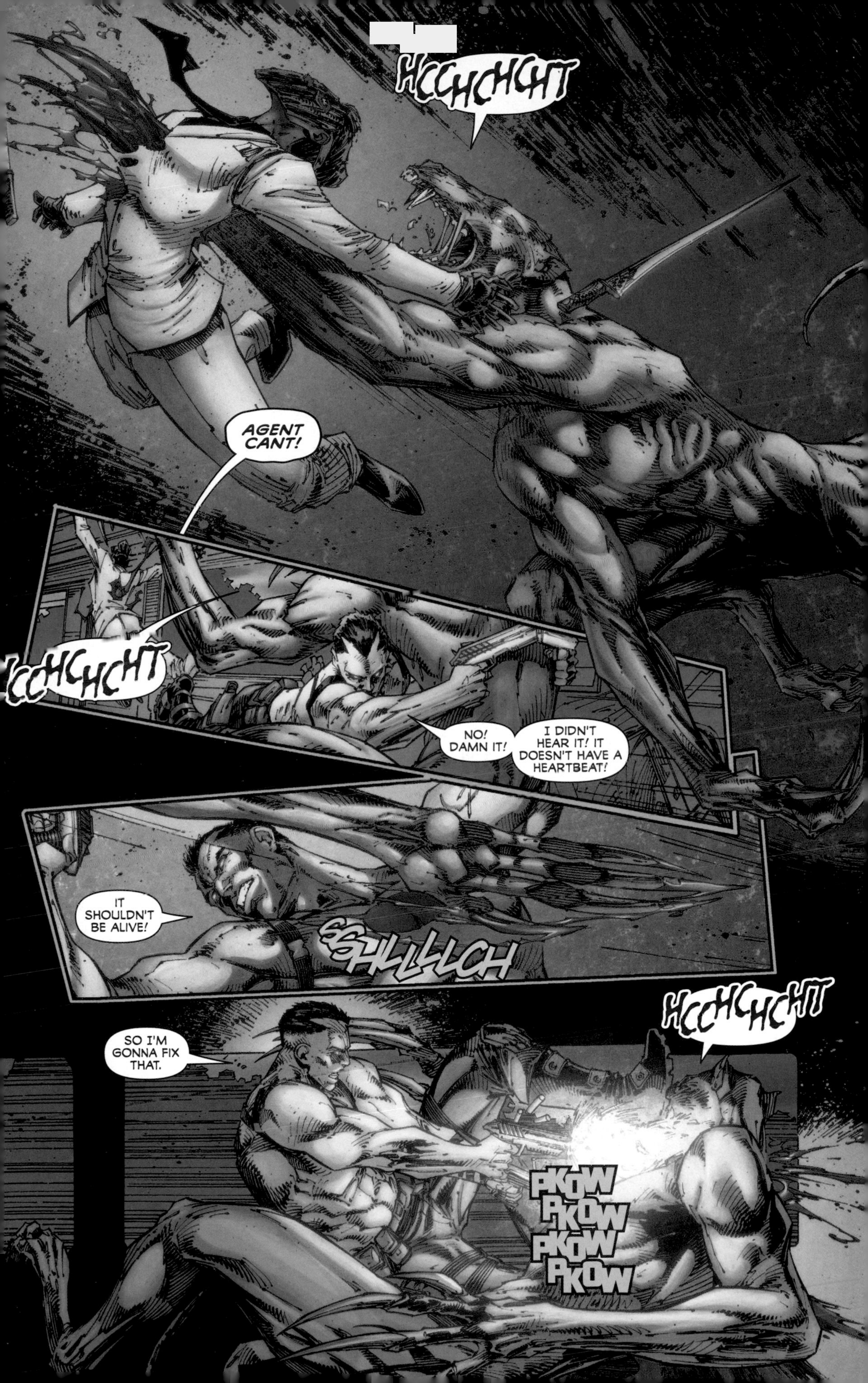
HCCHCHCHT
AGENT CANT!
CCHCHCHT
NO! DAMN IT!
I DIDN'T HEAR IT! IT DOESN'T HAVE A HEARTBEAT!
IT SHOULDN'T BE ALIVE!
SSHLLLLCH
SO I'M GONNA FIX THAT.
HCCHCHCHT
PKOW
PKOW
PKOW
PKOW

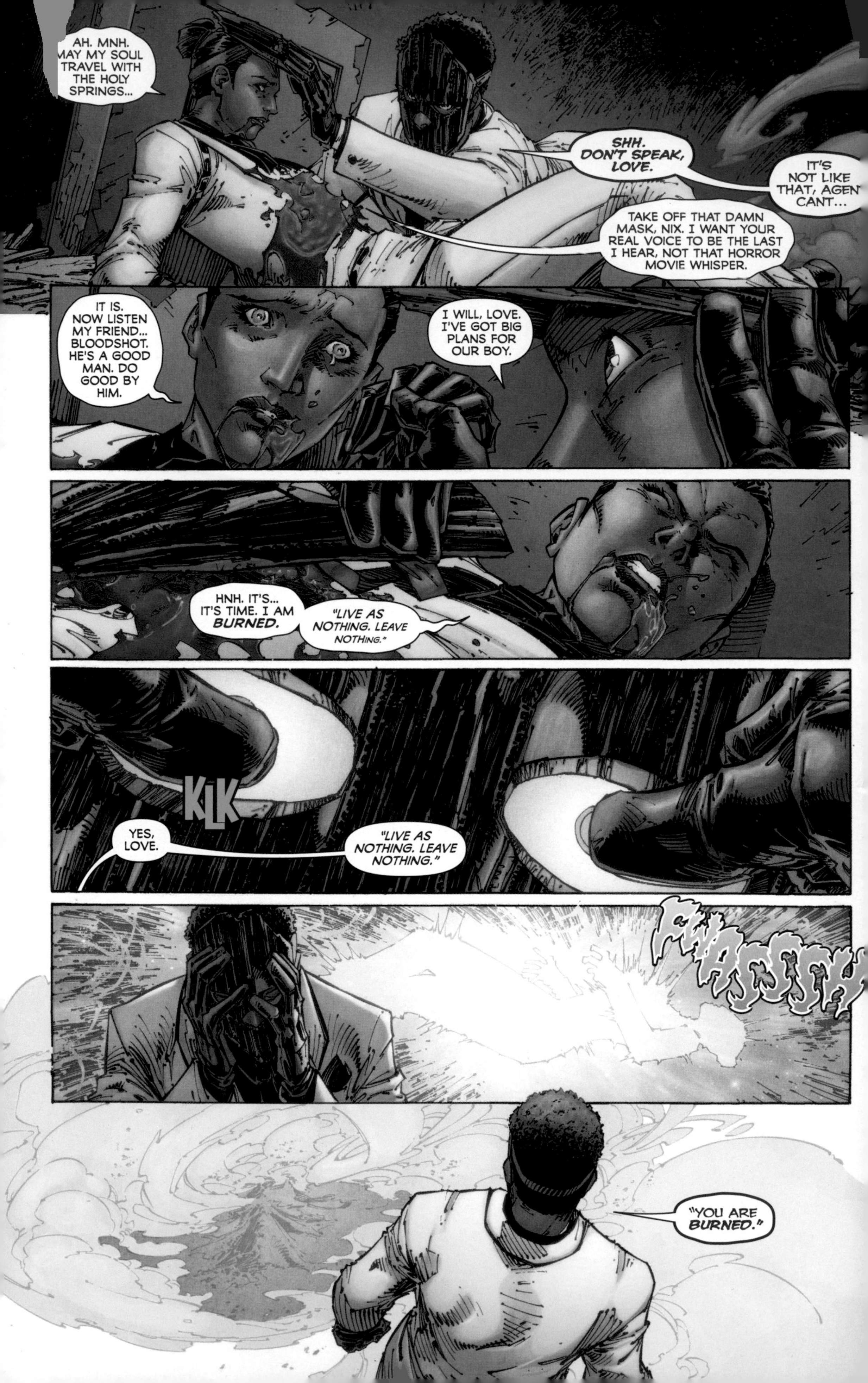
AH. MNH. MAY MY SOUL TRAVEL WITH THE HOLY SPRINGS...
SHH. DON'T SPEAK, LOVE.
IT'S NOT LIKE THAT, AGENT CANT...
TAKE OFF THAT DAMN MASK, NIX. I WANT YOUR REAL VOICE TO BE THE LAST I HEAR, NOT THAT HORROR MOVIE WHISPER.
IT IS. NOW LISTEN MY FRIEND... BLOODSHOT. HE'S A GOOD MAN. DO GOOD BY HIM.
I WILL, LOVE. I'VE GOT BIG PLANS FOR OUR BOY.
HNH. IT'S... IT'S TIME. I AM BURNED.
"LIVE AS NOTHING. LEAVE NOTHING."
KLK
YES, LOVE.
"LIVE AS NOTHING. LEAVE NOTHING."
FWASSSH
"YOU ARE BURNED."

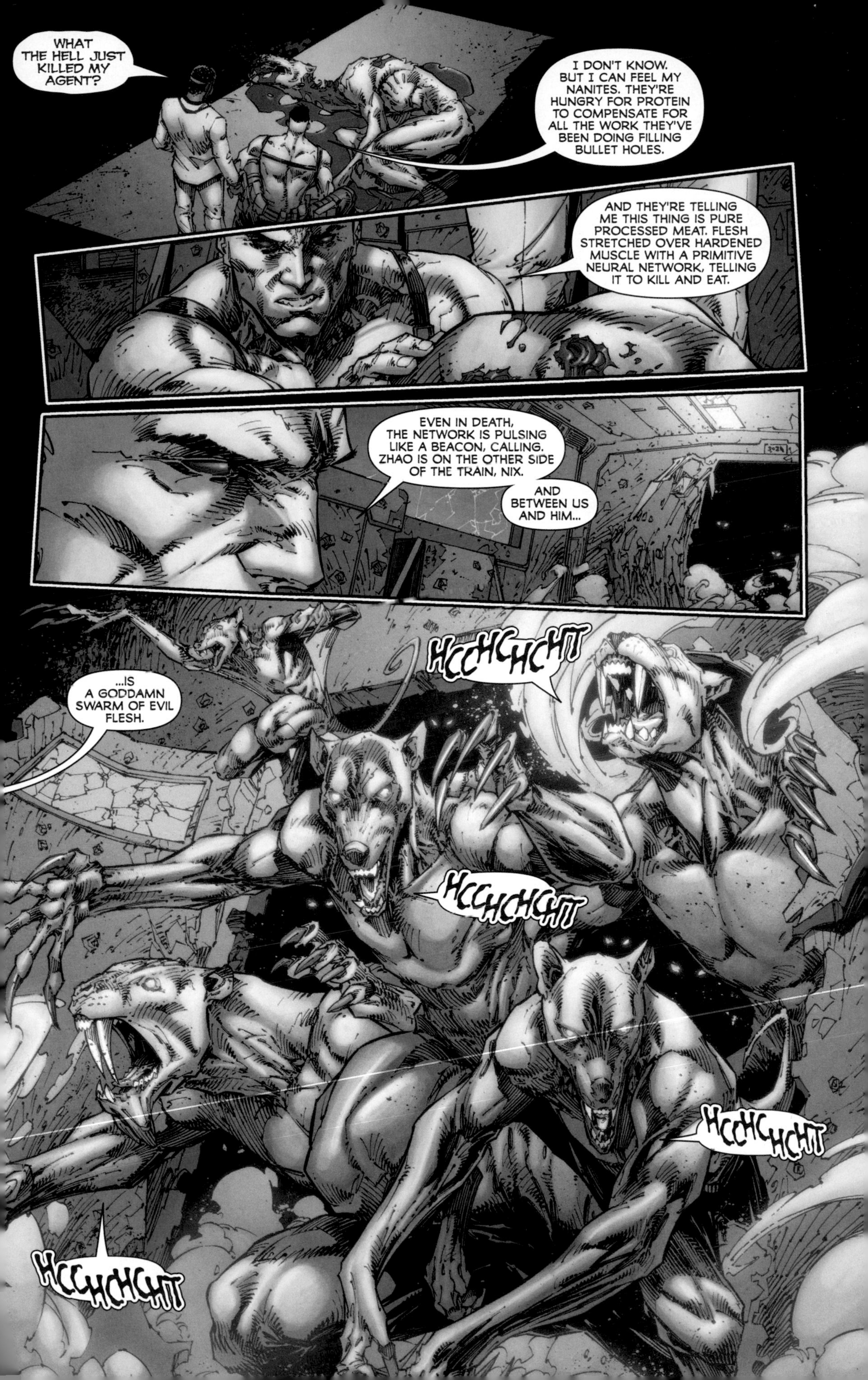
WHAT THE HELL JUST KILLED MY AGENT?
I DON'T KNOW. BUT I CAN FEEL MY NANITES. THEY'RE HUNGRY FOR PROTEIN TO COMPENSATE FOR ALL THE WORK THEY'VE BEEN DOING FILLING BULLET HOLES.
AND THEY'RE TELLING ME THIS THING IS PURE PROCESSED MEAT. FLESH STRETCHED OVER HARDENED MUSCLE WITH A PRIMITIVE NEURAL NETWORK, TELLING IT TO KILL AND EAT.
EVEN IN DEATH, THE NETWORK IS PULSING LIKE A BEACON, CALLING. ZHAO IS ON THE OTHER SIDE OF THE TRAIN, NIX.
AND BETWEEN US AND HIM...
...IS A GODDAMN SWARM OF EVIL FLESH.
HCCHCHCHT
HCCHCHCHT
HCCHCHCHT
HCCHCHCHT

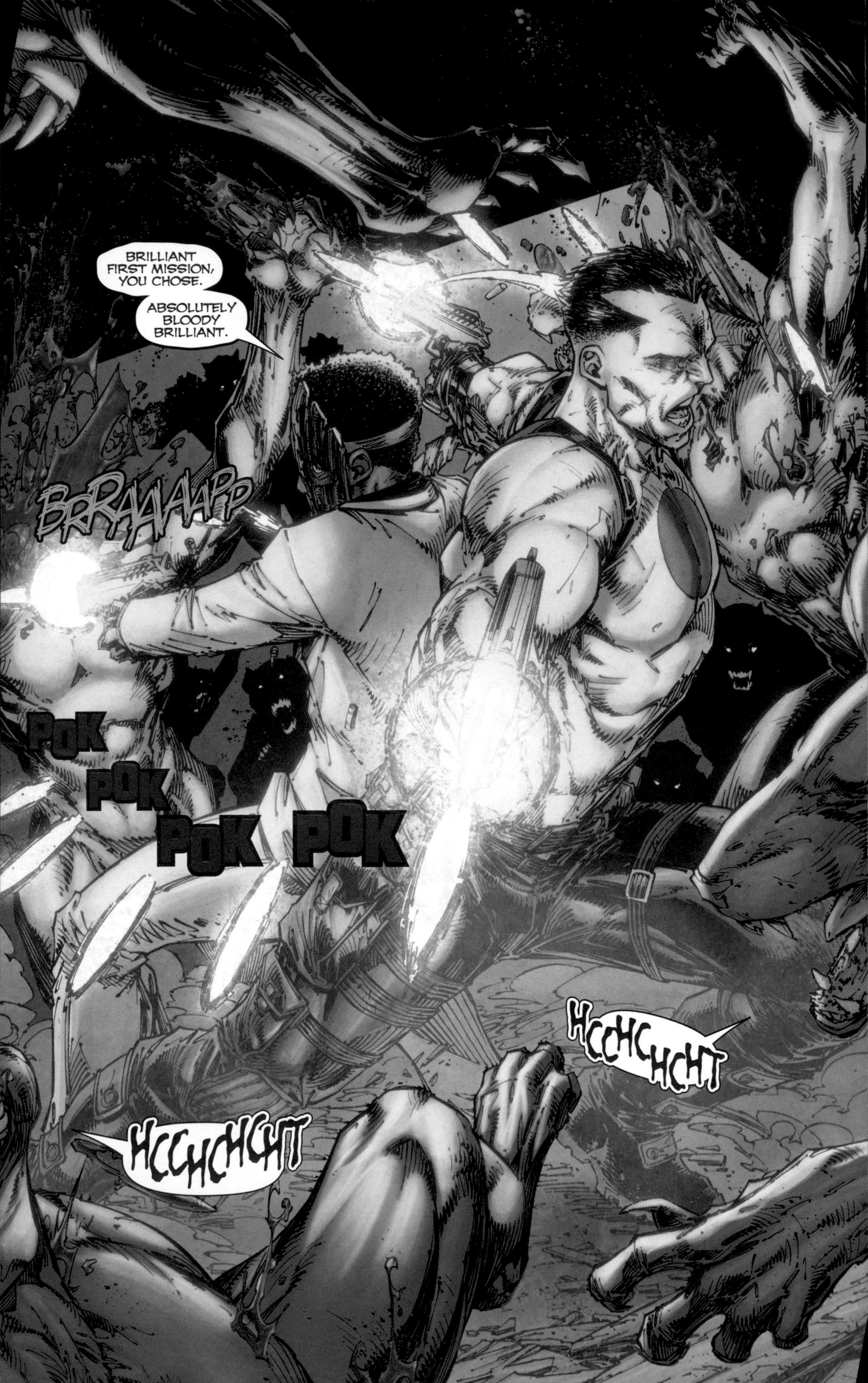
BRILLIANT FIRST MISSION, YOU CHOSE.
ABSOLUTELY BLOODY BRILLIANT.
BRRAAAAAPP
POK
POK
POK
POK
HCCHCHCHT
HCCHCHCHT

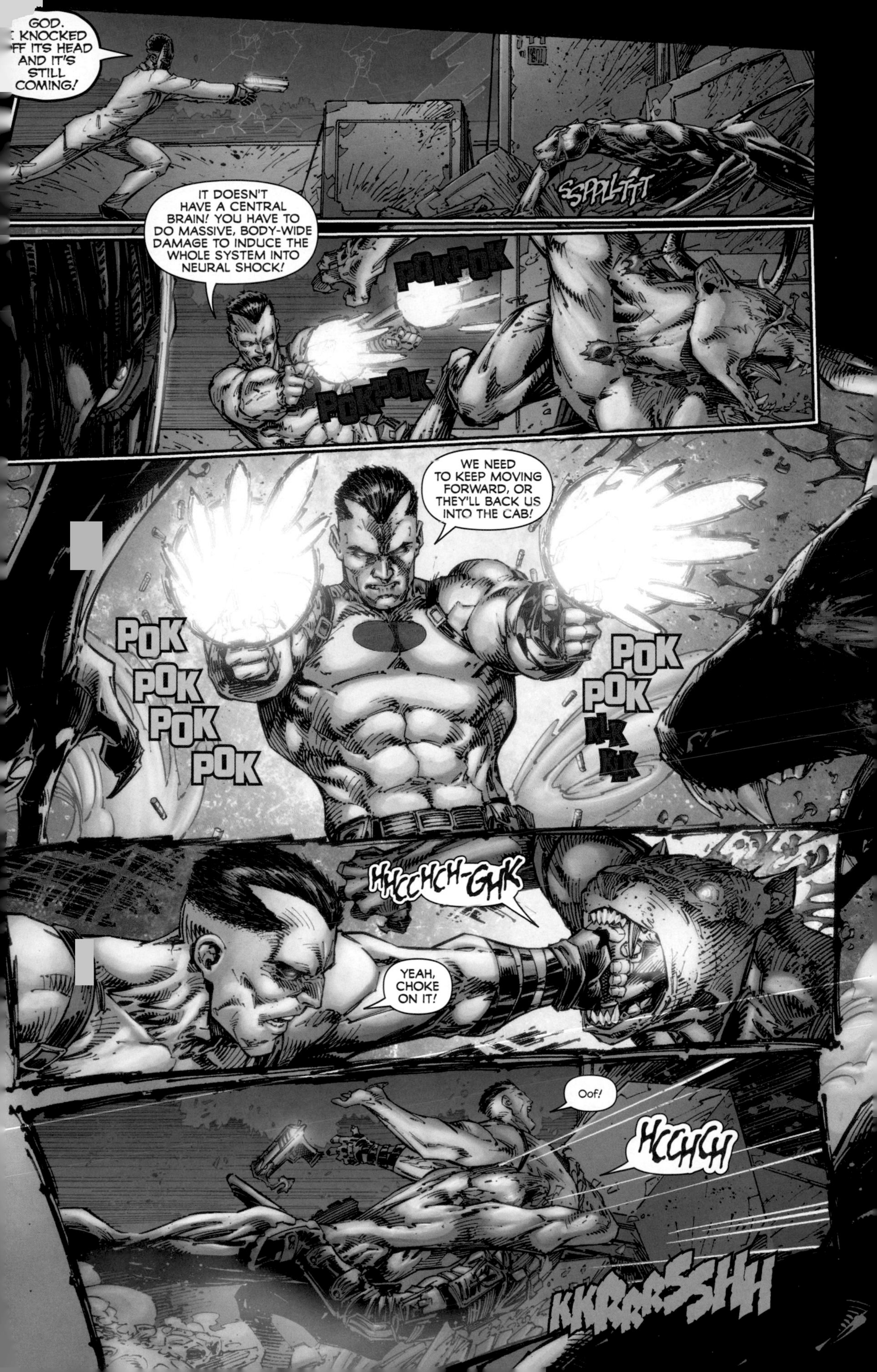

GOD. I KNOCKED OFF ITS HEAD AND IT'S STILL COMING!
SSPPL-TTT
IT DOESN'T HAVE A CENTRAL BRAIN! YOU HAVE TO DO MASSIVE, BODY-WIDE DAMAGE TO INDUCE THE WHOLE SYSTEM INTO NEURAL SHOCK!
POKPOK
POKPOK
WE NEED TO KEEP MOVING FORWARD, OR THEY'LL BACK US INTO THE CAB!
POK POK POK POK
POK POK KLIK KLIK
HHCCHCH-GHK
YEAH, CHOKE ON IT!
Oof!
HCCHCH
KKRRRSSHH

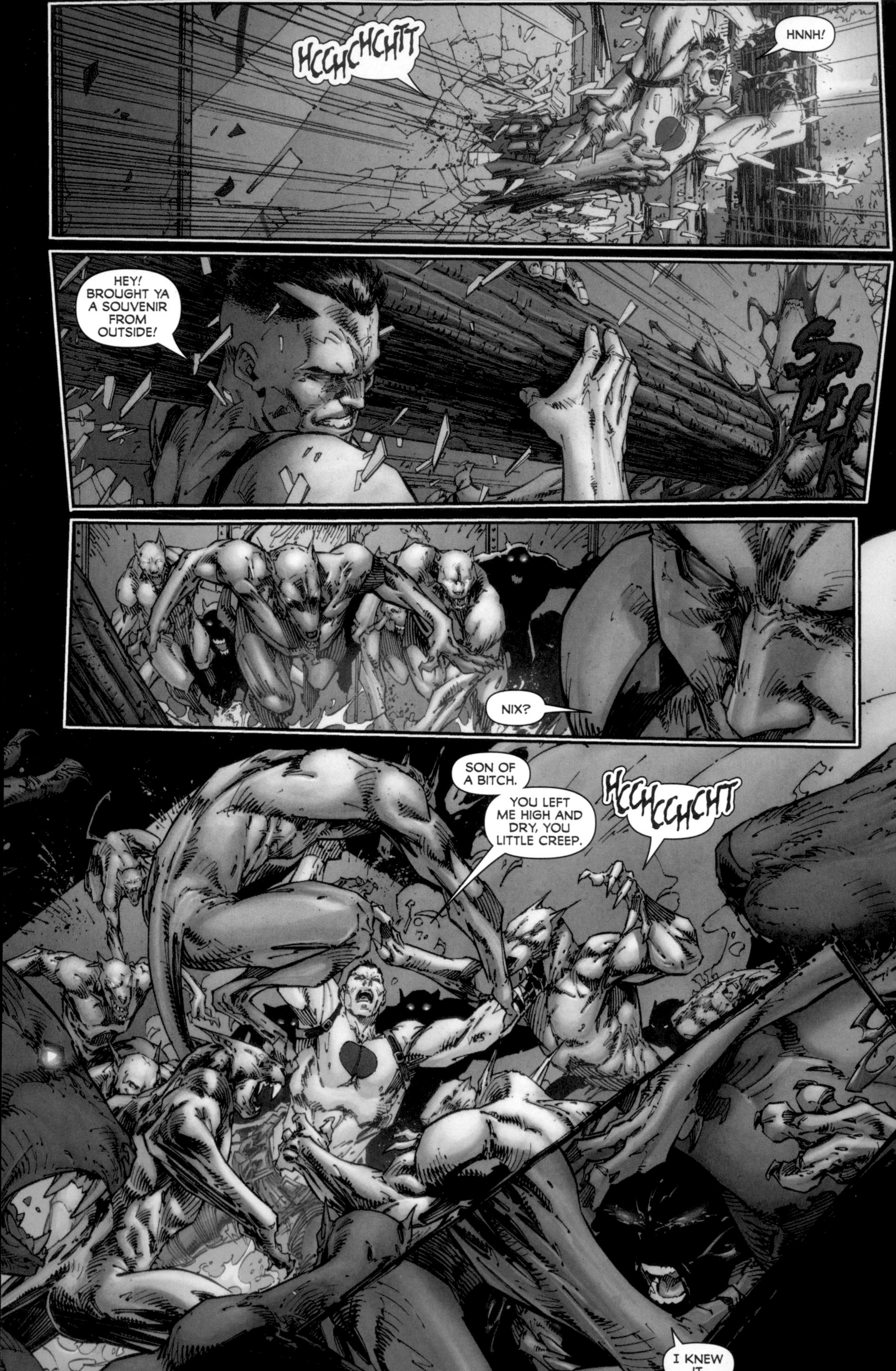
HCCHCHCHTT
HNNH!
HEY! BROUGHT YA A SOUVENIR FROM OUTSIDE!
NIX?
SON OF A BITCH.
YOU LEFT ME HIGH AND DRY, YOU LITTLE CREEP.
HCCHCCHCHT
I KNEW IT.

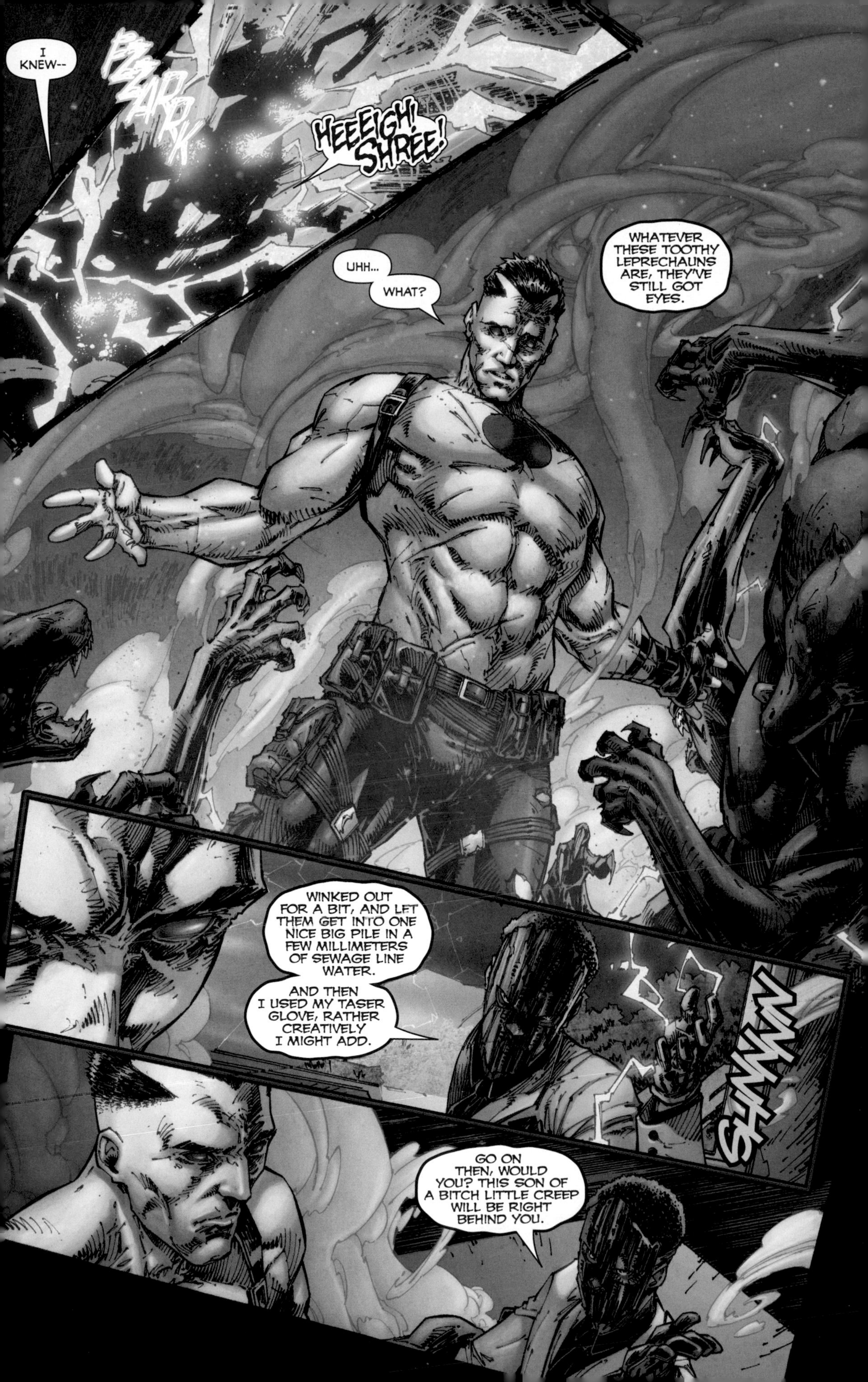
I KNEW--
PZZZARRK
HEEEIGH! SHREE!
UHH...
WHAT?
WHATEVER THESE TOOTHY LEPRECHAUNS ARE, THEY'VE STILL GOT EYES.
WINKED OUT FOR A BIT, AND LET THEM GET INTO ONE NICE BIG PILE IN A FEW MILLIMETERS OF SEWAGE LINE WATER.
AND THEN I USED MY TASER GLOVE, RATHER CREATIVELY I MIGHT ADD.
SHNNNNN
GO ON THEN, WOULD YOU? THIS SON OF A BITCH LITTLE CREEP WILL BE RIGHT BEHIND YOU.

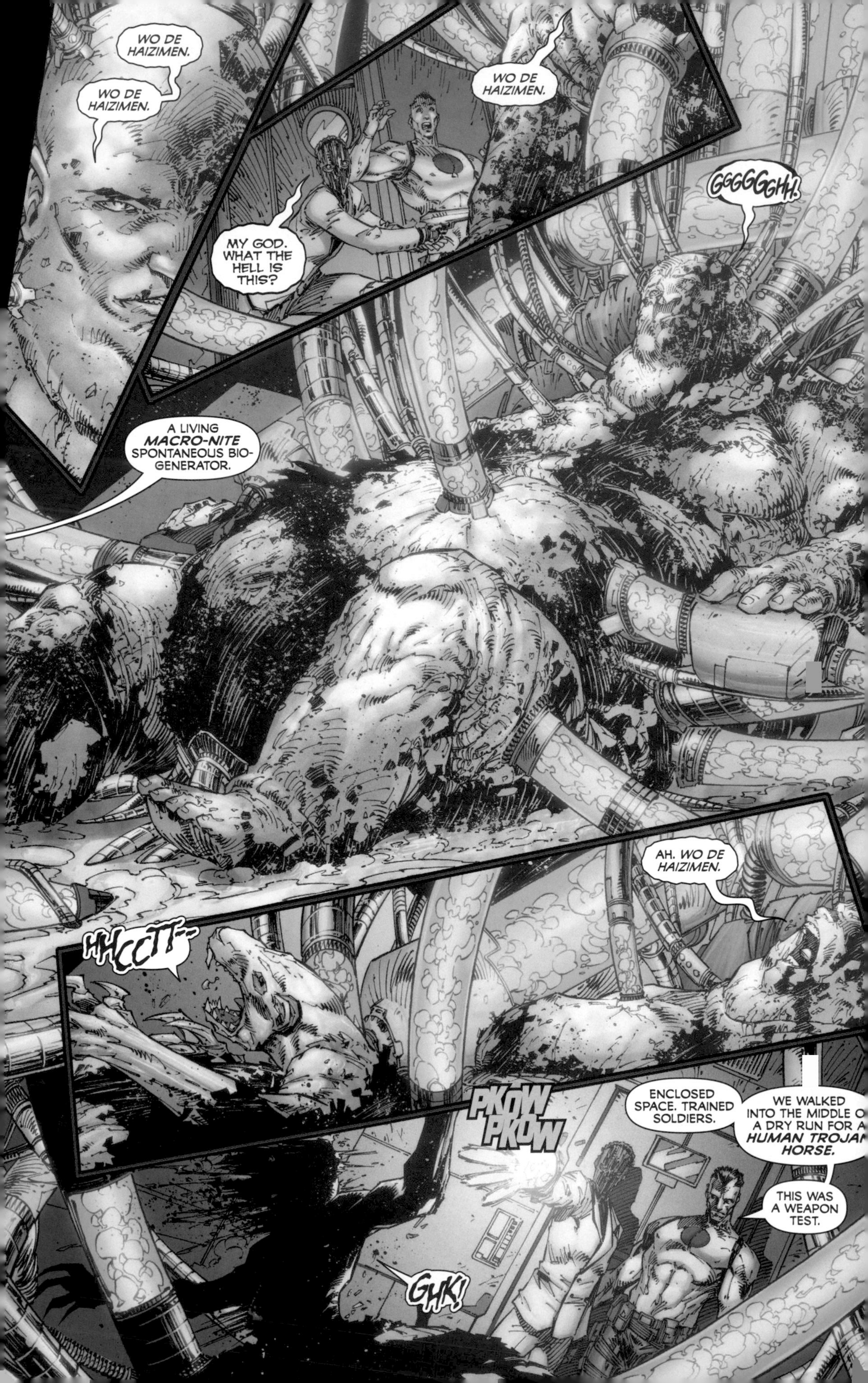
WO DE HAIZIMEN.
WO DE HAIZIMEN.
WO DE HAIZIMEN.
MY GOD. WHAT THE HELL IS THIS?
GGGGGGHH!
A LIVING MACRO-NITE SPONTANEOUS BIO-GENERATOR.
AH. WO DE HAIZIMEN.
HHCCTT--
PKOW PKOW
ENCLOSED SPACE. TRAINED SOLDIERS.
WE WALKED INTO THE MIDDLE O A DRY RUN FOR A HUMAN TROJA HORSE.
THIS WAS A WEAPON TEST.
GHK!

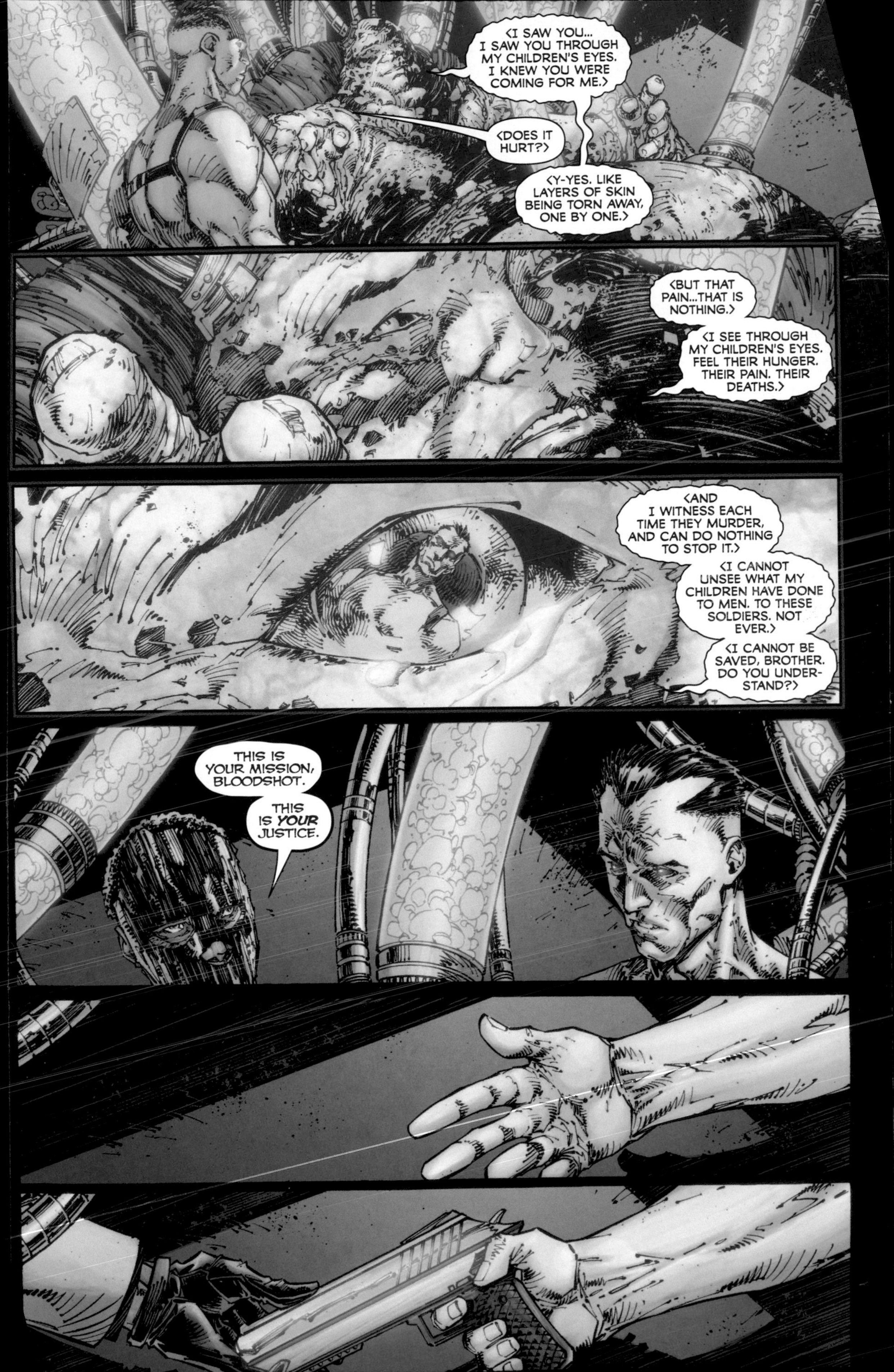

<I SAW YOU... I SAW YOU THROUGH MY CHILDREN'S EYES. I KNEW YOU WERE COMING FOR ME.>
<DOES IT HURT?>
<Y-YES. LIKE LAYERS OF SKIN BEING TORN AWAY, ONE BY ONE.>
<BUT THAT PAIN...THAT IS NOTHING.>
<I SEE THROUGH MY CHILDREN'S EYES. FEEL THEIR HUNGER. THEIR PAIN. THEIR DEATHS.>
<AND I WITNESS EACH TIME THEY MURDER, AND CAN DO NOTHING TO STOP IT.>
<I CANNOT UNSEE WHAT MY CHILDREN HAVE DONE TO MEN. TO THESE SOLDIERS. NOT EVER.>
<I CANNOT BE SAVED, BROTHER. DO YOU UNDER-STAND?>
THIS IS YOUR MISSION, BLOODSHOT.
THIS IS *YOUR* JUSTICE.

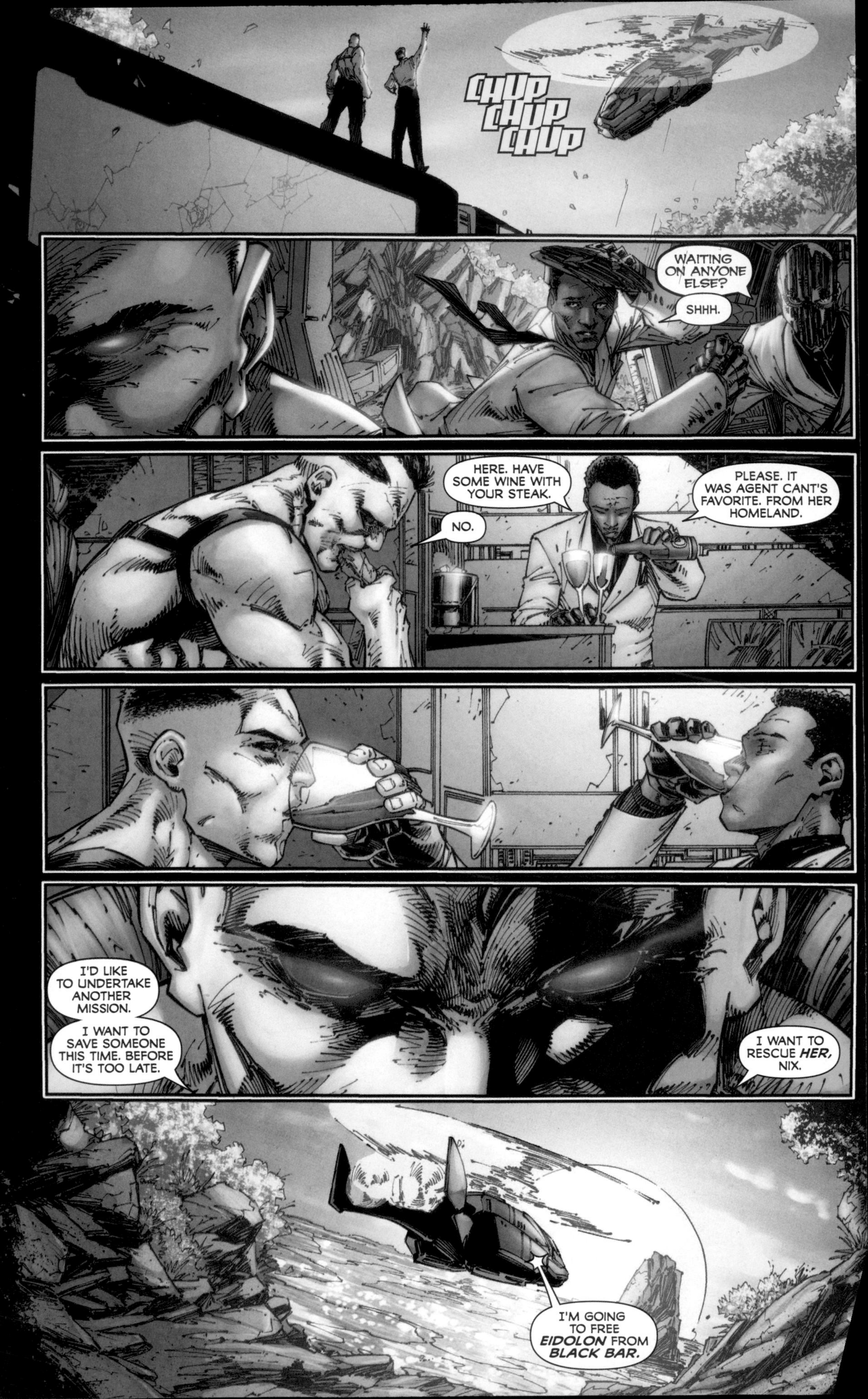
CHUP CHUP CHUP
WAITING ON ANYONE ELSE?
SHHH.
HERE. HAVE SOME WINE WITH YOUR STEAK.
NO.
PLEASE. IT WAS AGENT CANT'S FAVORITE. FROM HER HOMELAND.
I'D LIKE TO UNDERTAKE ANOTHER MISSION.
I WANT TO SAVE SOMEONE THIS TIME. BEFORE IT'S TOO LATE.
I WANT TO RESCUE *HER,* NIX.
I'M GOING TO FREE ***EIDOLON*** FROM ***BLACK BAR.***

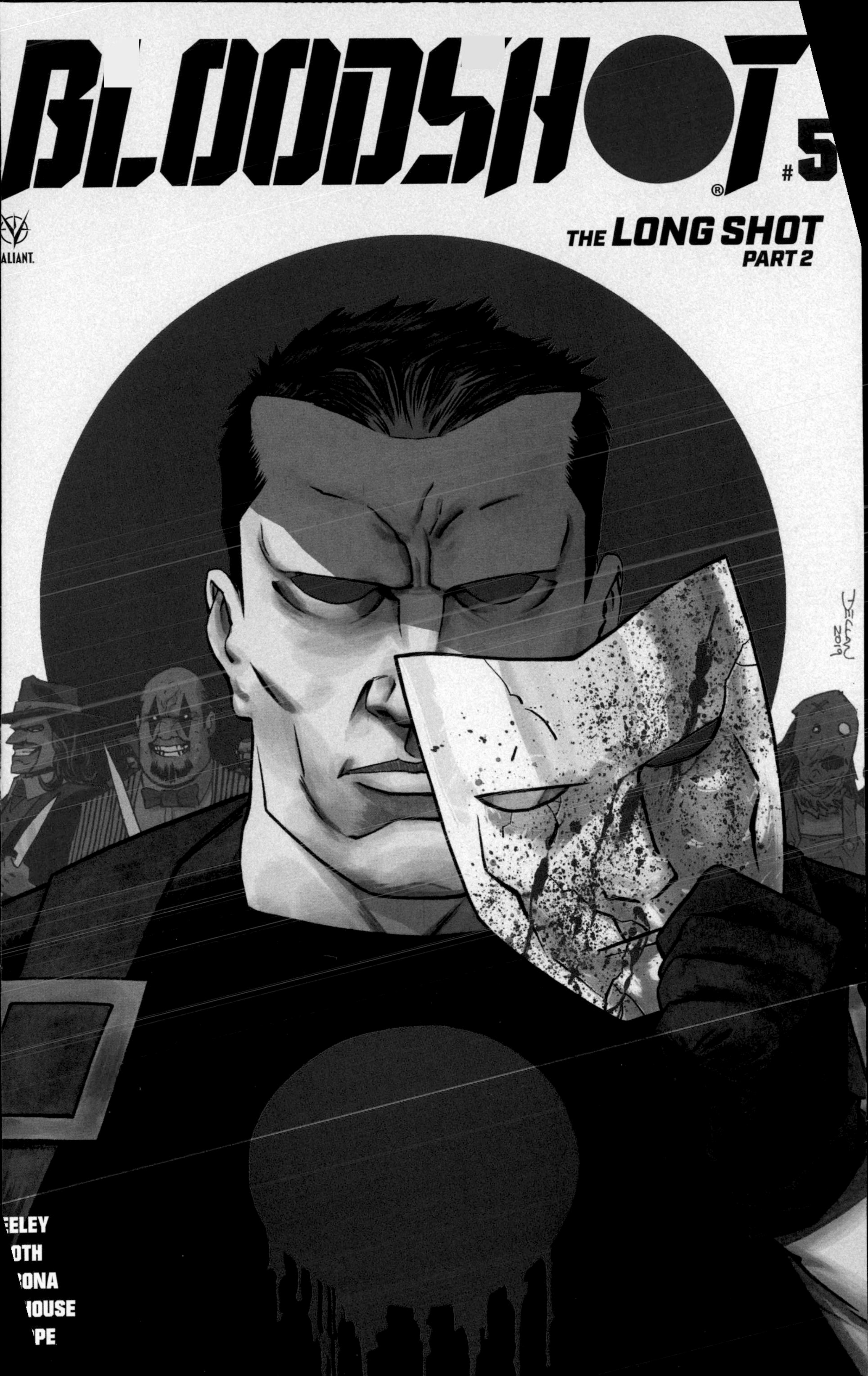
BLOODSHOT
#5
THE LONG SHOT
PART 2
DECLAN 2019

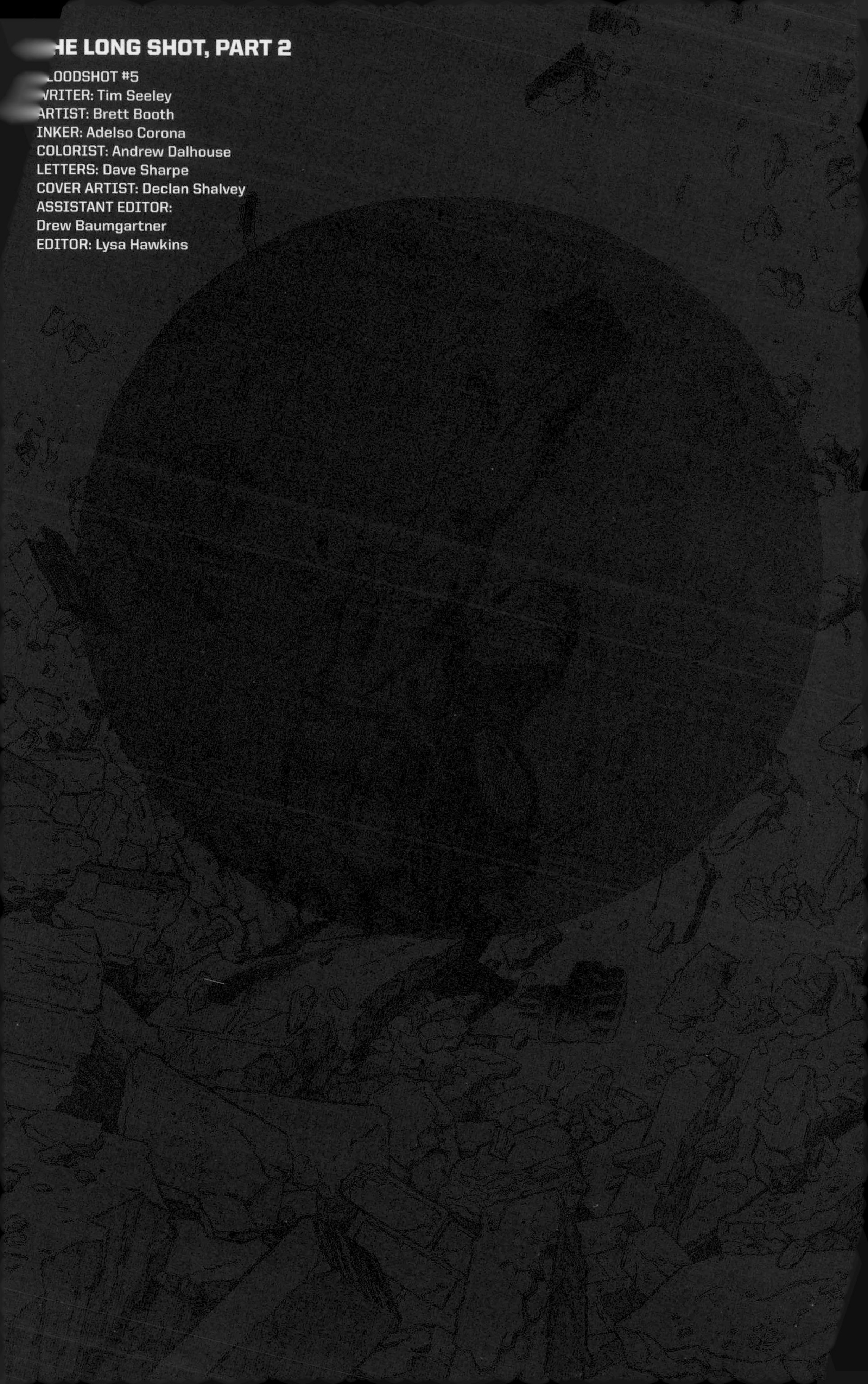

THE LONG SHOT, PART 2

BLOODSHOT #5
WRITER: Tim Seeley
ARTIST: Brett Booth
INKER: Adelso Corona
COLORIST: Andrew Dalhouse
LETTERS: Dave Sharpe
COVER ARTIST: Declan Shalvey
ASSISTANT EDITOR:
Drew Baumgartner
EDITOR: Lysa Hawkins

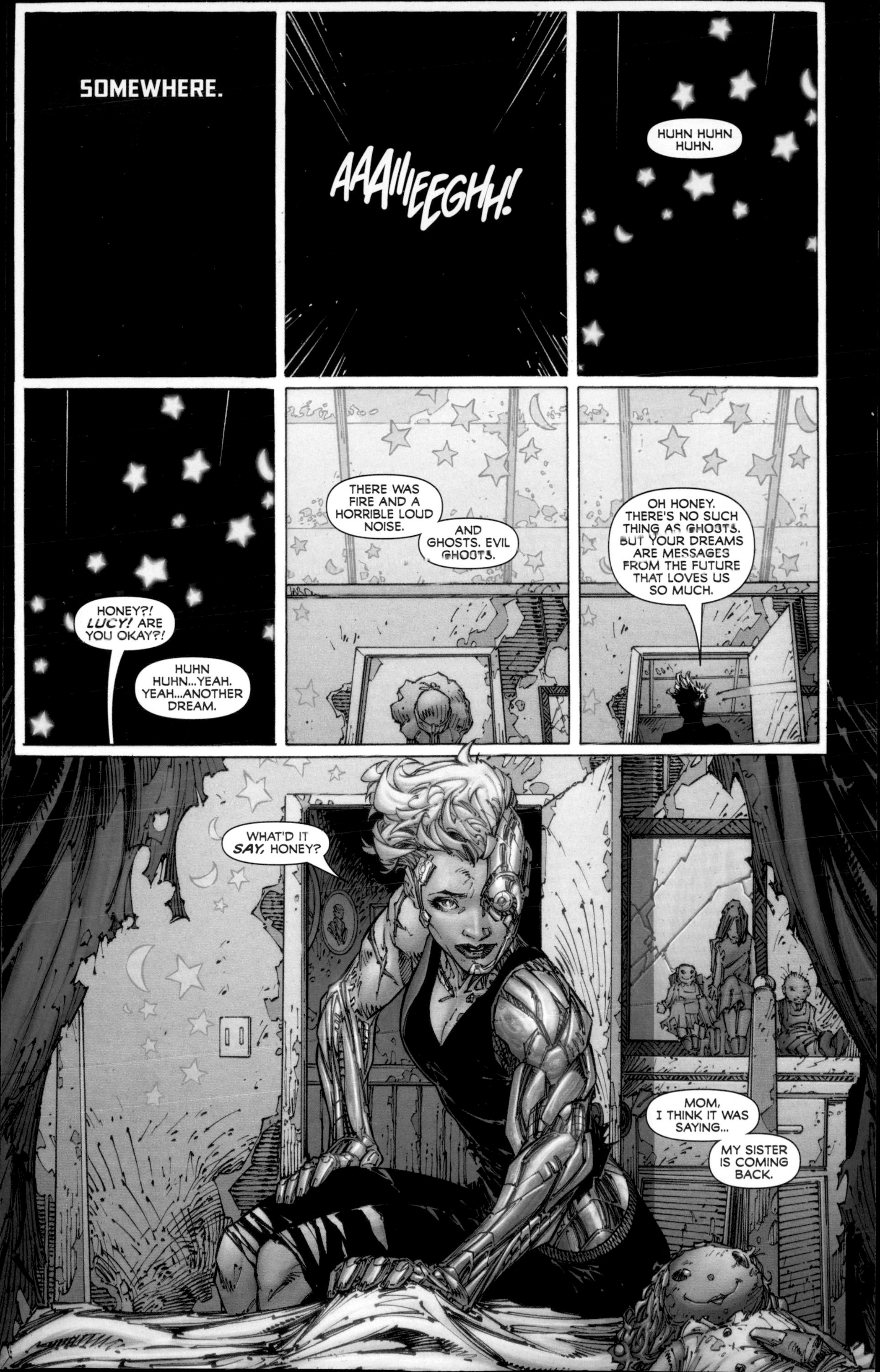
SOMEWHERE.
AAAIIIEEGHH!
HUHN HUHN HUHN.
HONEY?! LUCY! ARE YOU OKAY?!
HUHN HUHN...YEAH. YEAH...ANOTHER DREAM.
THERE WAS FIRE AND A HORRIBLE LOUD NOISE.
AND GHOSTS. EVIL GHOSTS.
OH HONEY. THERE'S NO SUCH THING AS GHOSTS. BUT YOUR DREAMS ARE MESSAGES FROM THE FUTURE THAT LOVES US SO MUCH.
WHAT'D IT SAY, HONEY?
MOM, I THINK IT WAS SAYING...
MY SISTER IS COMING BACK.

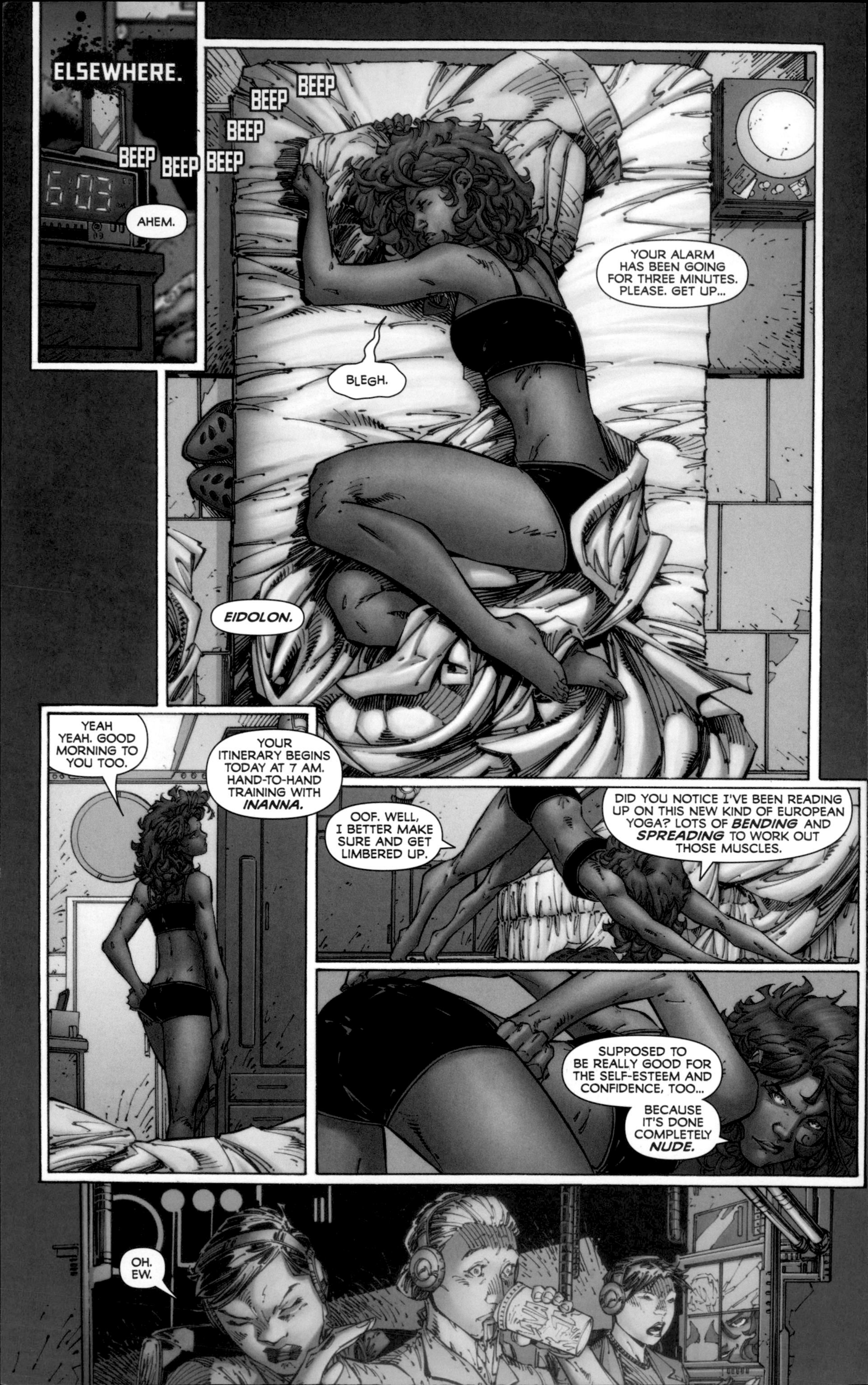
ELSEWHERE.
BEEP BEEP BEEP
BEEP BEEP BEEP
AHEM.
YOUR ALARM HAS BEEN GOING FOR THREE MINUTES. PLEASE. GET UP...
BLEGH.
EIDOLON.
YEAH YEAH. GOOD MORNING TO YOU TOO.
YOUR ITINERARY BEGINS TODAY AT 7 AM. HAND-TO-HAND TRAINING WITH *INANNA.*
OOF. WELL, I BETTER MAKE SURE AND GET LIMBERED UP.
DID YOU NOTICE I'VE BEEN READING UP ON THIS NEW KIND OF EUROPEAN YOGA? LOTS OF *BENDING* AND *SPREADING* TO WORK OUT THOSE MUSCLES.
SUPPOSED TO BE REALLY GOOD FOR THE SELF-ESTEEM AND CONFIDENCE, TOO...
BECAUSE IT'S DONE COMPLETELY *NUDE.*
OH. EW.

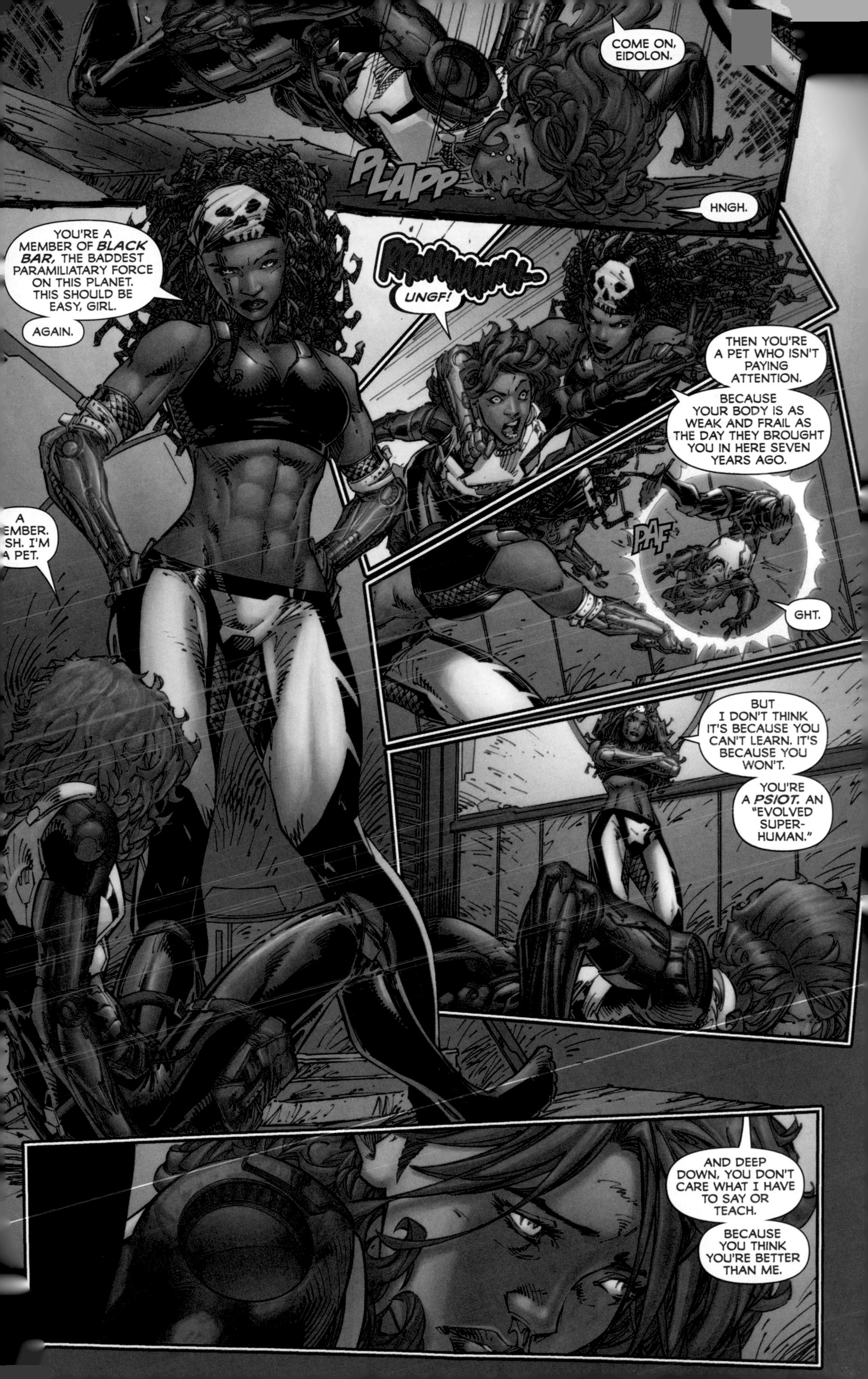
COME ON, EIDOLON.
PLAPP
HNGH.
YOU'RE A MEMBER OF BLACK BAR, THE BADDEST PARAMILIATARY FORCE ON THIS PLANET. THIS SHOULD BE EASY, GIRL.
AGAIN.
UNGF!
A EMBER. SH. I'M A PET.
THEN YOU'RE A PET WHO ISN'T PAYING ATTENTION.
BECAUSE YOUR BODY IS AS WEAK AND FRAIL AS THE DAY THEY BROUGHT YOU IN HERE SEVEN YEARS AGO.
PAF
GHT.
BUT I DON'T THINK IT'S BECAUSE YOU CAN'T LEARN. IT'S BECAUSE YOU WON'T.
YOU'RE A PSIOT. AN "EVOLVED SUPER-HUMAN."
AND DEEP DOWN, YOU DON'T CARE WHAT I HAVE TO SAY OR TEACH.
BECAUSE YOU THINK YOU'RE BETTER THAN ME.

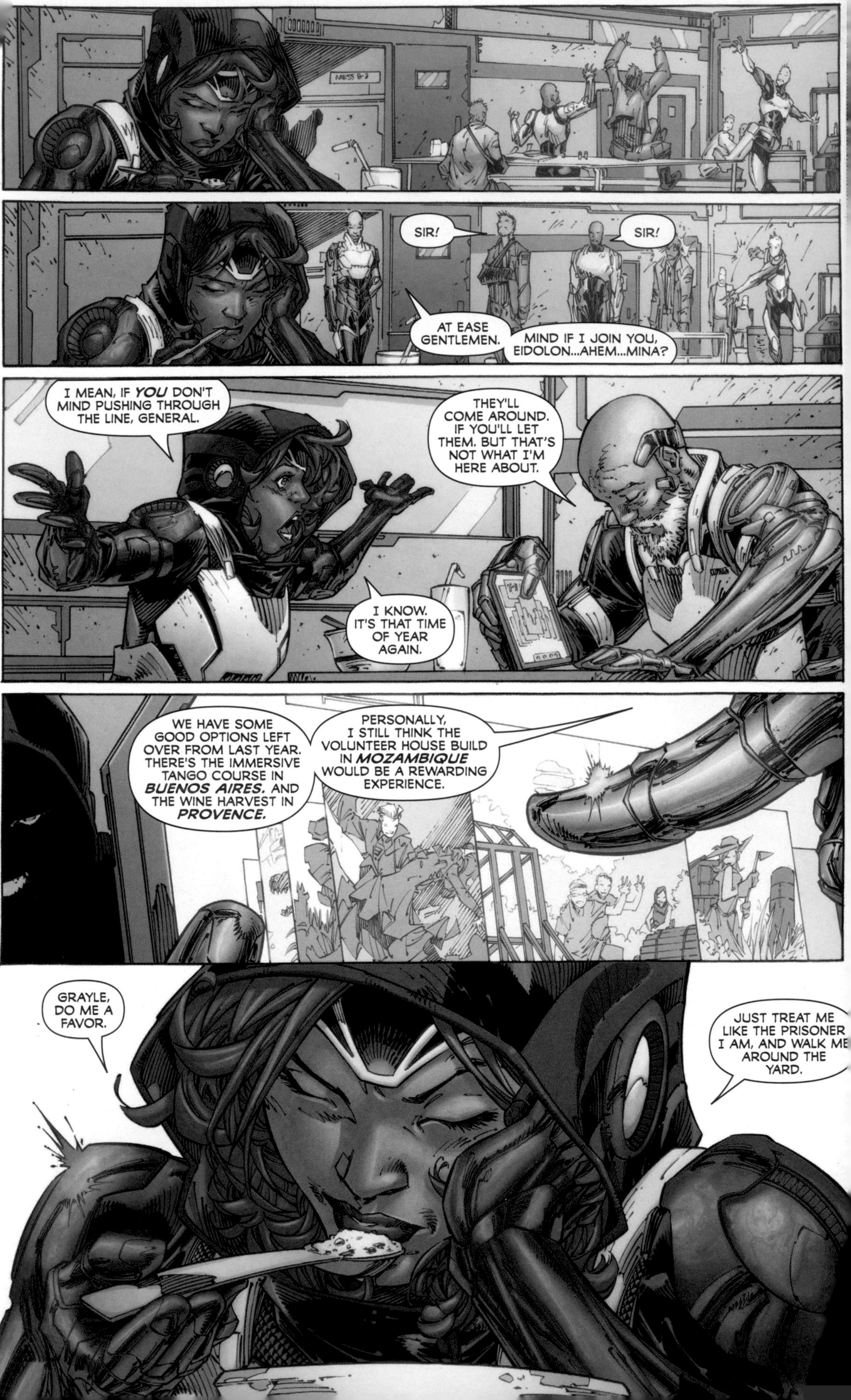
MESS B-2
SIR!
SIR!
AT EASE GENTLEMEN.
MIND IF I JOIN YOU, EIDOLON...AHEM...MINA?
I MEAN, IF YOU DON'T MIND PUSHING THROUGH THE LINE, GENERAL.
THEY'LL COME AROUND. IF YOU'LL LET THEM. BUT THAT'S NOT WHAT I'M HERE ABOUT.
I KNOW. IT'S THAT TIME OF YEAR AGAIN.
WE HAVE SOME GOOD OPTIONS LEFT OVER FROM LAST YEAR. THERE'S THE IMMERSIVE TANGO COURSE IN BUENOS AIRES. AND THE WINE HARVEST IN PROVENCE.
PERSONALLY, I STILL THINK THE VOLUNTEER HOUSE BUILD IN MOZAMBIQUE WOULD BE A REWARDING EXPERIENCE.
GRAYLE, DO ME A FAVOR.
JUST TREAT ME LIKE THE PRISONER I AM, AND WALK ME AROUND THE YARD.

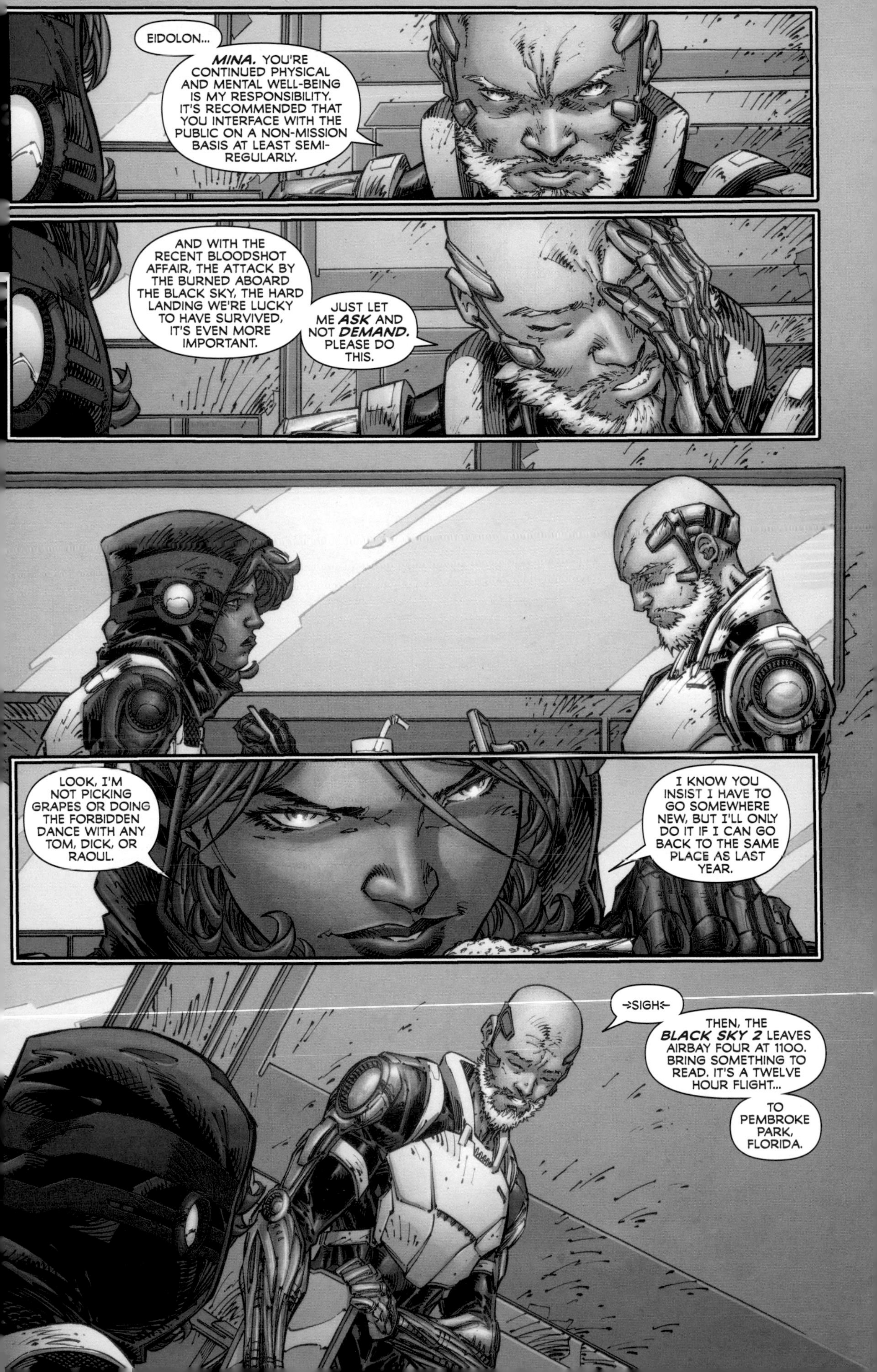
EIDOLON...
MINA. YOU'RE CONTINUED PHYSICAL AND MENTAL WELL-BEING IS MY RESPONSIBILITY. IT'S RECOMMENDED THAT YOU INTERFACE WITH THE PUBLIC ON A NON-MISSION BASIS AT LEAST SEMI-REGULARLY.
AND WITH THE RECENT BLOODSHOT AFFAIR, THE ATTACK BY THE BURNED ABOARD THE BLACK SKY, THE HARD LANDING WE'RE LUCKY TO HAVE SURVIVED, IT'S EVEN MORE IMPORTANT.
JUST LET ME ASK AND NOT DEMAND. PLEASE DO THIS.
LOOK, I'M NOT PICKING GRAPES OR DOING THE FORBIDDEN DANCE WITH ANY TOM, DICK, OR RAOUL.
I KNOW YOU INSIST I HAVE TO GO SOMEWHERE NEW, BUT I'LL ONLY DO IT IF I CAN GO BACK TO THE SAME PLACE AS LAST YEAR.
>SIGH<
THEN, THE BLACK SKY 2 LEAVES AIRBAY FOUR AT 1100. BRING SOMETHING TO READ. IT'S A TWELVE HOUR FLIGHT...
TO PEMBROKE PARK, FLORIDA.

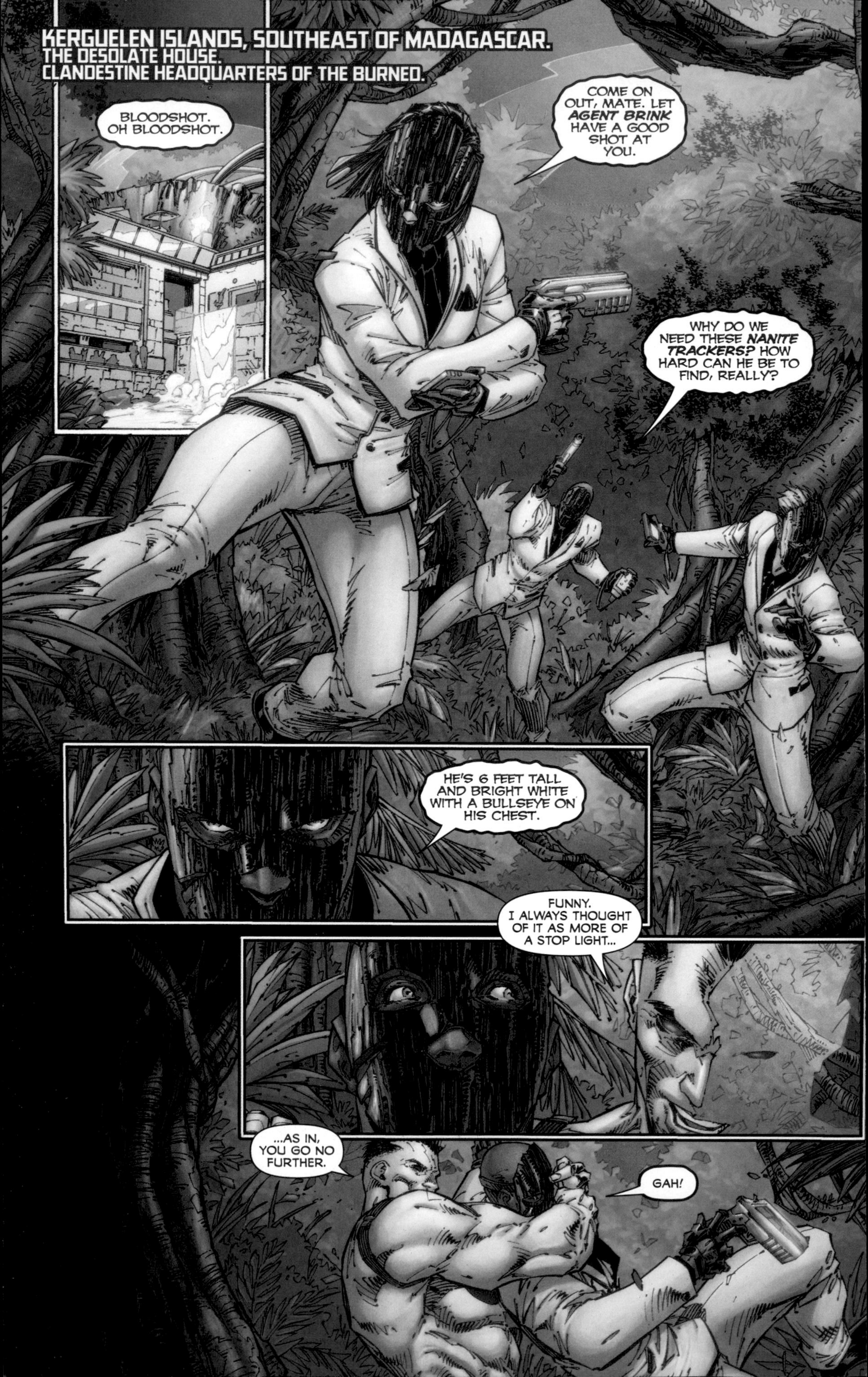
KERGUELEN ISLANDS, SOUTHEAST OF MADAGASCAR.
THE DESOLATE HOUSE.
CLANDESTINE HEADQUARTERS OF THE BURNED.
BLOODSHOT. OH BLOODSHOT.
COME ON OUT, MATE. LET AGENT BRINK HAVE A GOOD SHOT AT YOU.
WHY DO WE NEED THESE NANITE TRACKERS? HOW HARD CAN HE BE TO FIND, REALLY?
HE'S 6 FEET TALL AND BRIGHT WHITE WITH A BULLSEYE ON HIS CHEST.
FUNNY. I ALWAYS THOUGHT OF IT AS MORE OF A STOP LIGHT...
...AS IN, YOU GO NO FURTHER.
GAH!

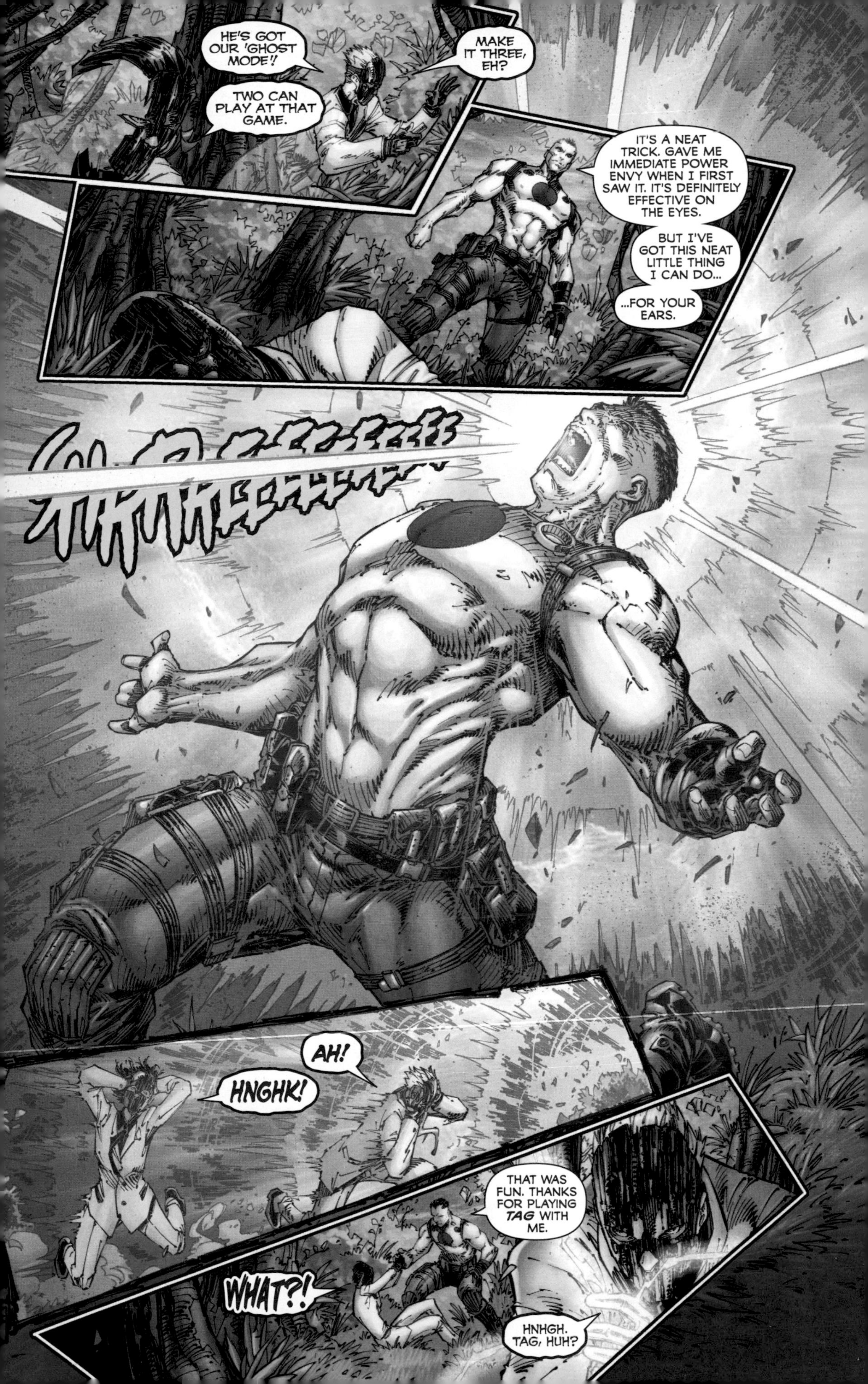
HE'S GOT OUR 'GHOST MODE'!
TWO CAN PLAY AT THAT GAME.
MAKE IT THREE, EH?
IT'S A NEAT TRICK. GAVE ME IMMEDIATE POWER ENVY WHEN I FIRST SAW IT. IT'S DEFINITELY EFFECTIVE ON THE EYES.
BUT I'VE GOT THIS NEAT LITTLE THING I CAN DO...
...FOR YOUR EARS.
AH!
HNGHK!
THAT WAS FUN. THANKS FOR PLAYING TAG WITH ME.
WHAT?!
HNHGH. TAG, HUH?

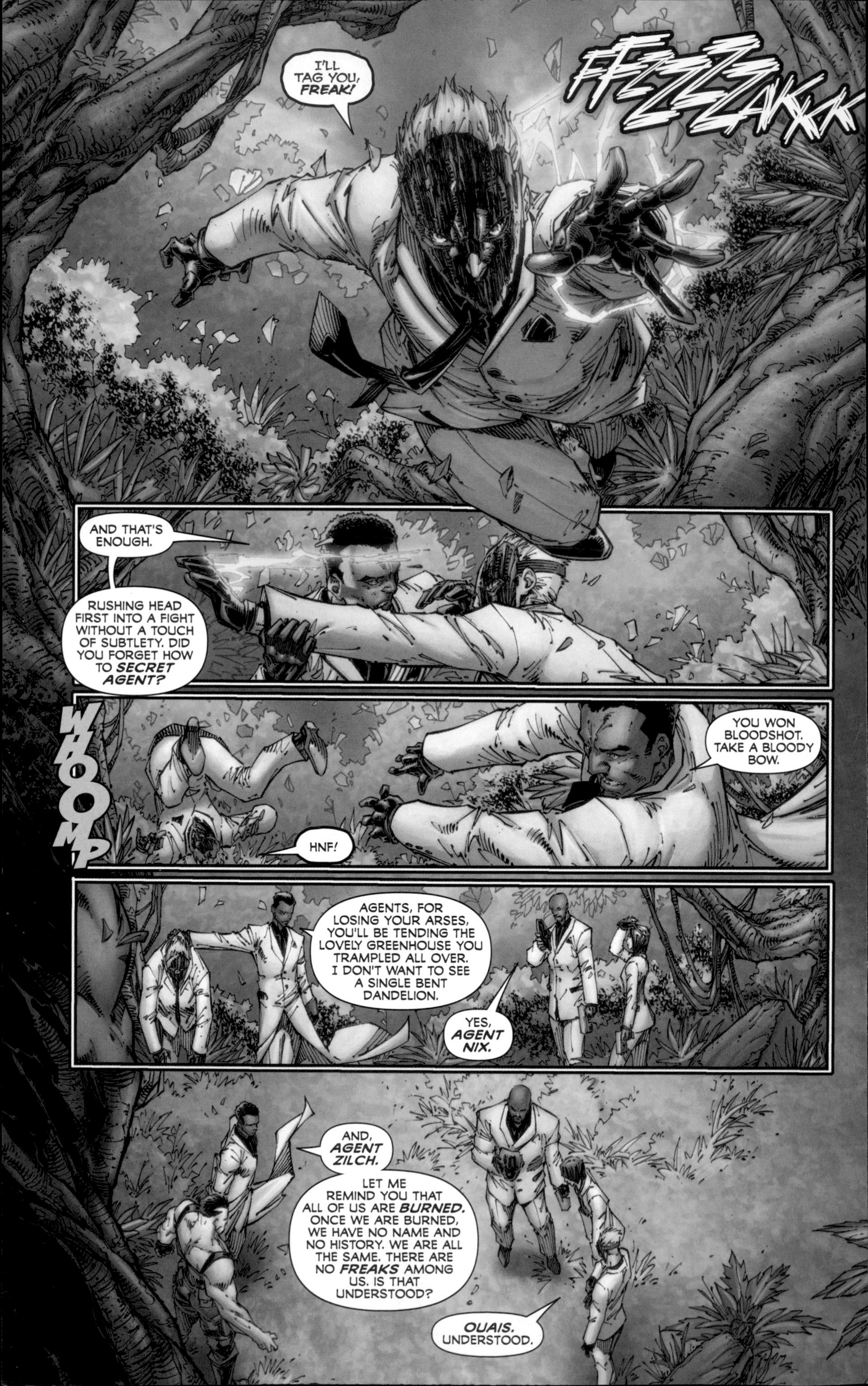

I'LL TAG YOU, FREAK!
FFFZZZAKKK
AND THAT'S ENOUGH.
RUSHING HEAD FIRST INTO A FIGHT WITHOUT A TOUCH OF SUBTLETY. DID YOU FORGET HOW TO SECRET AGENT?
WHOOMP
YOU WON BLOODSHOT. TAKE A BLOODY BOW.
HNF!
AGENTS, FOR LOSING YOUR ARSES, YOU'LL BE TENDING THE LOVELY GREENHOUSE YOU TRAMPLED ALL OVER. I DON'T WANT TO SEE A SINGLE BENT DANDELION.
YES, AGENT NIX.
AND, AGENT ZILCH.
LET ME REMIND YOU THAT ALL OF US ARE BURNED. ONCE WE ARE BURNED, WE HAVE NO NAME AND NO HISTORY. WE ARE ALL THE SAME. THERE ARE NO FREAKS AMONG US. IS THAT UNDERSTOOD?
OUAIS. UNDERSTOOD.

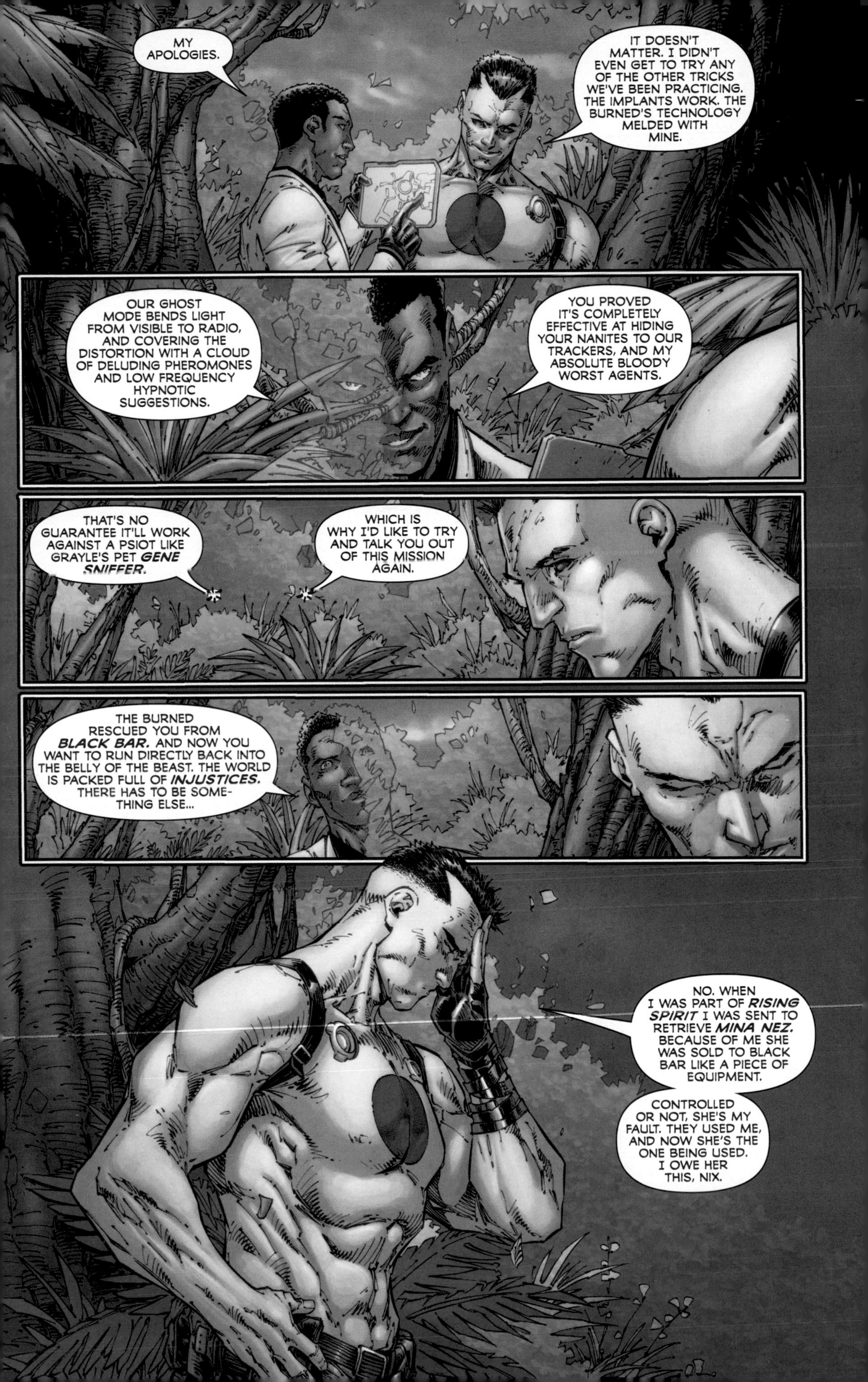
MY APOLOGIES.
IT DOESN'T MATTER. I DIDN'T EVEN GET TO TRY ANY OF THE OTHER TRICKS WE'VE BEEN PRACTICING. THE IMPLANTS WORK. THE BURNED'S TECHNOLOGY MELDED WITH MINE.
OUR GHOST MODE BENDS LIGHT FROM VISIBLE TO RADIO, AND COVERING THE DISTORTION WITH A CLOUD OF DELUDING PHEROMONES AND LOW FREQUENCY HYPNOTIC SUGGESTIONS.
YOU PROVED IT'S COMPLETELY EFFECTIVE AT HIDING YOUR NANITES TO OUR TRACKERS, AND MY ABSOLUTE BLOODY WORST AGENTS.
THAT'S NO GUARANTEE IT'LL WORK AGAINST A PSIOT LIKE GRAYLE'S PET GENE SNIFFER.
WHICH IS WHY I'D LIKE TO TRY AND TALK YOU OUT OF THIS MISSION AGAIN.
THE BURNED RESCUED YOU FROM BLACK BAR. AND NOW YOU WANT TO RUN DIRECTLY BACK INTO THE BELLY OF THE BEAST. THE WORLD IS PACKED FULL OF INJUSTICES. THERE HAS TO BE SOME-THING ELSE...
NO. WHEN I WAS PART OF RISING SPIRIT I WAS SENT TO RETRIEVE MINA NEZ. BECAUSE OF ME SHE WAS SOLD TO BLACK BAR LIKE A PIECE OF EQUIPMENT.
CONTROLLED OR NOT, SHE'S MY FAULT. THEY USED ME, AND NOW SHE'S THE ONE BEING USED. I OWE HER THIS, NIX.

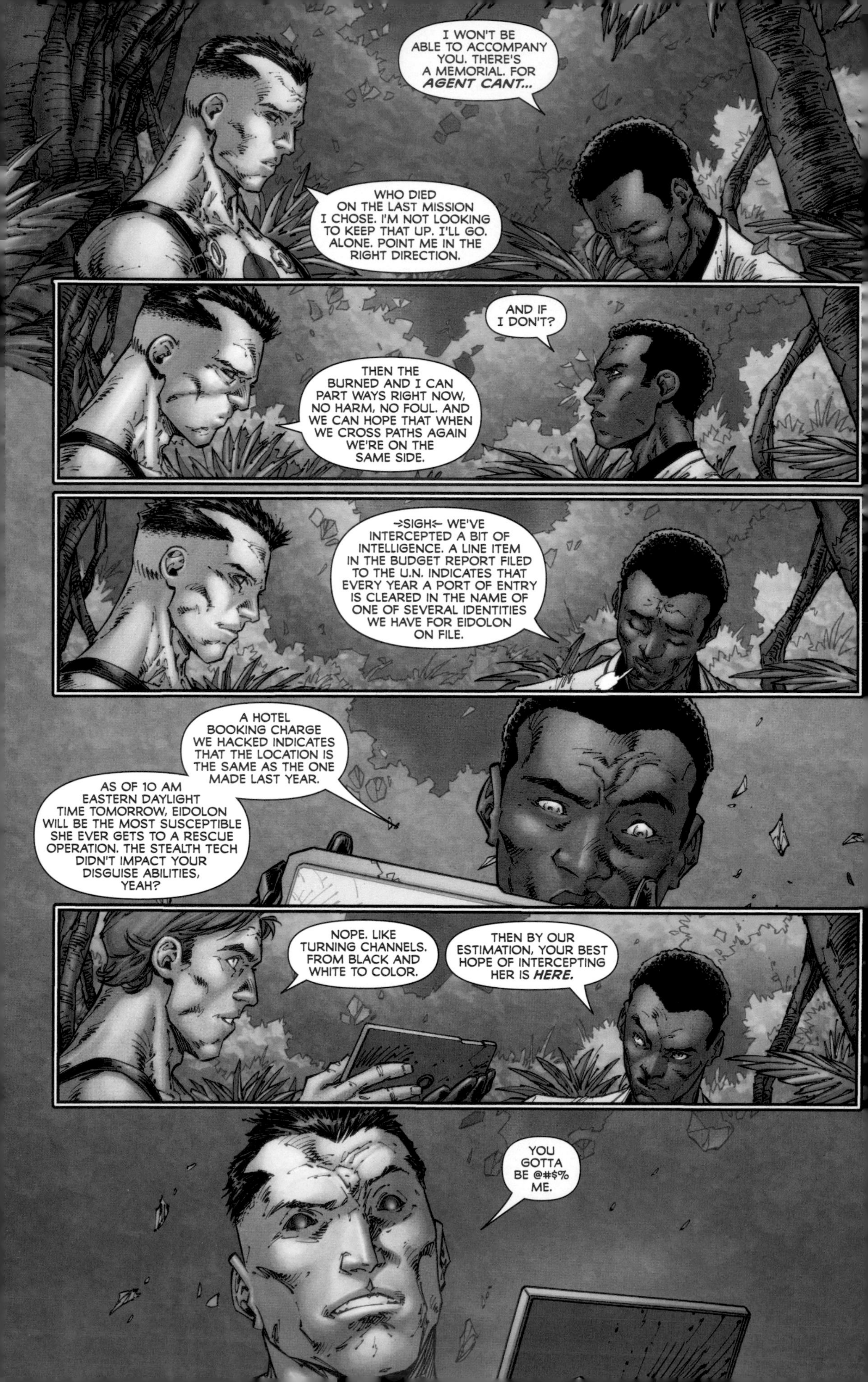
I WON'T BE ABLE TO ACCOMPANY YOU. THERE'S A MEMORIAL. FOR *AGENT CANT...*
WHO DIED ON THE LAST MISSION I CHOSE. I'M NOT LOOKING TO KEEP THAT UP. I'LL GO. ALONE. POINT ME IN THE RIGHT DIRECTION.
AND IF I DON'T?
THEN THE BURNED AND I CAN PART WAYS RIGHT NOW, NO HARM, NO FOUL. AND WE CAN HOPE THAT WHEN WE CROSS PATHS AGAIN WE'RE ON THE SAME SIDE.
➔SIGH← WE'VE INTERCEPTED A BIT OF INTELLIGENCE. A LINE ITEM IN THE BUDGET REPORT FILED TO THE U.N. INDICATES THAT EVERY YEAR A PORT OF ENTRY IS CLEARED IN THE NAME OF ONE OF SEVERAL IDENTITIES WE HAVE FOR EIDOLON ON FILE.
A HOTEL BOOKING CHARGE WE HACKED INDICATES THAT THE LOCATION IS THE SAME AS THE ONE MADE LAST YEAR.
AS OF 10 AM EASTERN DAYLIGHT TIME TOMORROW, EIDOLON WILL BE THE MOST SUSCEPTIBLE SHE EVER GETS TO A RESCUE OPERATION. THE STEALTH TECH DIDN'T IMPACT YOUR DISGUISE ABILITIES, YEAH?
NOPE. LIKE TURNING CHANNELS. FROM BLACK AND WHITE TO COLOR.
THEN BY OUR ESTIMATION, YOUR BEST HOPE OF INTERCEPTING HER IS *HERE.*
YOU GOTTA BE @#$% ME.

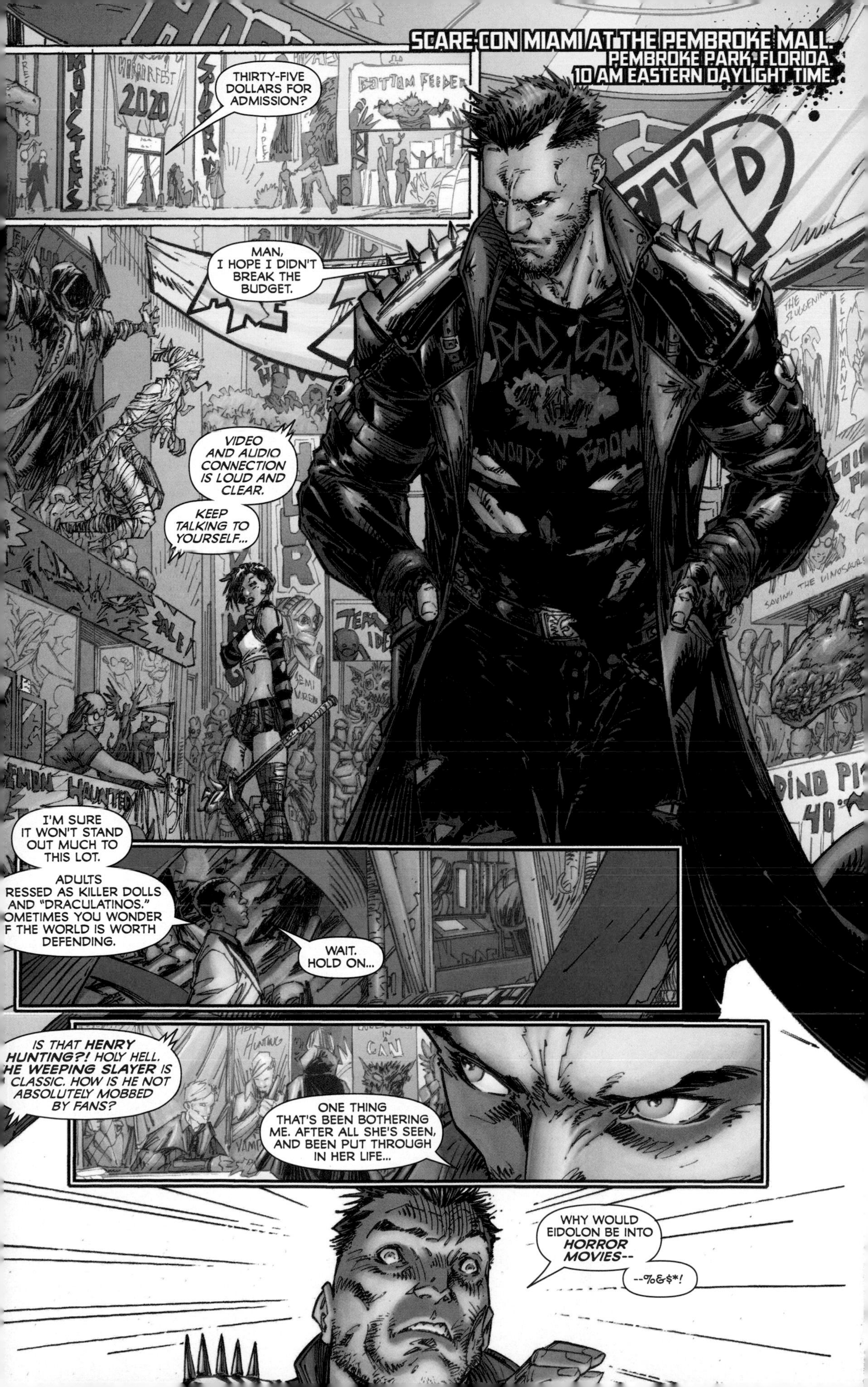
SCARE-CON MIAMI AT THE PEMBROKE MALL.
PEMBROKE PARK, FLORIDA.
10 AM EASTERN DAYLIGHT TIME.
THIRTY-FIVE DOLLARS FOR ADMISSION?
MAN, I HOPE I DIDN'T BREAK THE BUDGET.
VIDEO AND AUDIO CONNECTION IS LOUD AND CLEAR.
KEEP TALKING TO YOURSELF...
I'M SURE IT WON'T STAND OUT MUCH TO THIS LOT.
ADULTS RESSED AS KILLER DOLLS AND "DRACULATINOS." OMETIMES YOU WONDER F THE WORLD IS WORTH DEFENDING.
WAIT. HOLD ON...
IS THAT HENRY HUNTING?! HOLY HELL. HE WEEPING SLAYER IS CLASSIC. HOW IS HE NOT ABSOLUTELY MOBBED BY FANS?
ONE THING THAT'S BEEN BOTHERING ME. AFTER ALL SHE'S SEEN, AND BEEN PUT THROUGH IN HER LIFE...
WHY WOULD EIDOLON BE INTO HORROR MOVIES--
--%&$*!

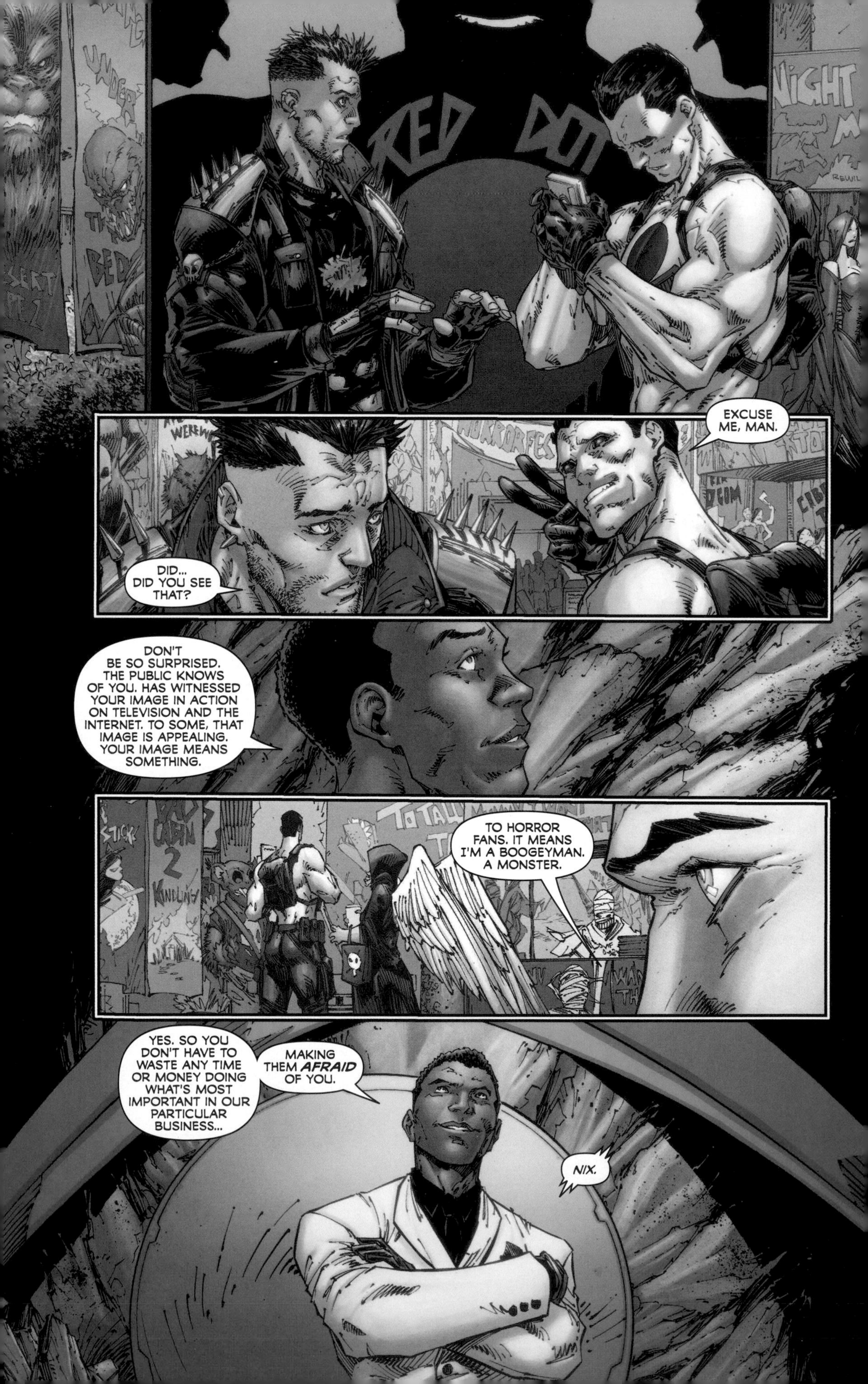
EXCUSE ME, MAN.
DID... DID YOU SEE THAT?
DON'T BE SO SURPRISED. THE PUBLIC KNOWS OF YOU. HAS WITNESSED YOUR IMAGE IN ACTION ON TELEVISION AND THE INTERNET. TO SOME, THAT IMAGE IS APPEALING. YOUR IMAGE MEANS SOMETHING.
TO HORROR FANS. IT MEANS I'M A BOOGEYMAN. A MONSTER.
YES. SO YOU DON'T HAVE TO WASTE ANY TIME OR MONEY DOING WHAT'S MOST IMPORTANT IN OUR PARTICULAR BUSINESS...
MAKING THEM *AFRAID* OF YOU.
NIX.

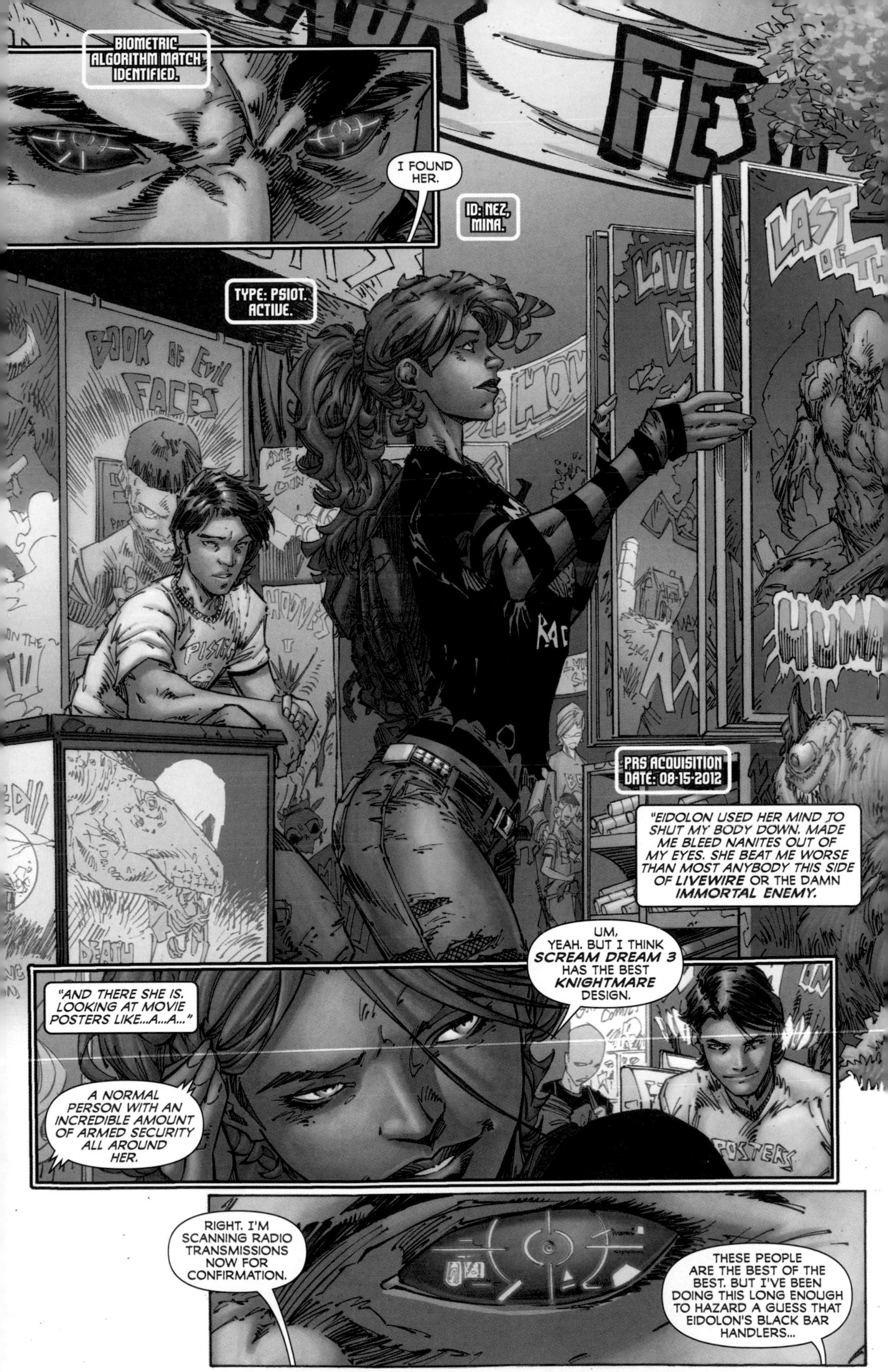
BIOMETRIC ALGORITHM MATCH IDENTIFIED.
I FOUND HER.
ID: NEZ, MINA.
TYPE: PSIOT. ACTIVE.
PRS ACQUISITION DATE: 08-15-2012
"EIDOLON USED HER MIND TO SHUT MY BODY DOWN. MADE ME BLEED NANITES OUT OF MY EYES. SHE BEAT ME WORSE THAN MOST ANYBODY THIS SIDE OF LIVEWIRE OR THE DAMN IMMORTAL ENEMY.
UM, YEAH. BUT I THINK SCREAM DREAM 3 HAS THE BEST KNIGHTMARE DESIGN.
"AND THERE SHE IS. LOOKING AT MOVIE POSTERS LIKE...A...A..."
A NORMAL PERSON WITH AN INCREDIBLE AMOUNT OF ARMED SECURITY ALL AROUND HER.
RIGHT. I'M SCANNING RADIO TRANSMISSIONS NOW FOR CONFIRMATION.
THESE PEOPLE ARE THE BEST OF THE BEST. BUT I'VE BEEN DOING THIS LONG ENOUGH TO HAZARD A GUESS THAT EIDOLON'S BLACK BAR HANDLERS...

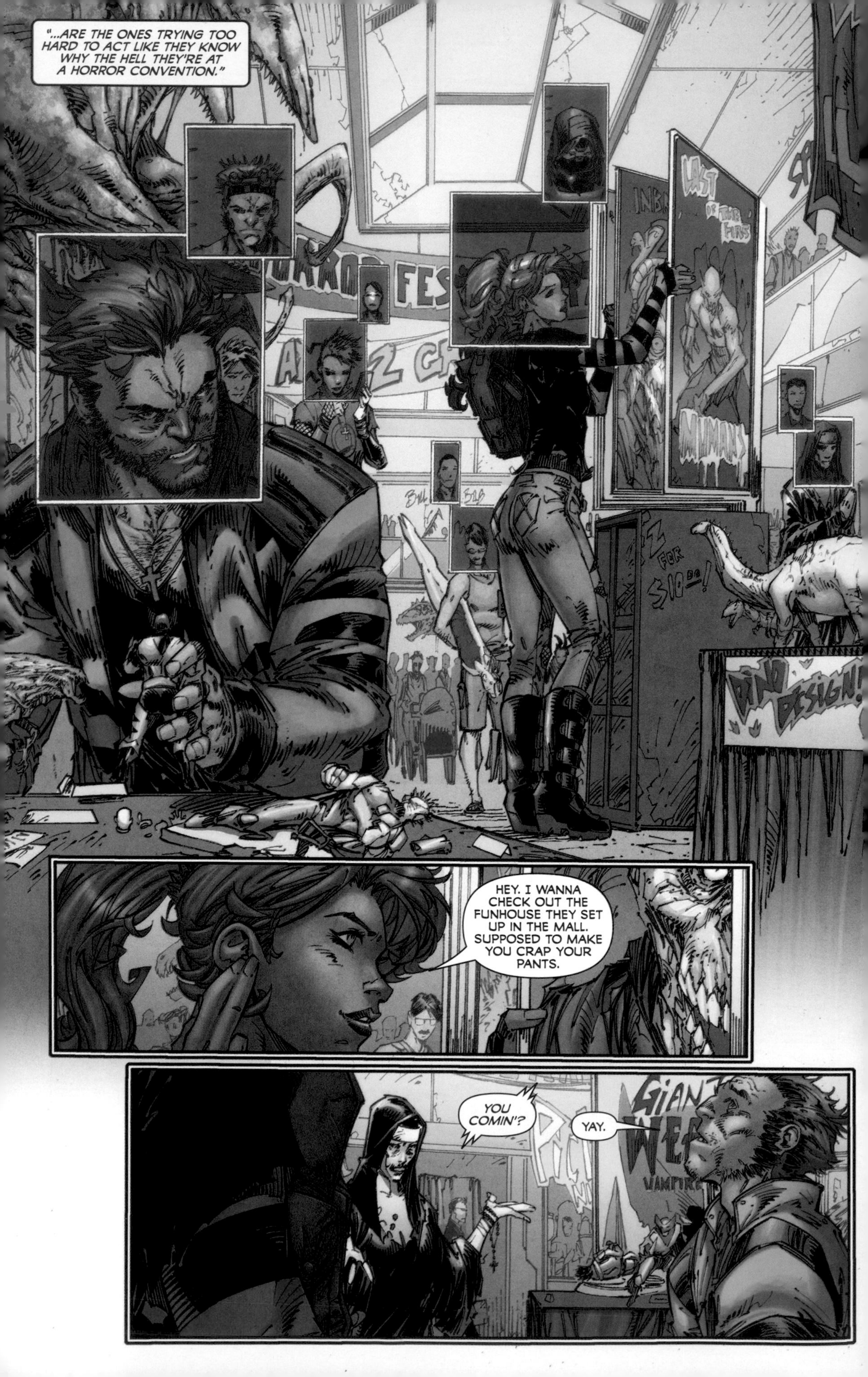
"...ARE THE ONES TRYING TOO HARD TO ACT LIKE THEY KNOW WHY THE HELL THEY'RE AT A HORROR CONVENTION."
HEY. I WANNA CHECK OUT THE FUNHOUSE THEY SET UP IN THE MALL. SUPPOSED TO MAKE YOU CRAP YOUR PANTS.
YOU COMIN'?
YAY.

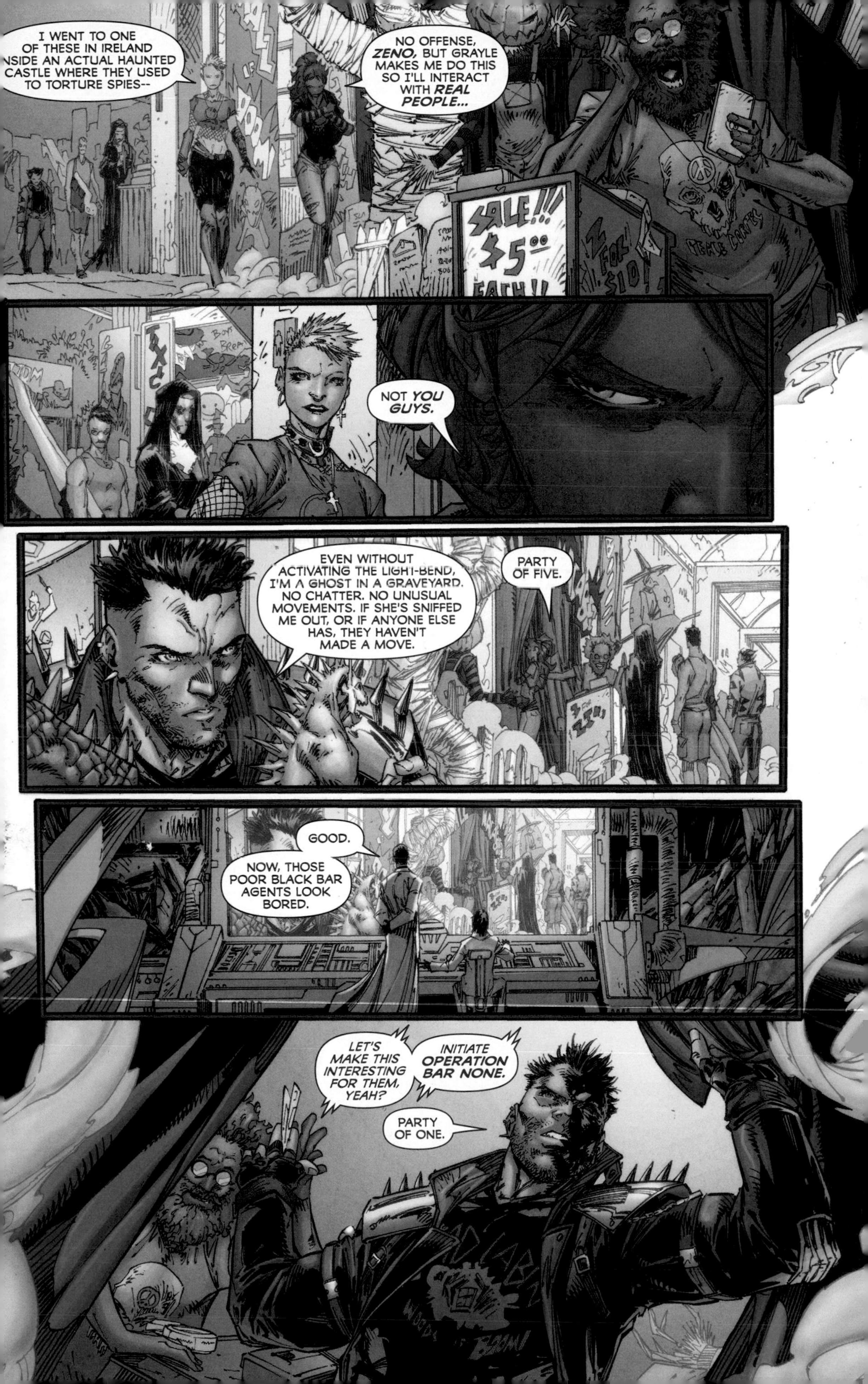
I WENT TO ONE OF THESE IN IRELAND INSIDE AN ACTUAL HAUNTED CASTLE WHERE THEY USED TO TORTURE SPIES--
NO OFFENSE, ZENO, BUT GRAYLE MAKES ME DO THIS SO I'LL INTERACT WITH REAL PEOPLE...
SALE!!! $5.00 EACH!!
2 FOR $10!
NOT YOU GUYS.
EVEN WITHOUT ACTIVATING THE LIGHT-BEND, I'M A GHOST IN A GRAVEYARD. NO CHATTER. NO UNUSUAL MOVEMENTS. IF SHE'S SNIFFED ME OUT, OR IF ANYONE ELSE HAS, THEY HAVEN'T MADE A MOVE.
PARTY OF FIVE.
GOOD.
NOW, THOSE POOR BLACK BAR AGENTS LOOK BORED.
LET'S MAKE THIS INTERESTING FOR THEM, YEAH?
INITIATE OPERATION BAR NONE.
PARTY OF ONE.

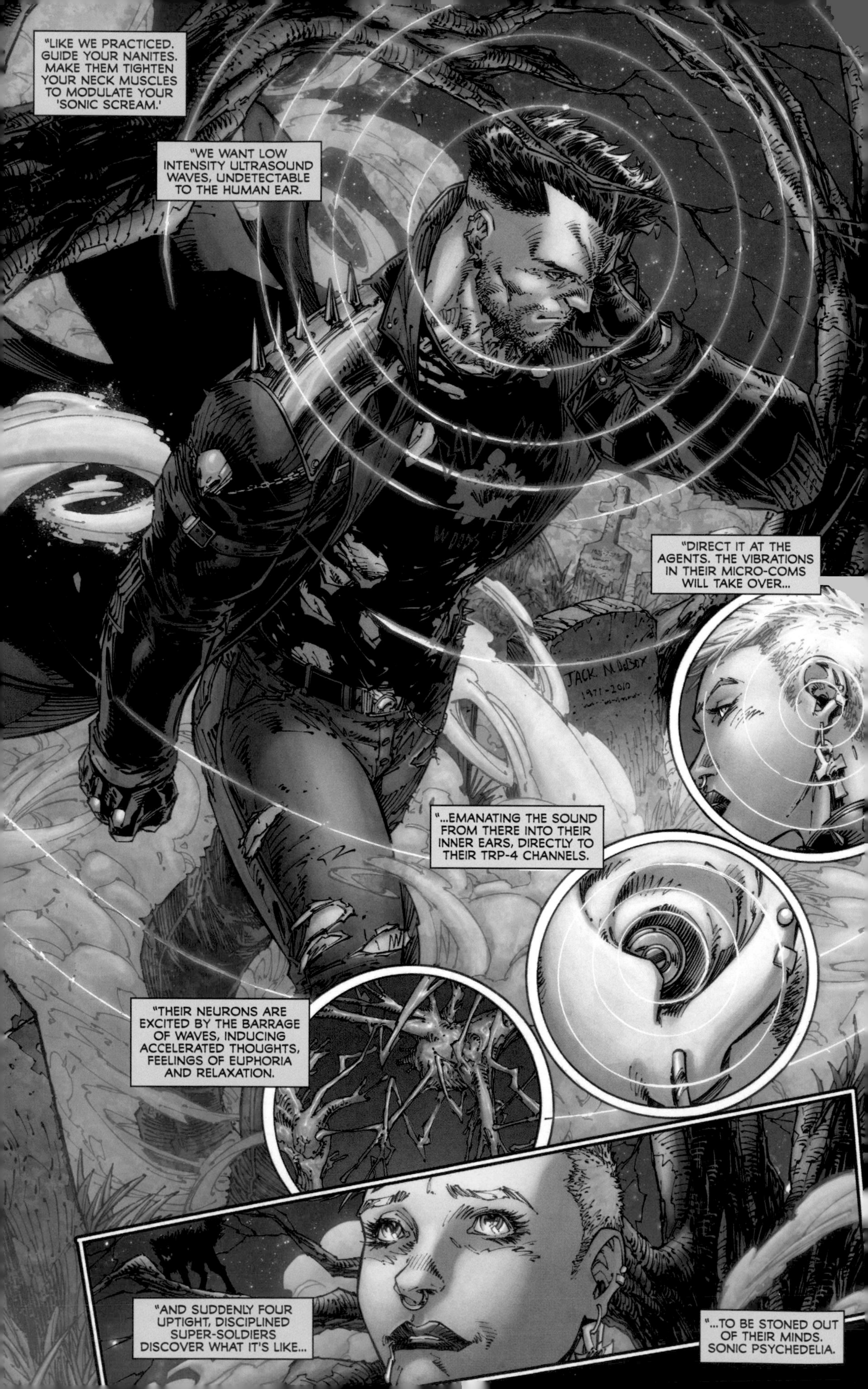
"LIKE WE PRACTICED. GUIDE YOUR NANITES. MAKE THEM TIGHTEN YOUR NECK MUSCLES TO MODULATE YOUR 'SONIC SCREAM.'
"WE WANT LOW INTENSITY ULTRASOUND WAVES, UNDETECTABLE TO THE HUMAN EAR.
"DIRECT IT AT THE AGENTS. THE VIBRATIONS IN THEIR MICRO-COMS WILL TAKE OVER...
"...EMANATING THE SOUND FROM THERE INTO THEIR INNER EARS, DIRECTLY TO THEIR TRP-4 CHANNELS.
"THEIR NEURONS ARE EXCITED BY THE BARRAGE OF WAVES, INDUCING ACCELERATED THOUGHTS, FEELINGS OF EUPHORIA AND RELAXATION.
"AND SUDDENLY FOUR UPTIGHT, DISCIPLINED SUPER-SOLDIERS DISCOVER WHAT IT'S LIKE...
"...TO BE STONED OUT OF THEIR MINDS. SONIC PSYCHEDELIA.

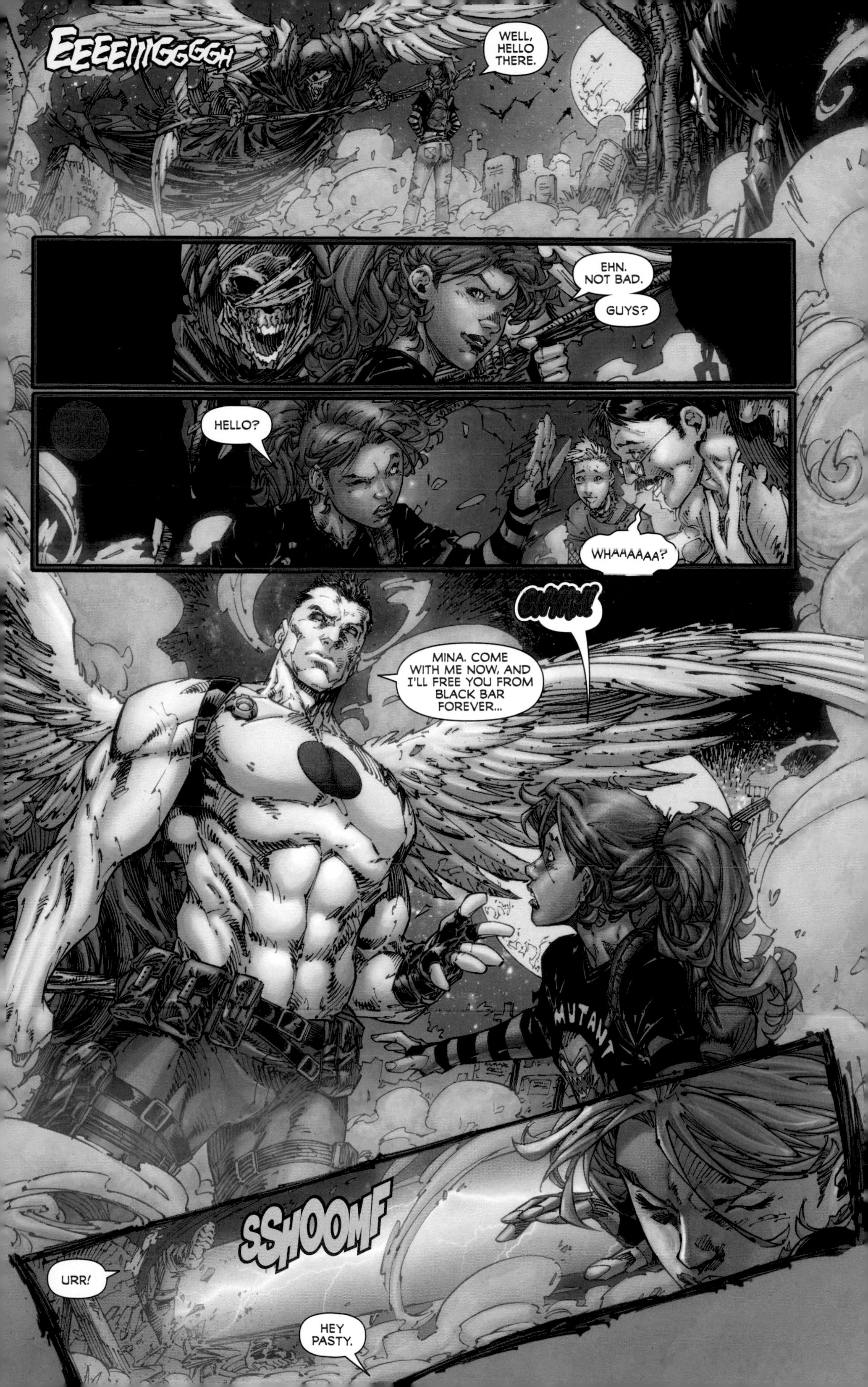
EEEEIIIGGGGH
WELL, HELLO THERE.
EHN. NOT BAD.
GUYS?
HELLO?
WHAAAAAA?
MINA. COME WITH ME NOW, AND I'LL FREE YOU FROM BLACK BAR FOREVER...
SSHOOMF
URR!
HEY PASTY.

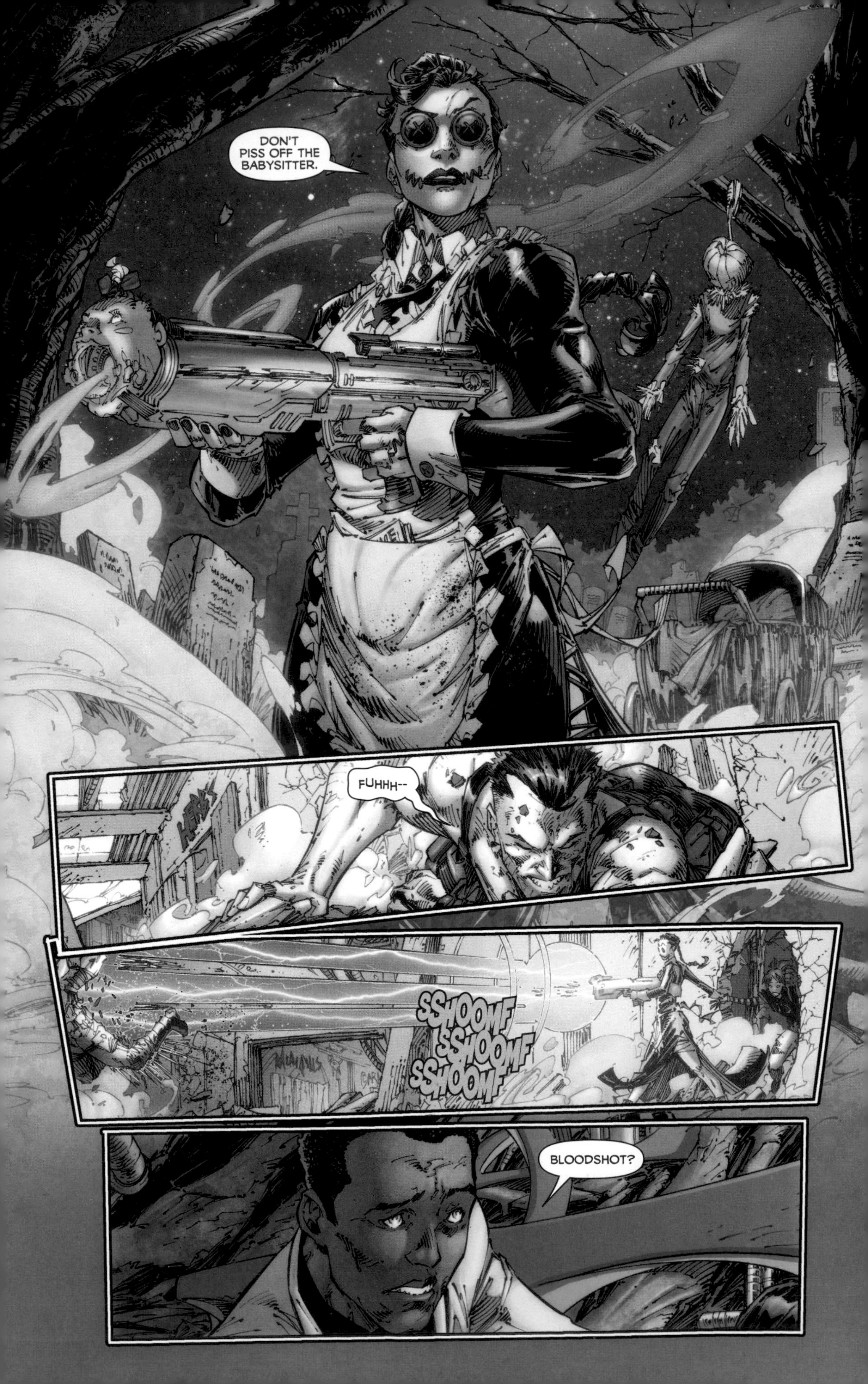
DON'T PISS OFF THE BABYSITTER.
FUHHH--
SSHOOMF SSHOOMF SSHOOMF
BLOODSHOT?

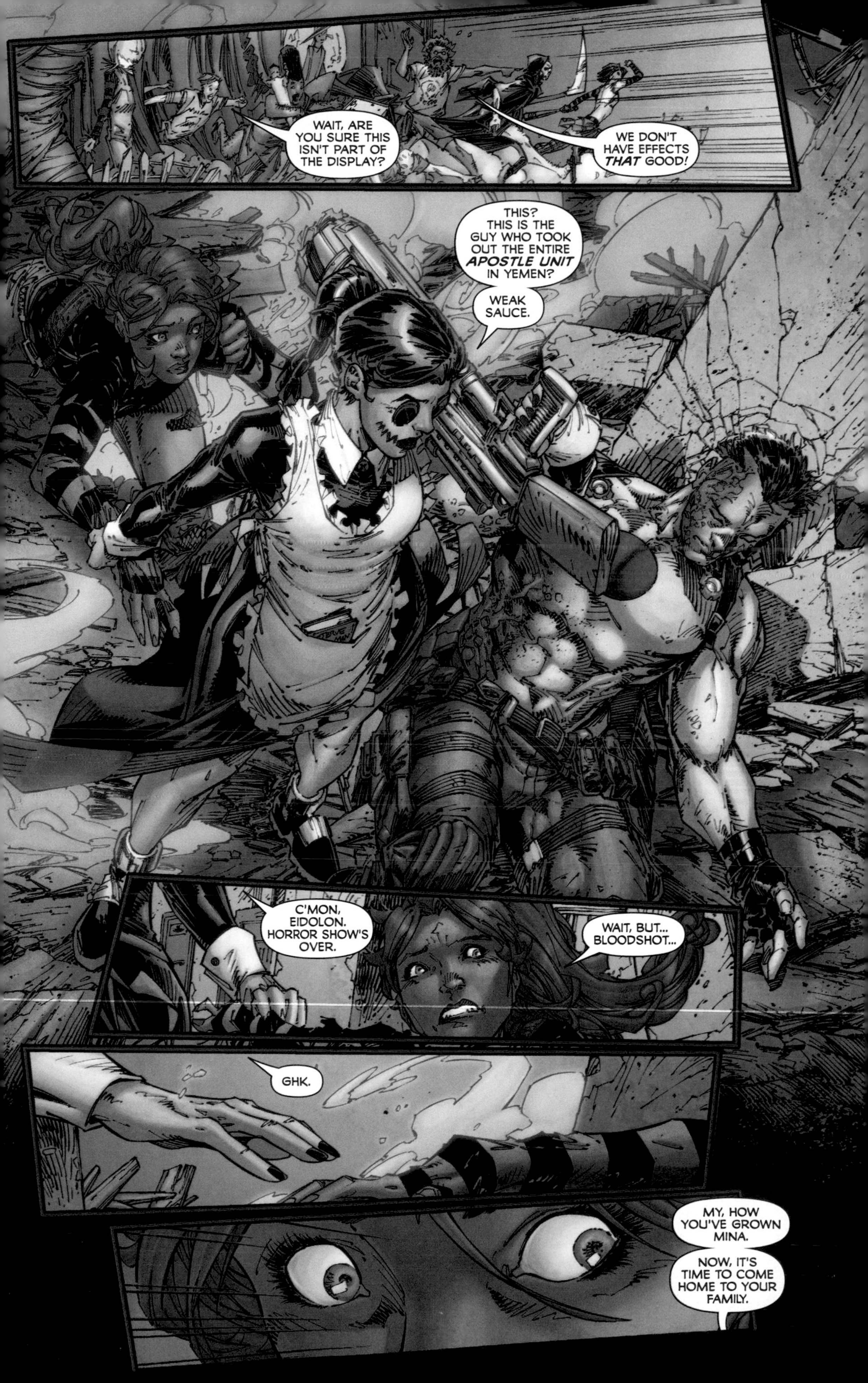
WAIT, ARE YOU SURE THIS ISN'T PART OF THE DISPLAY?
WE DON'T HAVE EFFECTS *THAT* GOOD!
THIS? THIS IS THE GUY WHO TOOK OUT THE ENTIRE ***APOSTLE UNIT*** IN YEMEN?
WEAK SAUCE.
C'MON, EIDOLON. HORROR SHOW'S OVER.
WAIT, BUT... BLOODSHOT...
GHK.
MY, HOW YOU'VE GROWN MINA.
NOW, IT'S TIME TO COME HOME TO YOUR FAMILY.

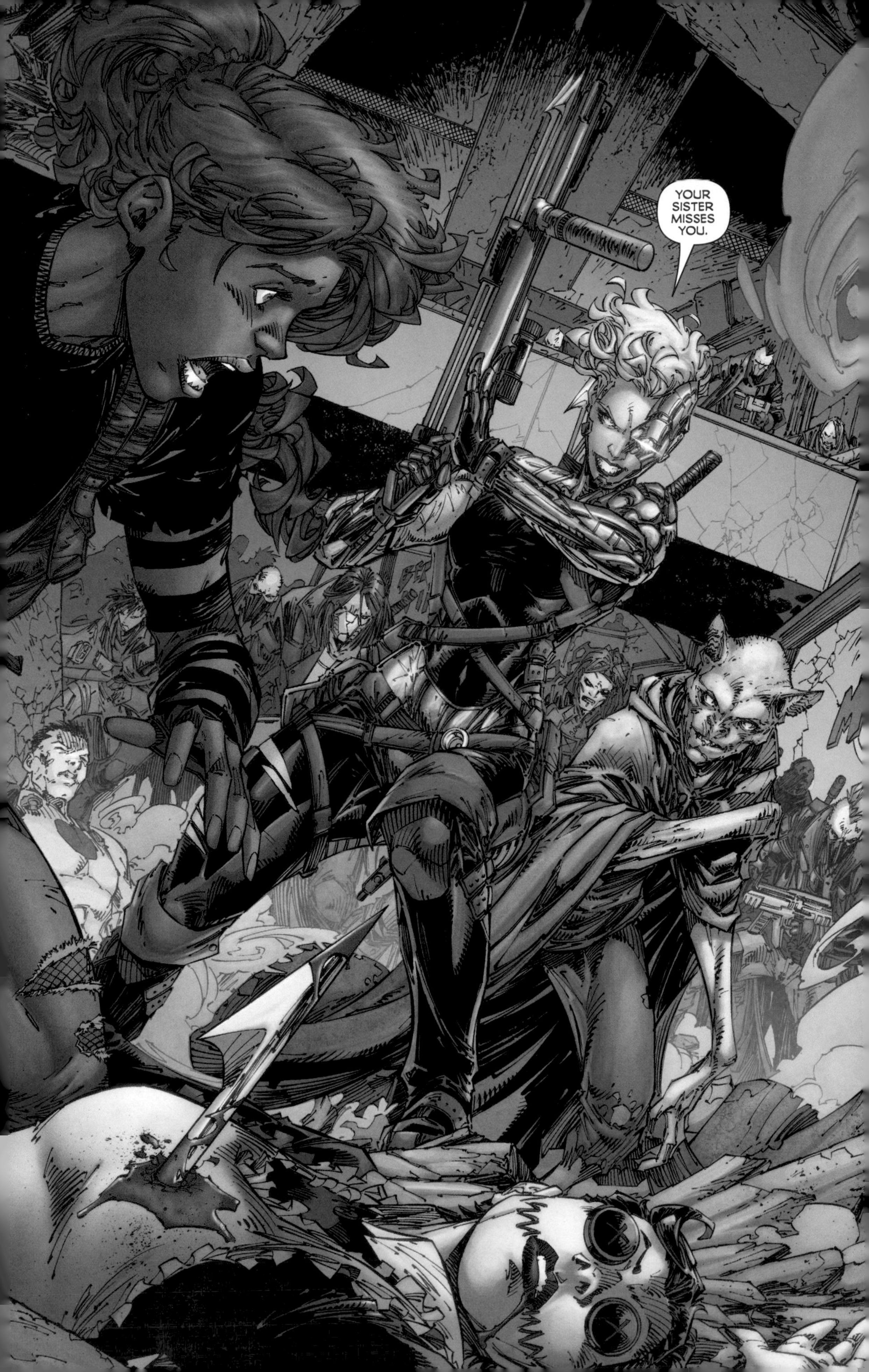
YOUR SISTER MISSES YOU.

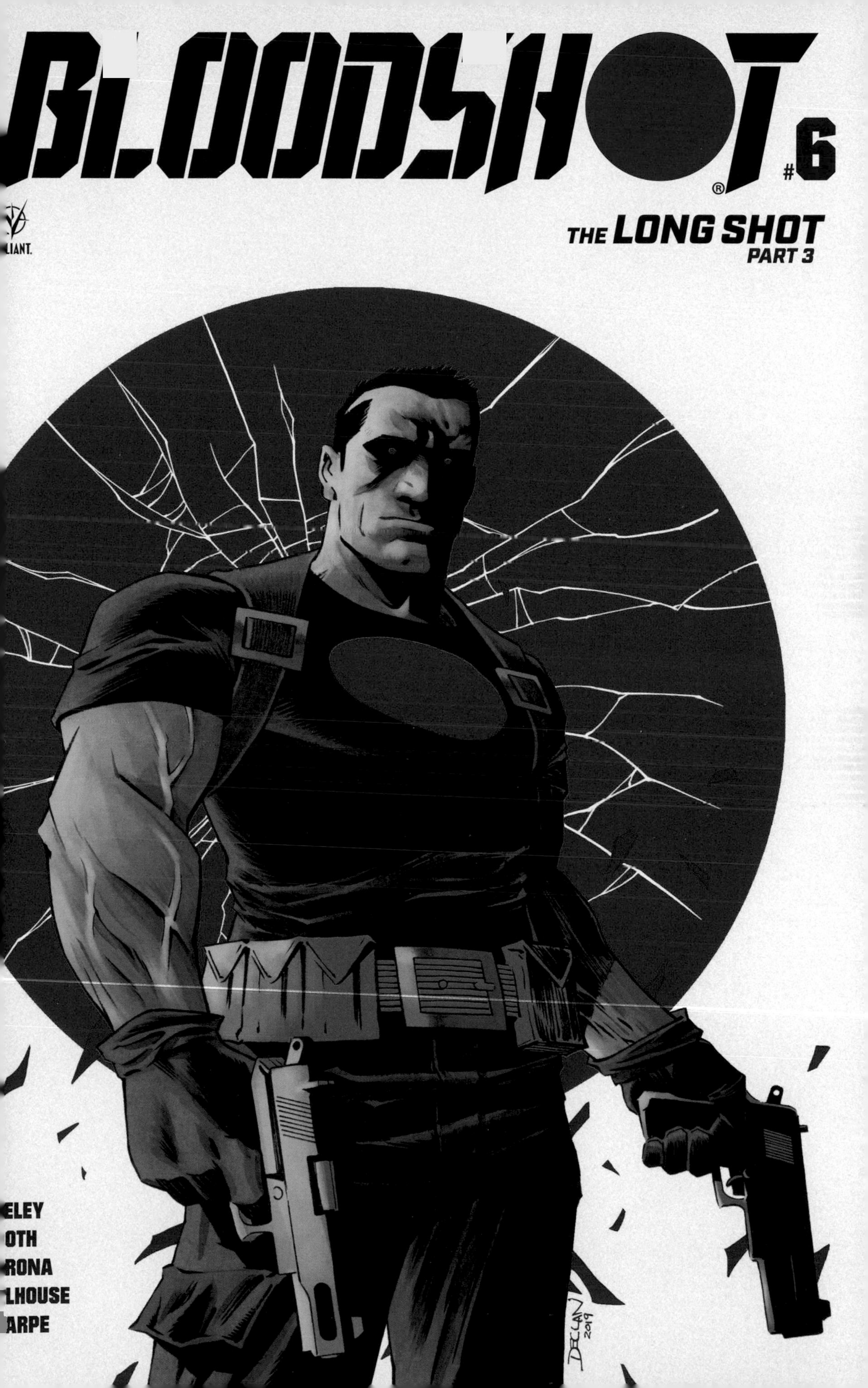
BLOODSHOT
#6
THE LONG SHOT
PART 3

THE LONG SHOT, PART 3

BLOODSHOT #6
WRITER: Tim Seeley
ARTIST: Brett Booth
INKER: Adelso Corona
COLORIST: Andrew Dalhouse
LETTERS: Dave Sharpe
COVER ARTIST: Declan Shalvey
ASSISTANT EDITOR:
Drew Baumgartner
EDITOR: Lysa Hawkins

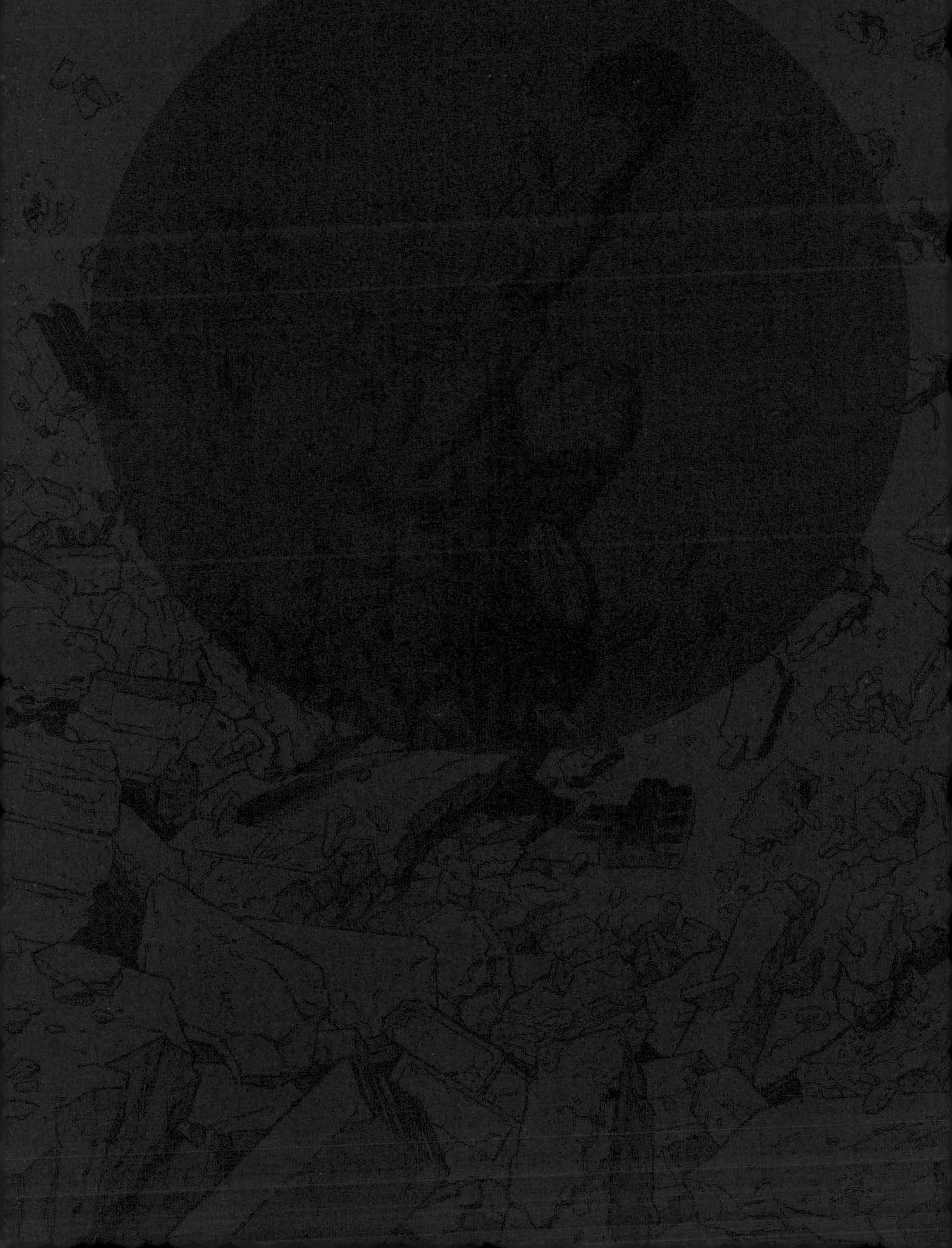

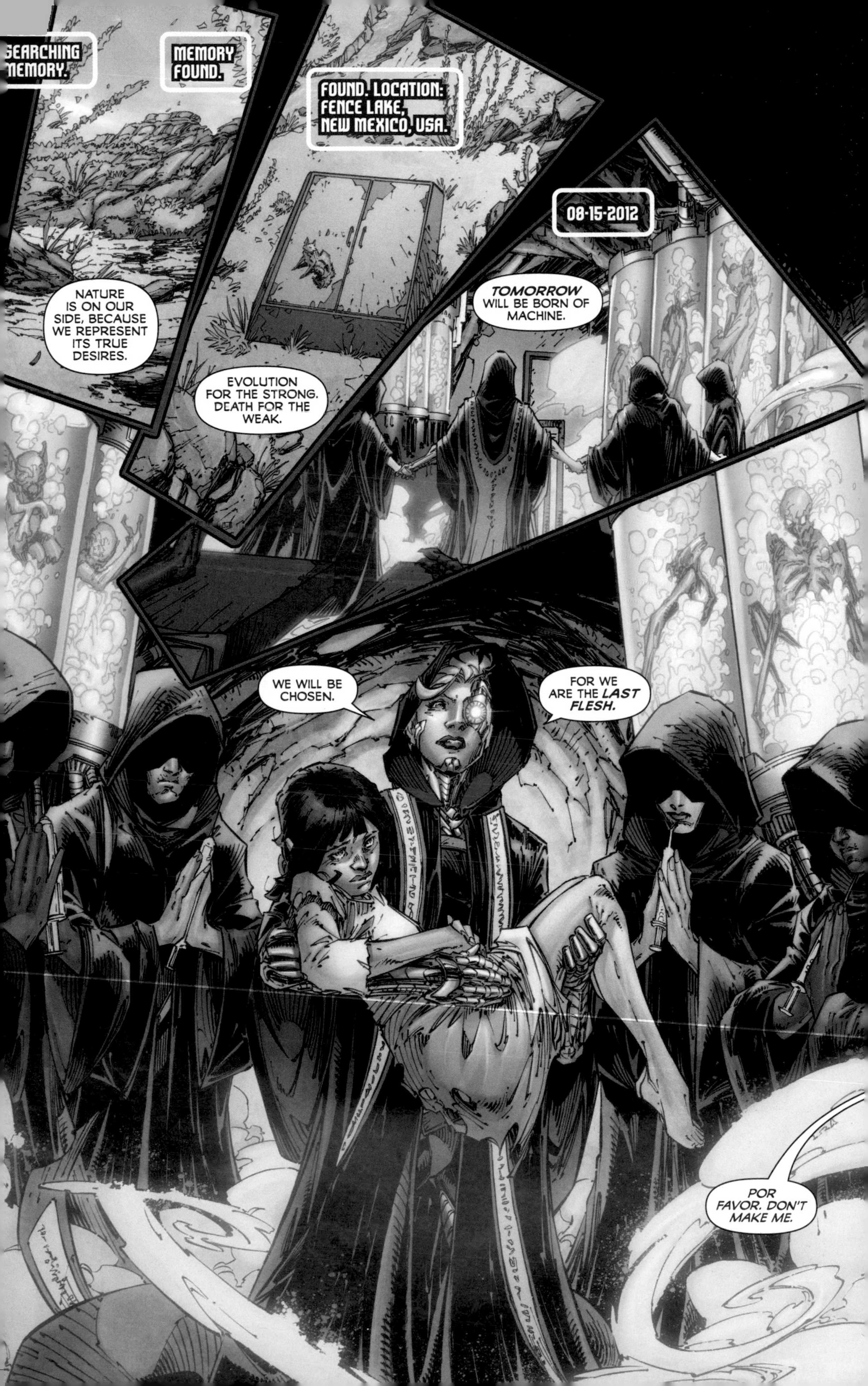
SEARCHING MEMORY.
MEMORY FOUND.
FOUND. LOCATION: FENCE LAKE, NEW MEXICO, USA.
NATURE IS ON OUR SIDE, BECAUSE WE REPRESENT ITS TRUE DESIRES.
EVOLUTION FOR THE STRONG. DEATH FOR THE WEAK.
08-15-2012
TOMORROW WILL BE BORN OF MACHINE.
WE WILL BE CHOSEN.
FOR WE ARE THE LAST FLESH.
POR FAVOR. DON'T MAKE ME.

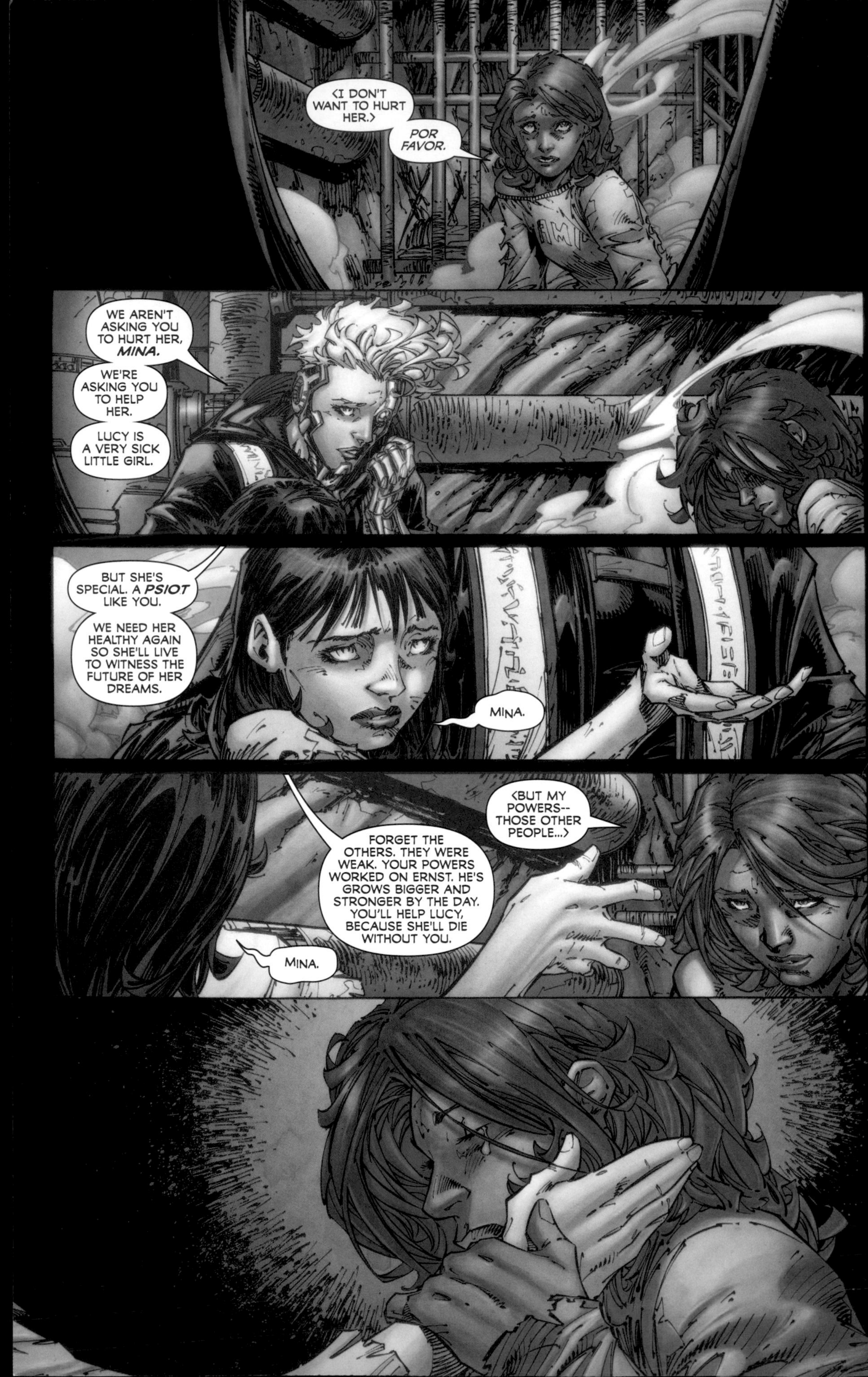

<I DON'T WANT TO HURT HER.>
POR FAVOR.
WE AREN'T ASKING YOU TO HURT HER, MINA.
WE'RE ASKING YOU TO HELP HER.
LUCY IS A VERY SICK LITTLE GIRL.
BUT SHE'S SPECIAL. A PSIOT LIKE YOU.
WE NEED HER HEALTHY AGAIN SO SHE'LL LIVE TO WITNESS THE FUTURE OF HER DREAMS.
MINA.
<BUT MY POWERS-- THOSE OTHER PEOPLE...>
FORGET THE OTHERS. THEY WERE WEAK. YOUR POWERS WORKED ON ERNST. HE'S GROWS BIGGER AND STRONGER BY THE DAY. YOU'LL HELP LUCY, BECAUSE SHE'LL DIE WITHOUT YOU.
MINA.

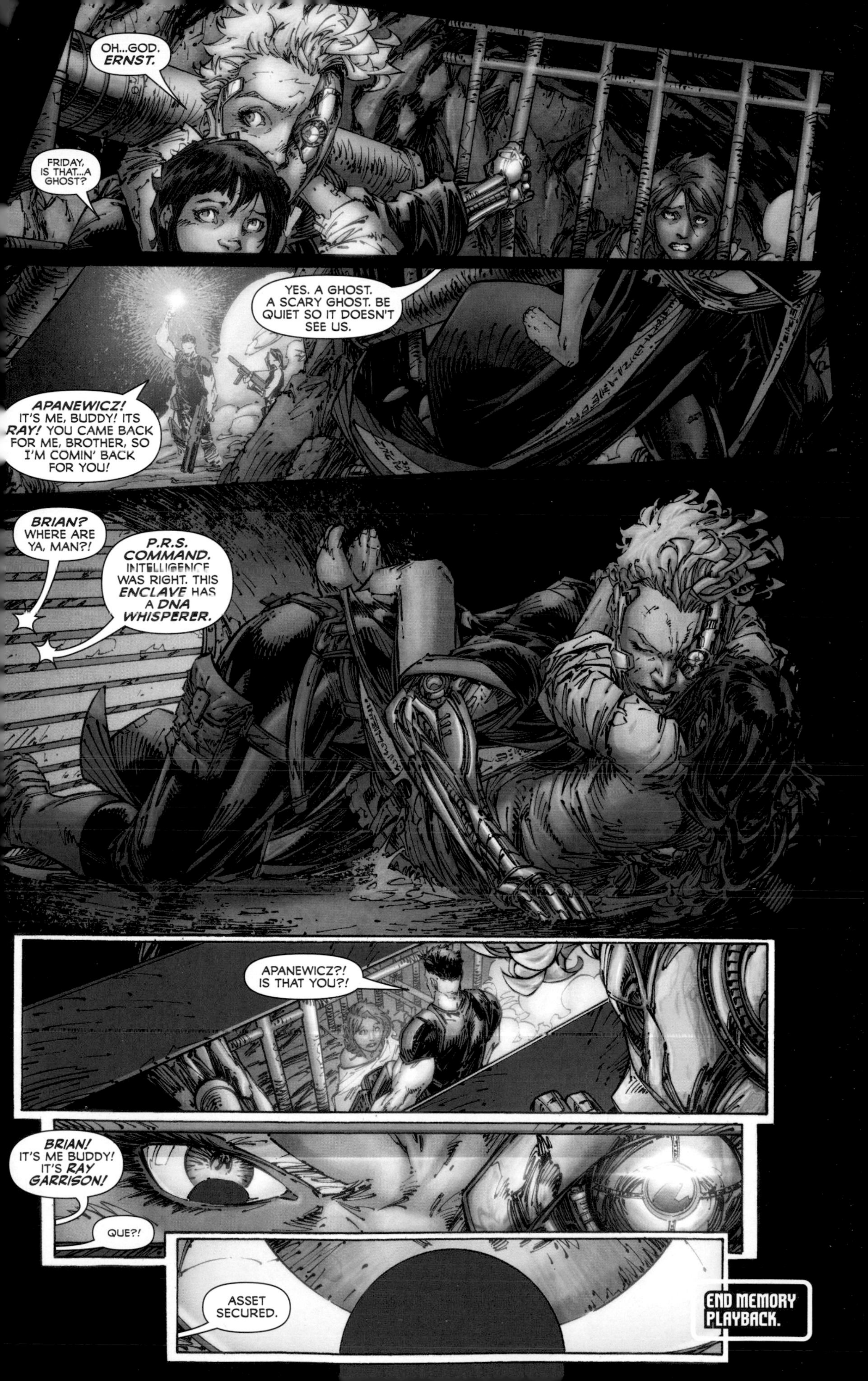
OH...GOD. ERNST.
FRIDAY, IS THAT...A GHOST?
YES. A GHOST. A SCARY GHOST. BE QUIET SO IT DOESN'T SEE US.
APANEWICZ! IT'S ME, BUDDY! ITS RAY! YOU CAME BACK FOR ME, BROTHER, SO I'M COMIN' BACK FOR YOU!
BRIAN? WHERE ARE YA, MAN?!
P.R.S. COMMAND. INTELLIGENCE WAS RIGHT. THIS ENCLAVE HAS A DNA WHISPERER.
APANEWICZ?! IS THAT YOU?!
BRIAN! IT'S ME BUDDY! IT'S RAY GARRISON!
QUE?!
ASSET SECURED.
END MEMORY PLAYBACK.

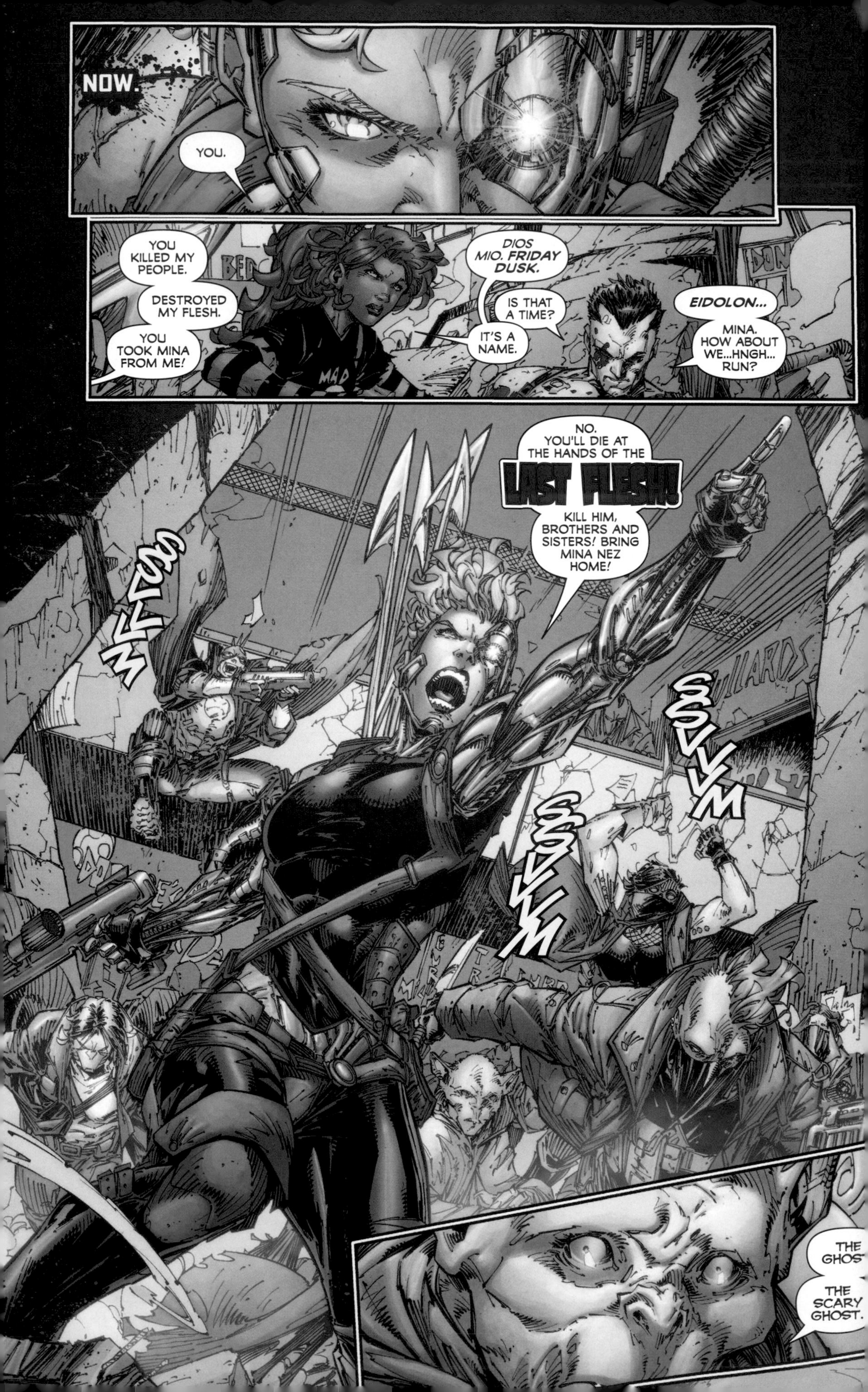
NOW.
YOU.
YOU KILLED MY PEOPLE.
DESTROYED MY FLESH.
YOU TOOK MINA FROM ME!
DIOS MIO. FRIDAY DUSK.
IS THAT A TIME?
IT'S A NAME.
EIDOLON...
MINA. HOW ABOUT WE...HNGH... RUN?
NO. YOU'LL DIE AT THE HANDS OF THE
LAST FLESH!
KILL HIM, BROTHERS AND SISTERS! BRING MINA NEZ HOME!
SSSVVM
SSSVVM
SSSVVM
THE GHOS
THE SCARY GHOST.

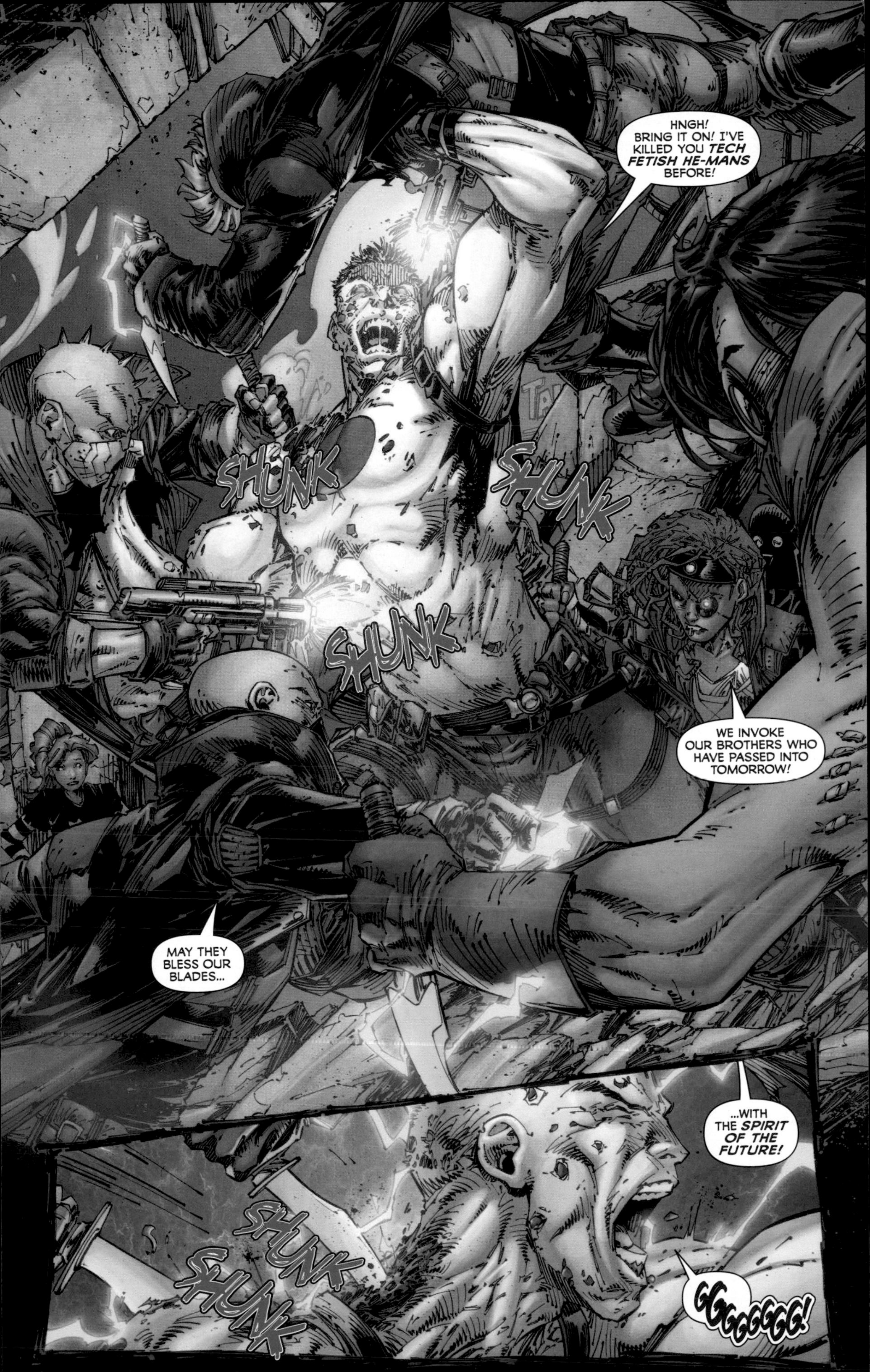
HNGH! BRING IT ON! I'VE KILLED YOU *TECH FETISH HE-MANS* BEFORE!
SHUNK
SHUNK
SHUNK
WE INVOKE OUR BROTHERS WHO HAVE PASSED INTO TOMORROW!
MAY THEY BLESS OUR BLADES...
...WITH THE *SPIRIT OF THE FUTURE!*
SHUNK
SHUNK
GGGGGGGG!

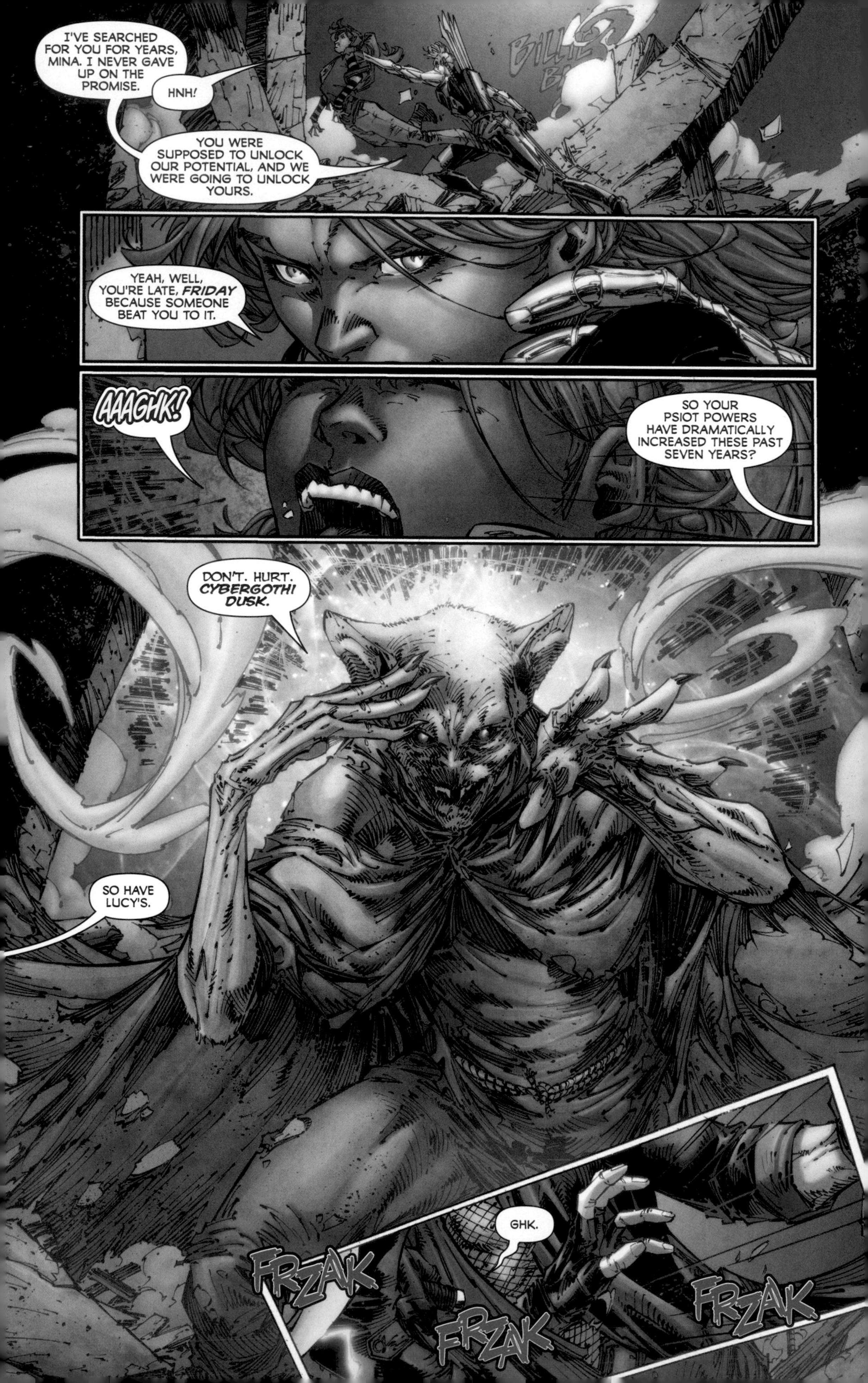
I'VE SEARCHED FOR YOU FOR YEARS, MINA. I NEVER GAVE UP ON THE PROMISE.
HNH!
YOU WERE SUPPOSED TO UNLOCK OUR POTENTIAL, AND WE WERE GOING TO UNLOCK YOURS.
YEAH, WELL, YOU'RE LATE, FRIDAY BECAUSE SOMEONE BEAT YOU TO IT.
AAAGHK!
SO YOUR PSIOT POWERS HAVE DRAMATICALLY INCREASED THESE PAST SEVEN YEARS?
DON'T. HURT. CYBERGOTHI DUSK.
SO HAVE LUCY'S.
GHK.
FRZAK
FRZAK
FRZAK

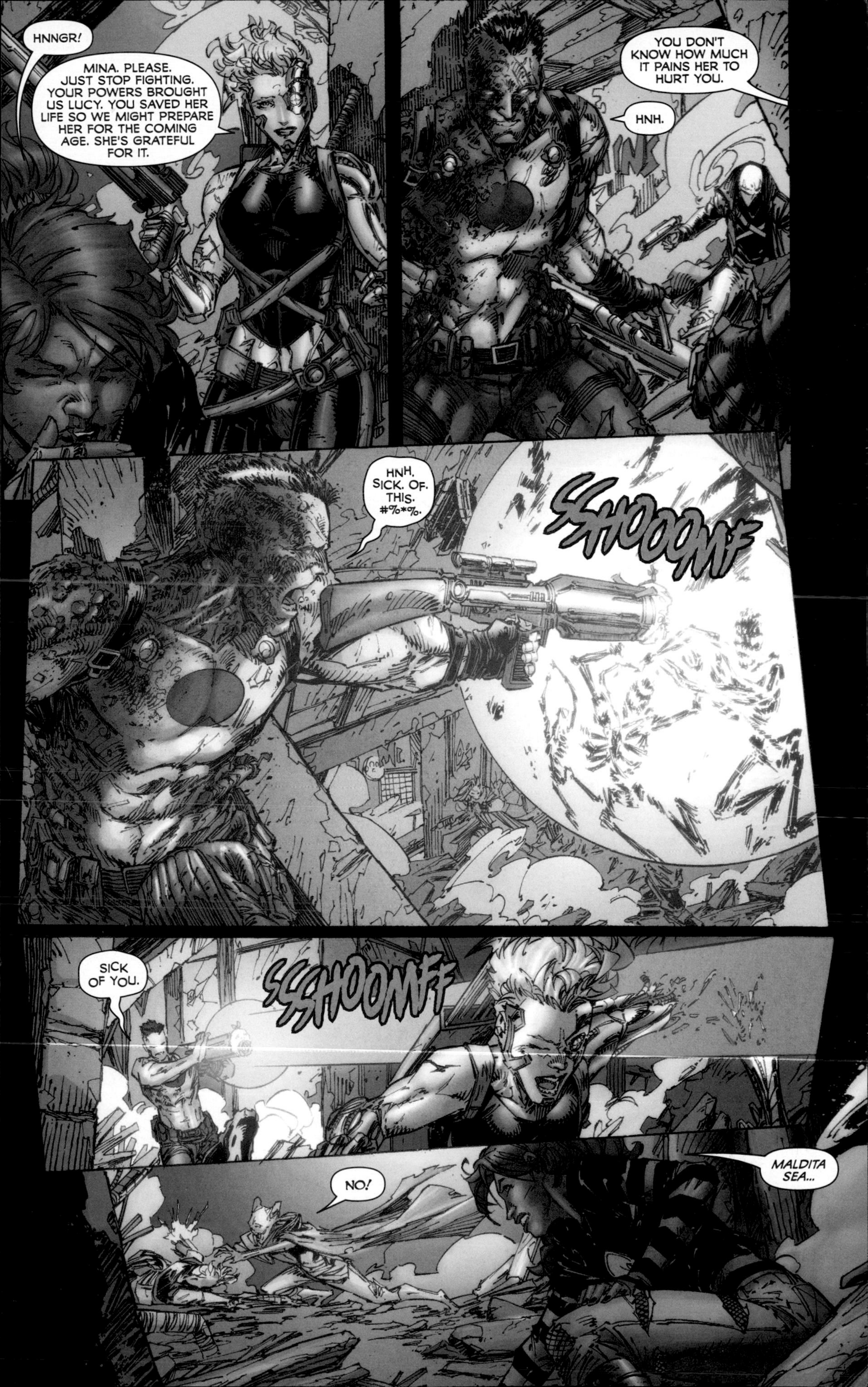
HNNGR!
MINA. PLEASE. JUST STOP FIGHTING. YOUR POWERS BROUGHT US LUCY. YOU SAVED HER LIFE SO WE MIGHT PREPARE HER FOR THE COMING AGE. SHE'S GRATEFUL FOR IT.
YOU DON'T KNOW HOW MUCH IT PAINS HER TO HURT YOU.
HNH.
HNH. SICK. OF. THIS. #%*%.
SSHOOOMF
SICK OF YOU.
SSSHOOMFF
MALDITA SEA...
NO!

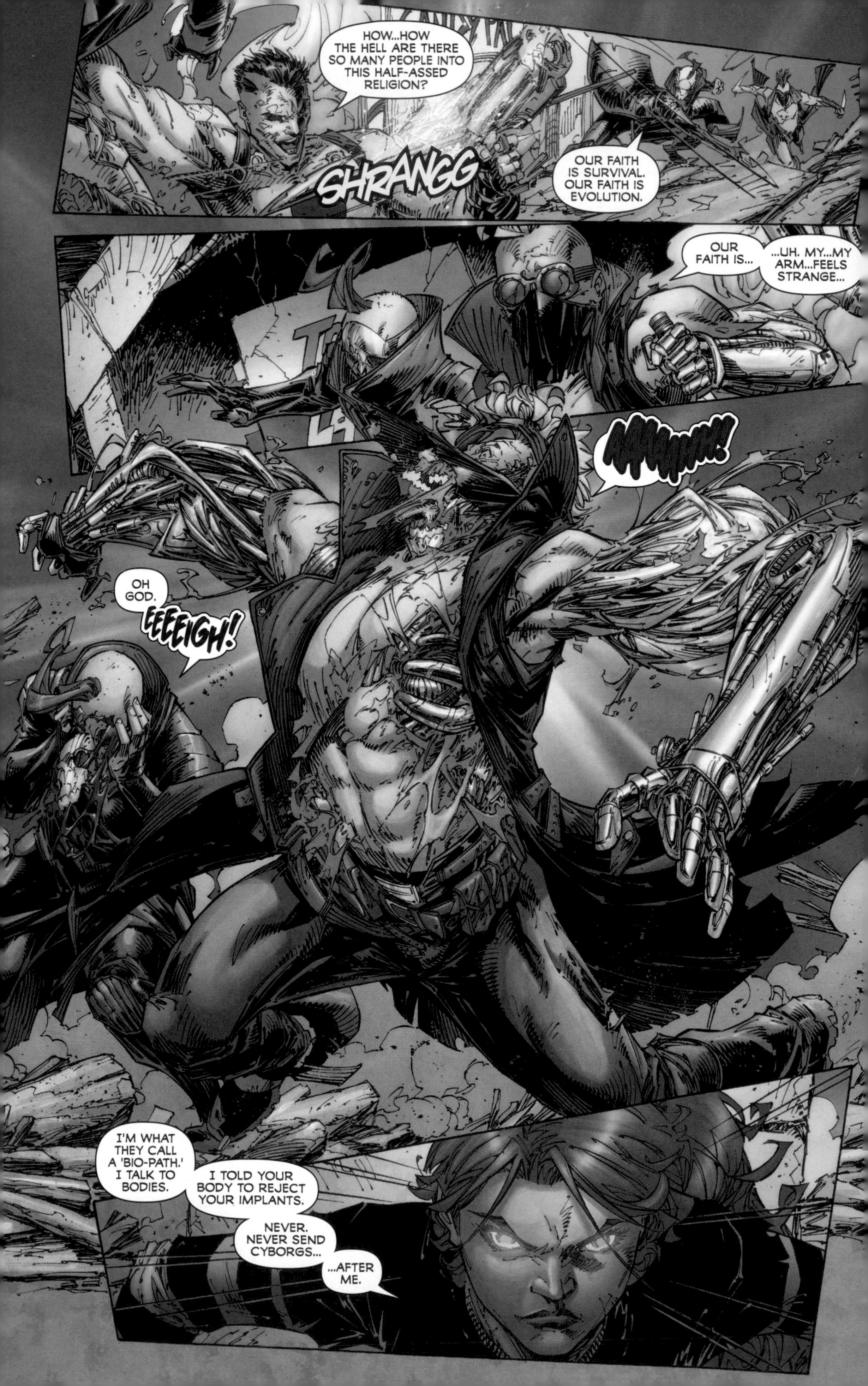
HOW...HOW THE HELL ARE THERE SO MANY PEOPLE INTO THIS HALF-ASSED RELIGION?
SHRANGG
OUR FAITH IS SURVIVAL. OUR FAITH IS EVOLUTION.
OUR FAITH IS...
...UH. MY...MY ARM...FEELS STRANGE...
AAAAAHHH!
OH GOD.
EEEEIGH!
I'M WHAT THEY CALL A 'BIO-PATH.' I TALK TO BODIES.
I TOLD YOUR BODY TO REJECT YOUR IMPLANTS.
NEVER. NEVER SEND CYBORGS...
...AFTER ME.

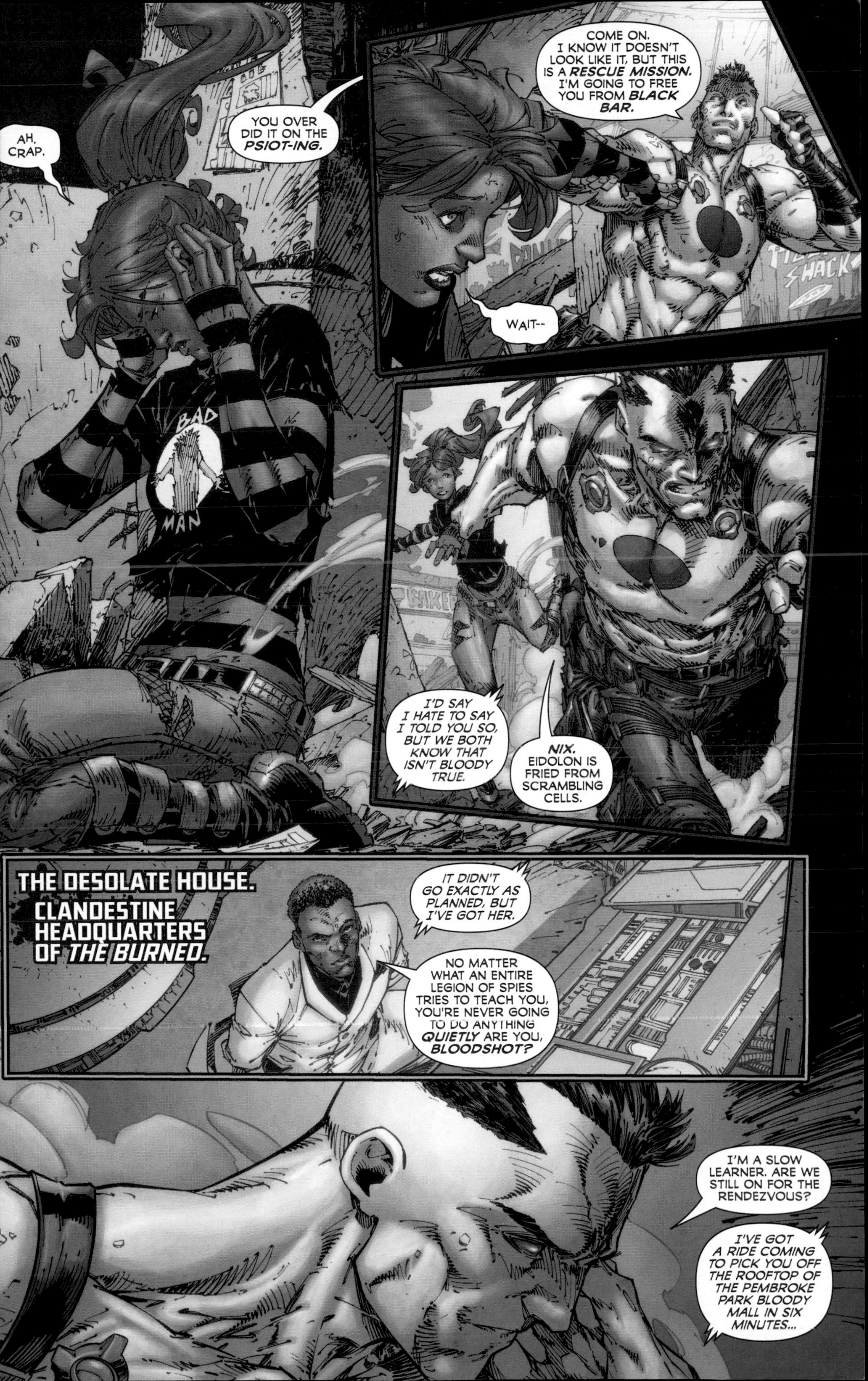
AH. CRAP.
YOU OVER DID IT ON THE PSIOT-ING.
COME ON. I KNOW IT DOESN'T LOOK LIKE IT, BUT THIS IS A RESCUE MISSION. I'M GOING TO FREE YOU FROM BLACK BAR.
WAIT--
I'D SAY I HATE TO SAY I TOLD YOU SO, BUT WE BOTH KNOW THAT ISN'T BLOODY TRUE.
NIX. EIDOLON IS FRIED FROM SCRAMBLING CELLS.
THE DESOLATE HOUSE. CLANDESTINE HEADQUARTERS OF THE BURNED.
IT DIDN'T GO EXACTLY AS PLANNED, BUT I'VE GOT HER.
NO MATTER WHAT AN ENTIRE LEGION OF SPIES TRIES TO TEACH YOU, YOU'RE NEVER GOING TO DO ANYTHING QUIETLY ARE YOU, BLOODSHOT?
I'M A SLOW LEARNER. ARE WE STILL ON FOR THE RENDEZVOUS?
I'VE GOT A RIDE COMING TO PICK YOU OFF THE ROOFTOP OF THE PEMBROKE PARK BLOODY MALL IN SIX MINUTES...

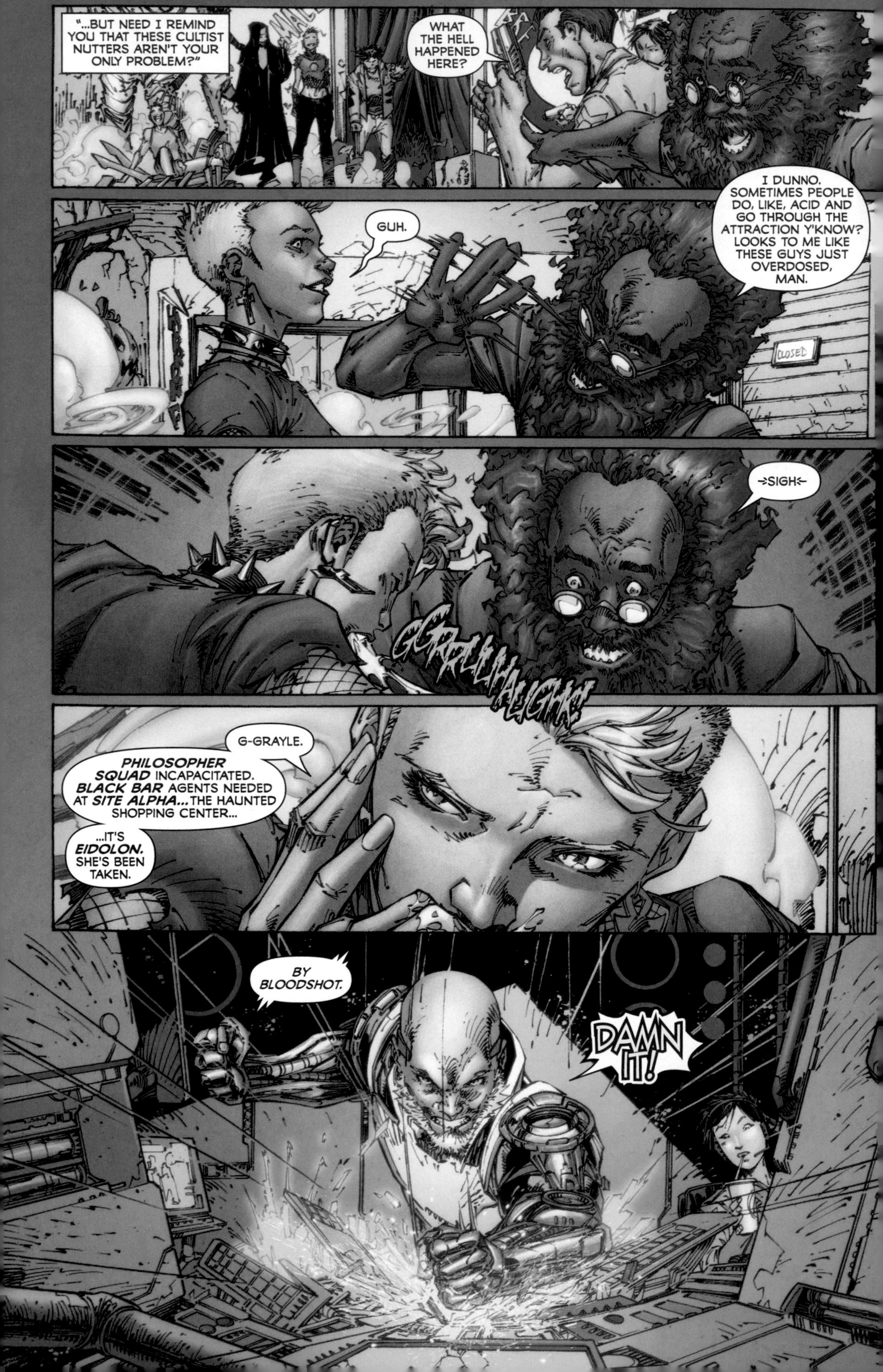
"...BUT NEED I REMIND YOU THAT THESE CULTIST NUTTERS AREN'T YOUR ONLY PROBLEM?"
WHAT THE HELL HAPPENED HERE?
GUH.
I DUNNO. SOMETIMES PEOPLE DO, LIKE, ACID AND GO THROUGH THE ATTRACTION Y'KNOW? LOOKS TO ME LIKE THESE GUYS JUST OVERDOSED, MAN.
CLOSED
SIGH
GGRUUHAUGH!
G-GRAYLE.
PHILOSOPHER SQUAD INCAPACITATED. BLACK BAR AGENTS NEEDED AT SITE ALPHA... THE HAUNTED SHOPPING CENTER...
...IT'S EIDOLON. SHE'S BEEN TAKEN.
BY BLOODSHOT.
DAMN IT!

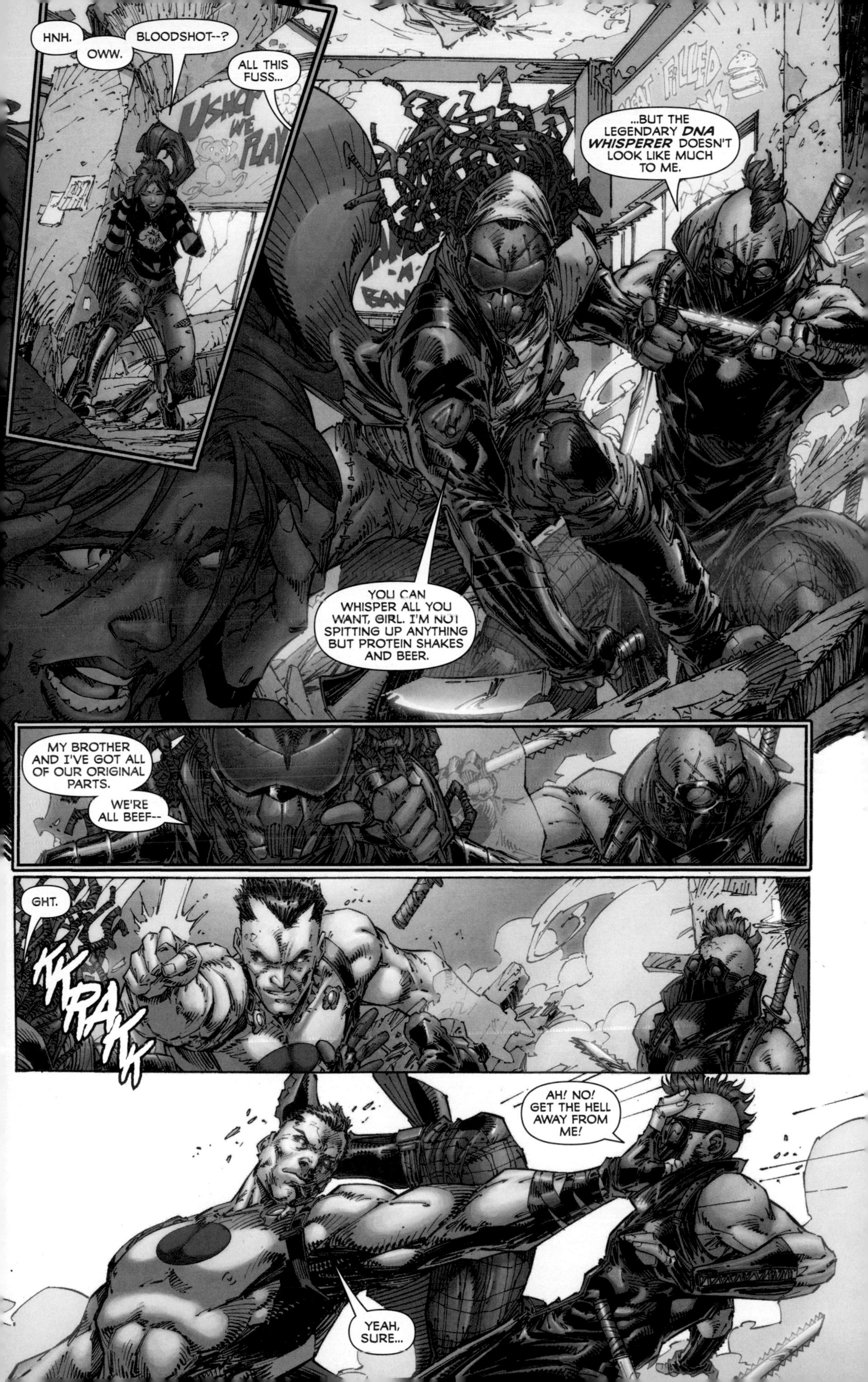
HNH.
OWW.
BLOODSHOT--?
ALL THIS FUSS...
...BUT THE LEGENDARY *DNA WHISPERER* DOESN'T LOOK LIKE MUCH TO ME.
YOU CAN WHISPER ALL YOU WANT, GIRL. I'M NOT SPITTING UP ANYTHING BUT PROTEIN SHAKES AND BEER.
MY BROTHER AND I'VE GOT ALL OF OUR ORIGINAL PARTS.
WE'RE ALL BEEF--
GHT.
KKRAKK
AH! NO! GET THE HELL AWAY FROM ME!
YEAH, SURE...

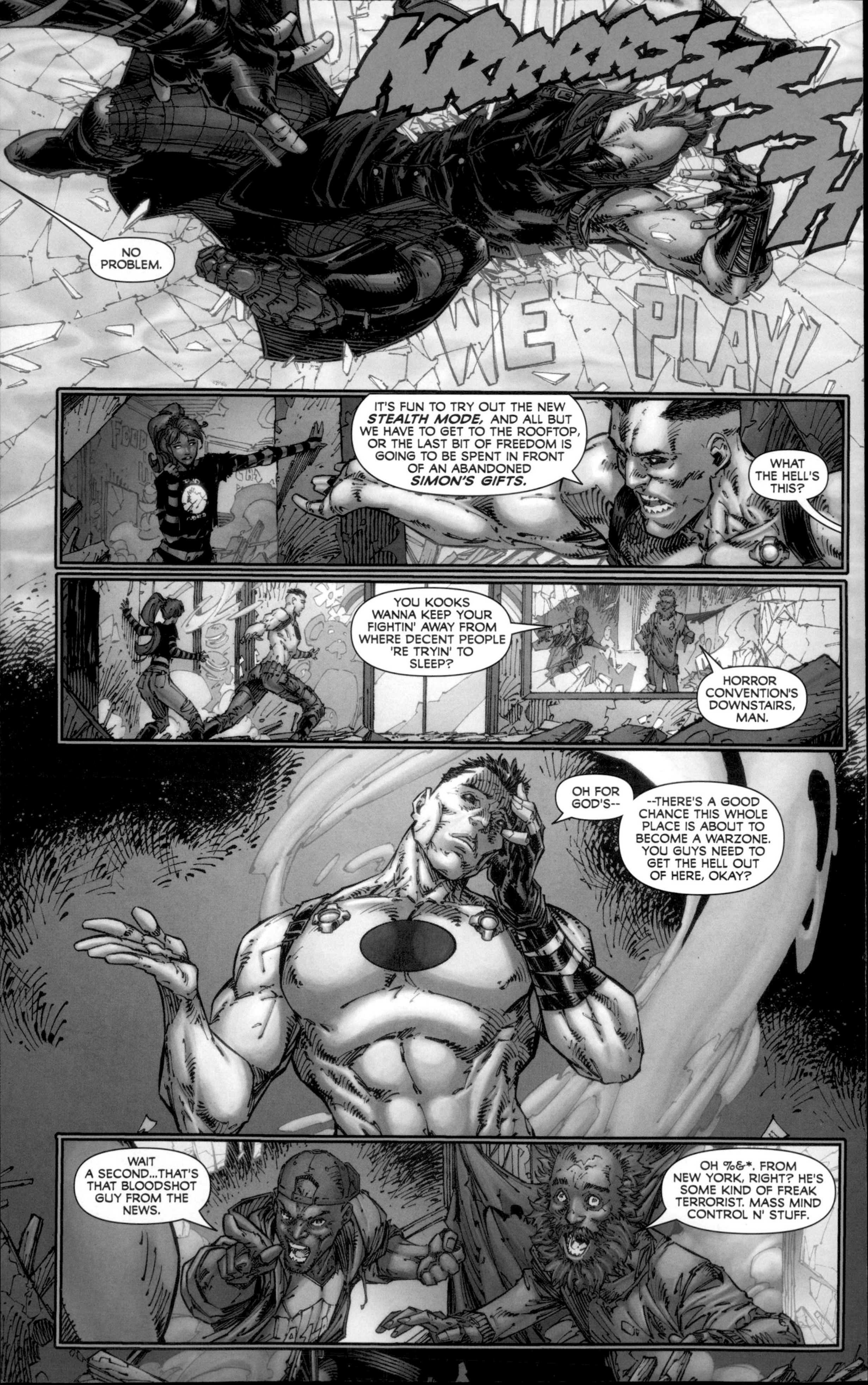
KRASSSH
WE PLAY!
NO PROBLEM.
IT'S FUN TO TRY OUT THE NEW STEALTH MODE, AND ALL BUT WE HAVE TO GET TO THE ROOFTOP, OR THE LAST BIT OF FREEDOM IS GOING TO BE SPENT IN FRONT OF AN ABANDONED SIMON'S GIFTS.
WHAT THE HELL'S THIS?
YOU KOOKS WANNA KEEP YOUR FIGHTIN' AWAY FROM WHERE DECENT PEOPLE 'RE TRYIN' TO SLEEP?
HORROR CONVENTION'S DOWNSTAIRS, MAN.
OH FOR GOD'S--
--THERE'S A GOOD CHANCE THIS WHOLE PLACE IS ABOUT TO BECOME A WARZONE. YOU GUYS NEED TO GET THE HELL OUT OF HERE, OKAY?
WAIT A SECOND...THAT'S THAT BLOODSHOT GUY FROM THE NEWS.
OH %&*. FROM NEW YORK, RIGHT? HE'S SOME KIND OF FREAK TERRORIST. MASS MIND CONTROL N' STUFF.

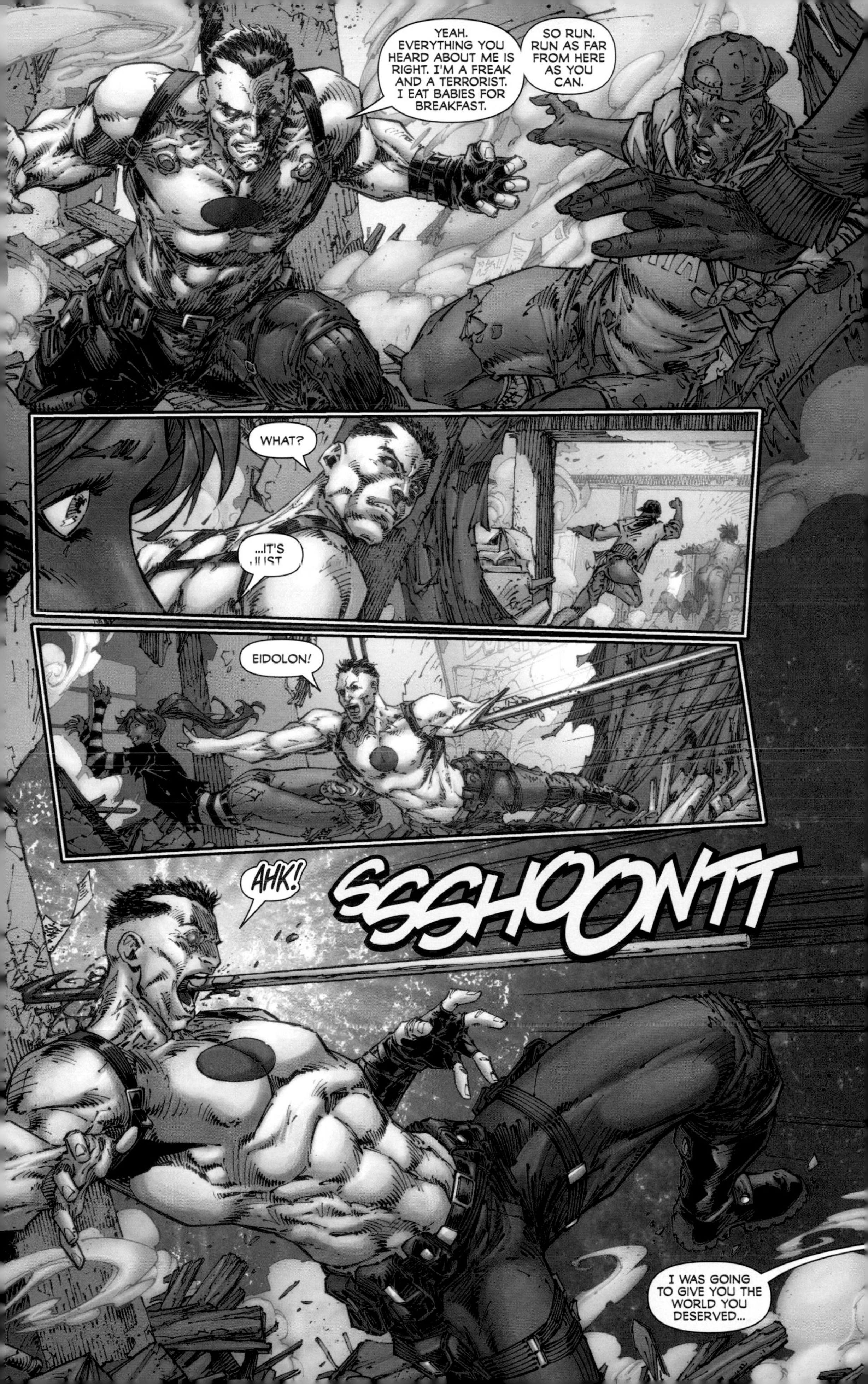
YEAH. EVERYTHING YOU HEARD ABOUT ME IS RIGHT. I'M A FREAK AND A TERRORIST. I EAT BABIES FOR BREAKFAST.
SO RUN. RUN AS FAR FROM HERE AS YOU CAN.
WHAT?
...IT'S JUST
EIDOLON!
AHK!
SSSHOONTT
I WAS GOING TO GIVE YOU THE WORLD YOU DESERVED...

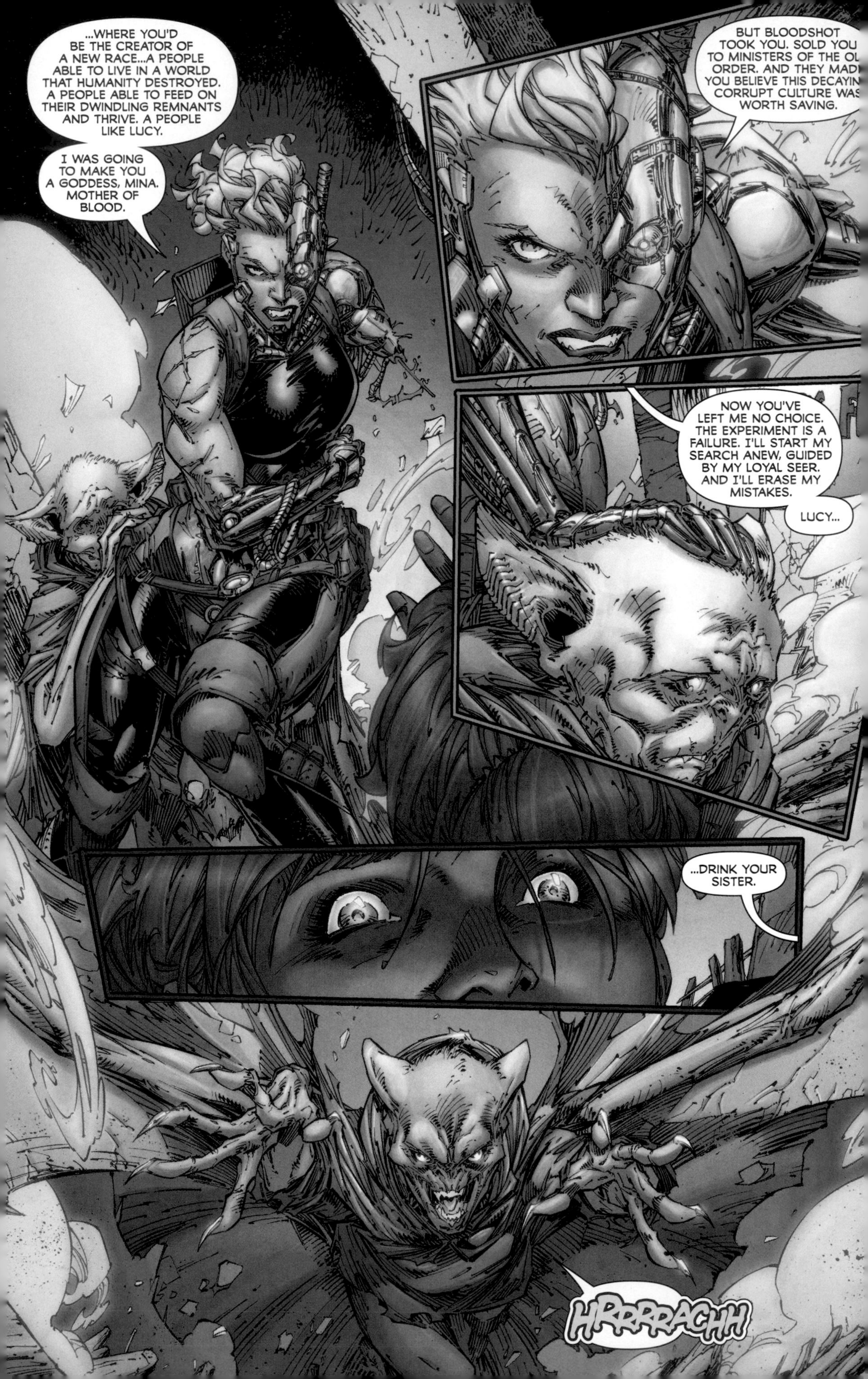
...WHERE YOU'D BE THE CREATOR OF A NEW RACE...A PEOPLE ABLE TO LIVE IN A WORLD THAT HUMANITY DESTROYED. A PEOPLE ABLE TO FEED ON THEIR DWINDLING REMNANTS AND THRIVE. A PEOPLE LIKE LUCY.
I WAS GOING TO MAKE YOU A GODDESS, MINA. MOTHER OF BLOOD.
BUT BLOODSHOT TOOK YOU. SOLD YOU TO MINISTERS OF THE OL ORDER. AND THEY MAD YOU BELIEVE THIS DECAYIN CORRUPT CULTURE WAS WORTH SAVING.
NOW YOU'VE LEFT ME NO CHOICE. THE EXPERIMENT IS A FAILURE. I'LL START MY SEARCH ANEW, GUIDED BY MY LOYAL SEER. AND I'LL ERASE MY MISTAKES.
LUCY...
...DRINK YOUR SISTER.
HRRRRACHH

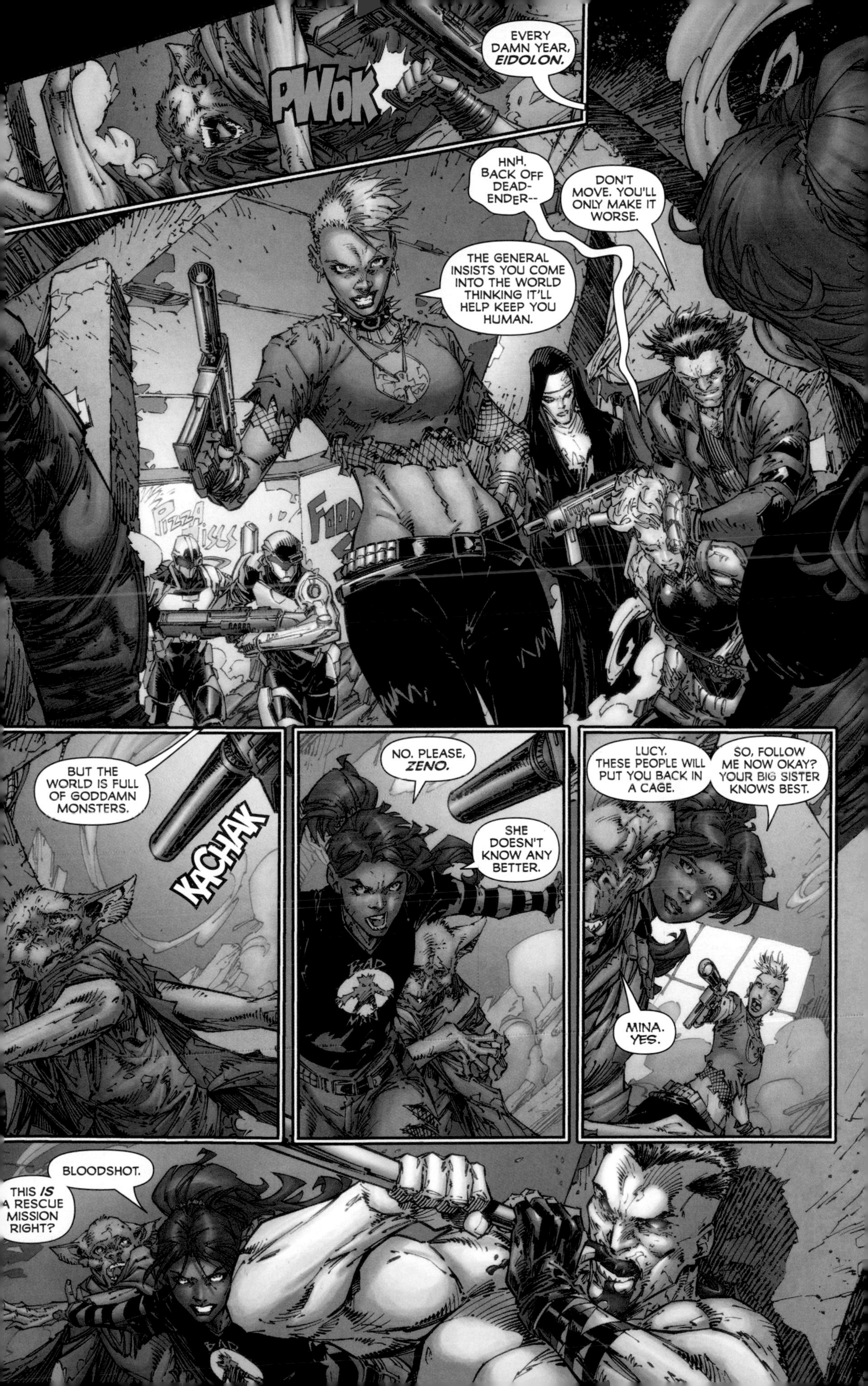
EVERY DAMN YEAR, *EIDOLON.*
PWOK
HNH. BACK OFF DEAD-ENDER--
DON'T MOVE. YOU'LL ONLY MAKE IT WORSE.
THE GENERAL INSISTS YOU COME INTO THE WORLD THINKING IT'LL HELP KEEP YOU HUMAN.
BUT THE WORLD IS FULL OF GODDAMN MONSTERS.
KACHAK
NO. PLEASE, *ZENO.*
SHE DOESN'T KNOW ANY BETTER.
LUCY. THESE PEOPLE WILL PUT YOU BACK IN A CAGE.
SO, FOLLOW ME NOW OKAY? YOUR BIG SISTER KNOWS BEST.
MINA. YES.
BLOODSHOT.
THIS *IS* A RESCUE MISSION RIGHT?

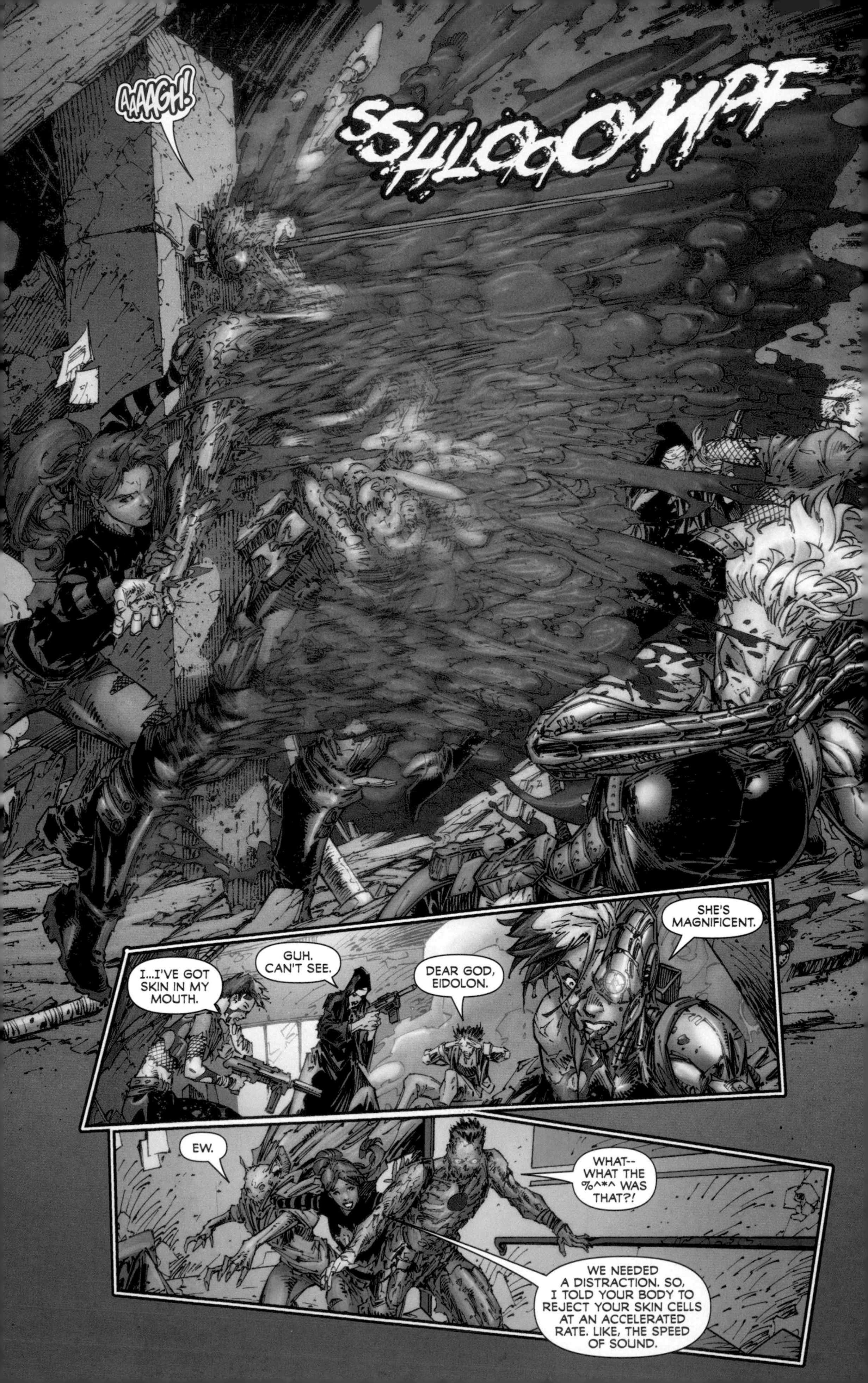

AAAAGH!
SSHLOOOOMPF
SHE'S MAGNIFICENT.
I...I'VE GOT SKIN IN MY MOUTH.
GUH. CAN'T SEE.
DEAR GOD, EIDOLON.
EW.
WHAT-- WHAT THE %^*^ WAS THAT?!
WE NEEDED A DISTRACTION. SO, I TOLD YOUR BODY TO REJECT YOUR SKIN CELLS AT AN ACCELERATED RATE. LIKE, THE SPEED OF SOUND.

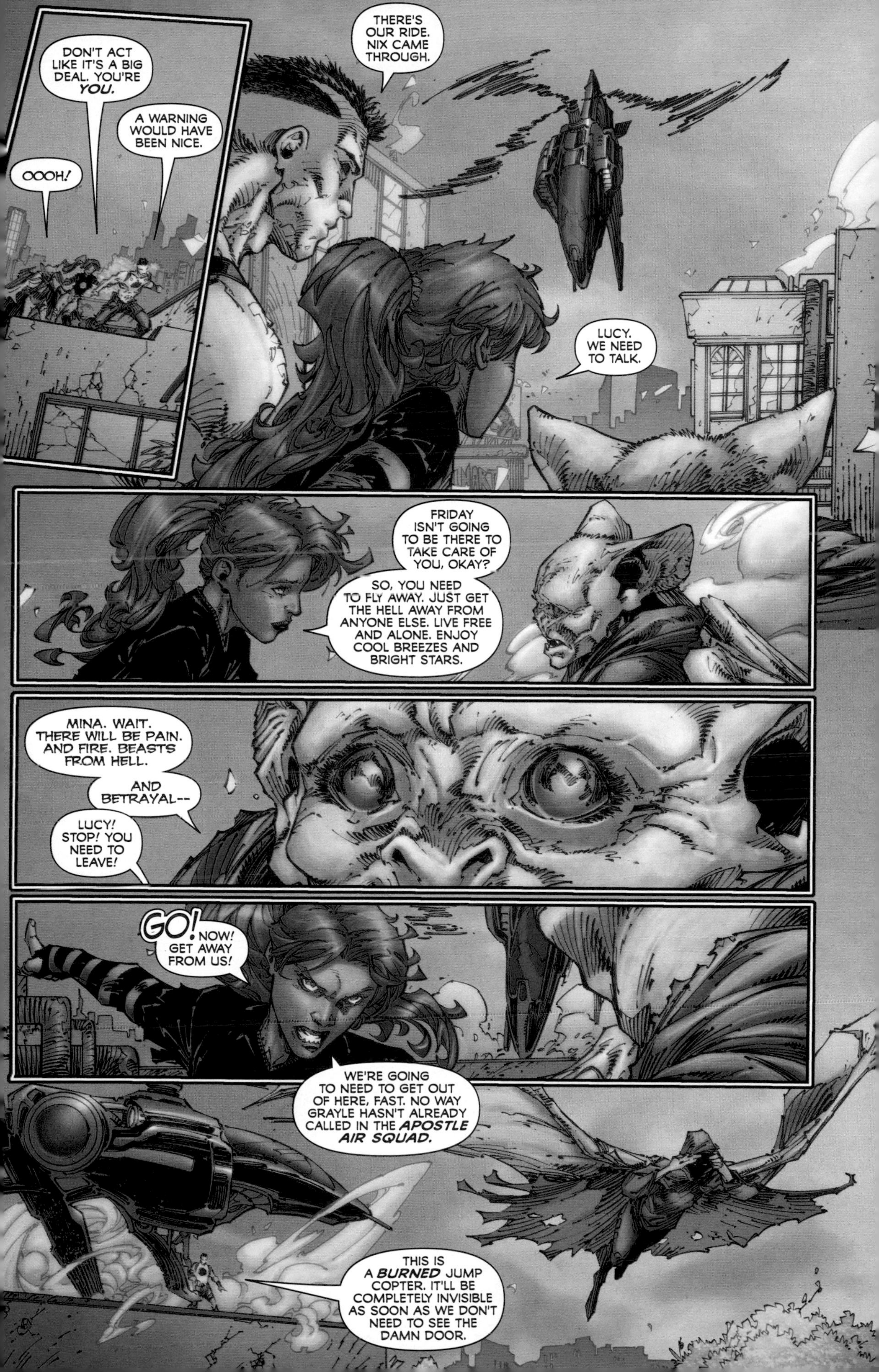
DON'T ACT LIKE IT'S A BIG DEAL. YOU'RE *YOU.*
A WARNING WOULD HAVE BEEN NICE.
OOOH!
THERE'S OUR RIDE. NIX CAME THROUGH.
LUCY. WE NEED TO TALK.
FRIDAY ISN'T GOING TO BE THERE TO TAKE CARE OF YOU, OKAY?
SO, YOU NEED TO FLY AWAY. JUST GET THE HELL AWAY FROM ANYONE ELSE. LIVE FREE AND ALONE. ENJOY COOL BREEZES AND BRIGHT STARS.
MINA. WAIT. THERE WILL BE PAIN. AND FIRE. BEASTS FROM HELL.
AND BETRAYAL--
LUCY! STOP! YOU NEED TO LEAVE!
GO! NOW! GET AWAY FROM US!
WE'RE GOING TO NEED TO GET OUT OF HERE, FAST. NO WAY GRAYLE HASN'T ALREADY CALLED IN THE *APOSTLE AIR SQUAD.*
THIS IS A *BURNED* JUMP COPTER. IT'LL BE COMPLETELY INVISIBLE AS SOON AS WE DON'T NEED TO SEE THE DAMN DOOR.

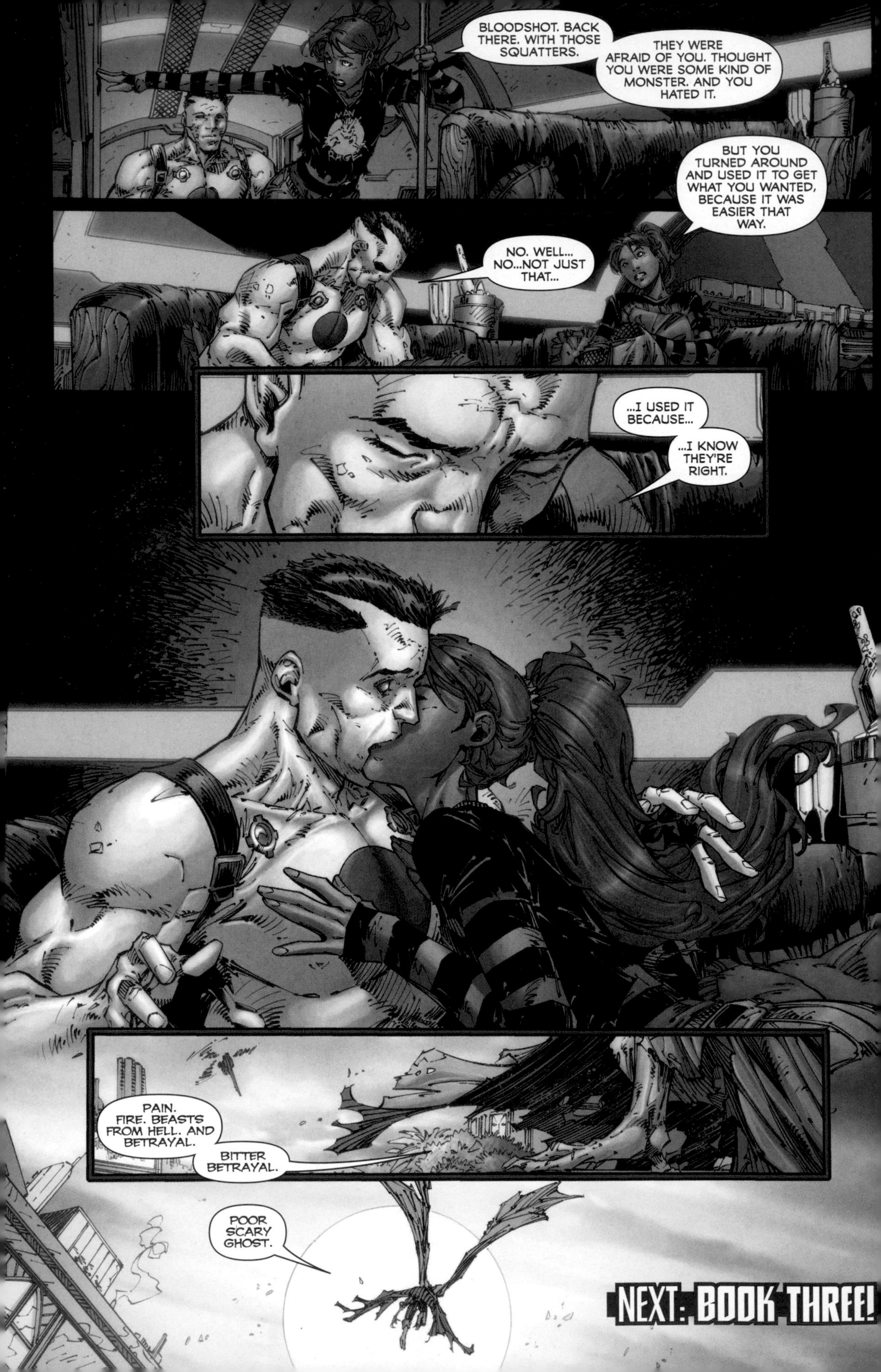
BLOODSHOT. BACK THERE. WITH THOSE SQUATTERS.
THEY WERE AFRAID OF YOU. THOUGHT YOU WERE SOME KIND OF MONSTER. AND YOU HATED IT.
BUT YOU TURNED AROUND AND USED IT TO GET WHAT YOU WANTED, BECAUSE IT WAS EASIER THAT WAY.
NO. WELL... NO...NOT JUST THAT...
...I USED IT BECAUSE...
...I KNOW THEY'RE RIGHT.
PAIN. FIRE. BEASTS FROM HELL. AND BETRAYAL.
BITTER BETRAYAL.
POOR SCARY GHOST.
NEXT: BOOK THREE!

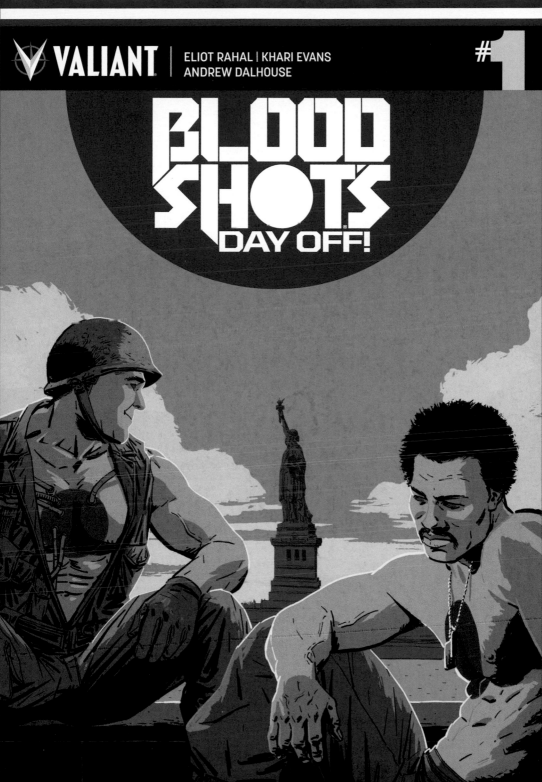

VALIANT | ELIOT RAHAL | KHARI EVANS
ANDREW DALHOUSE

#1

BLOOD SHOTS
DAY OFF!

BLOODSHOT'S DAY OFF #1

WRITER: Eliot Rahal
ARTIST: Khari Evans
COLORIST: Andrew Dalhouse
LETTERS: Dave Lanphear
COVER ARTIST: Kano
EDITOR: Charlotte Greenbaum

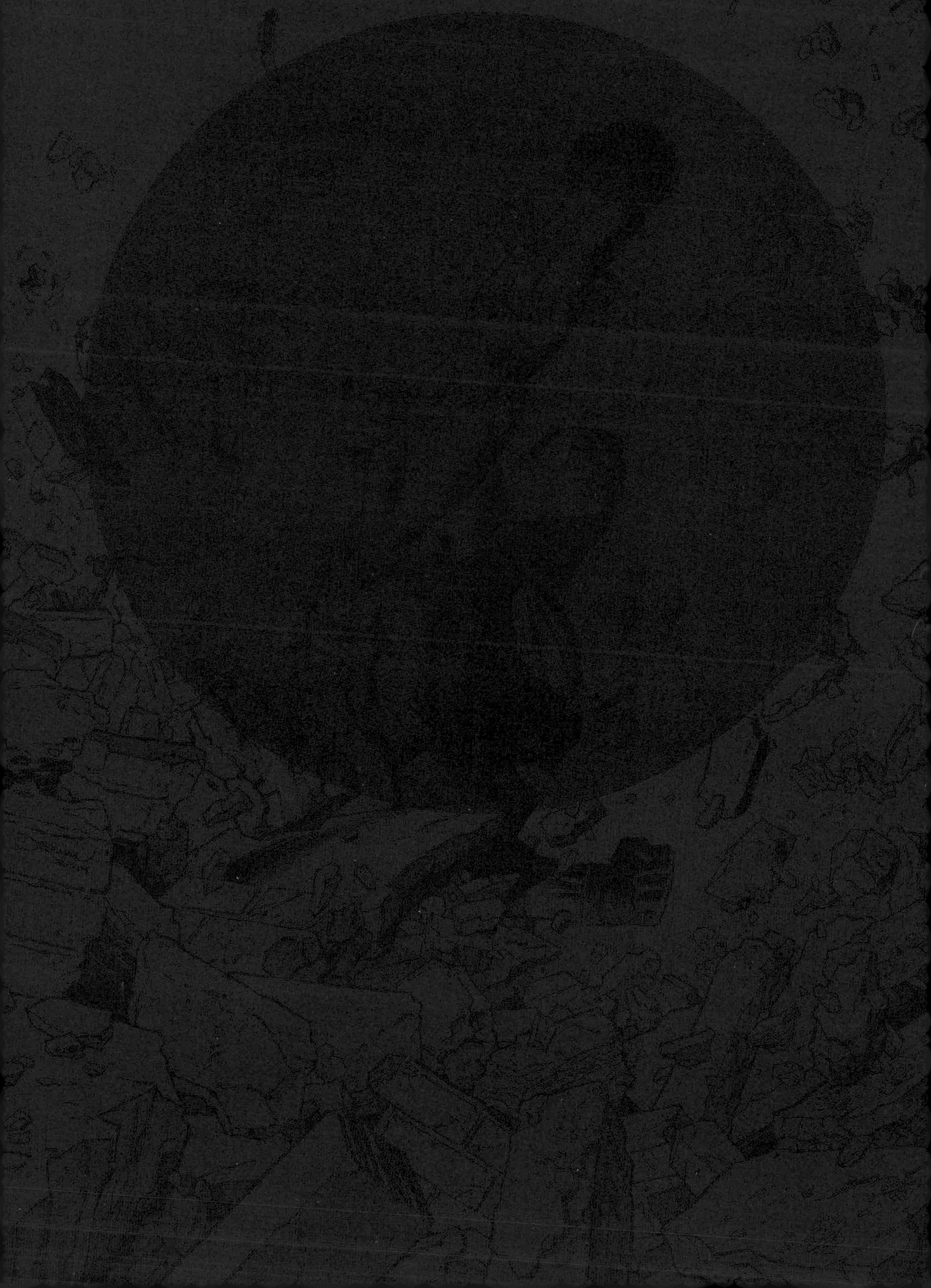

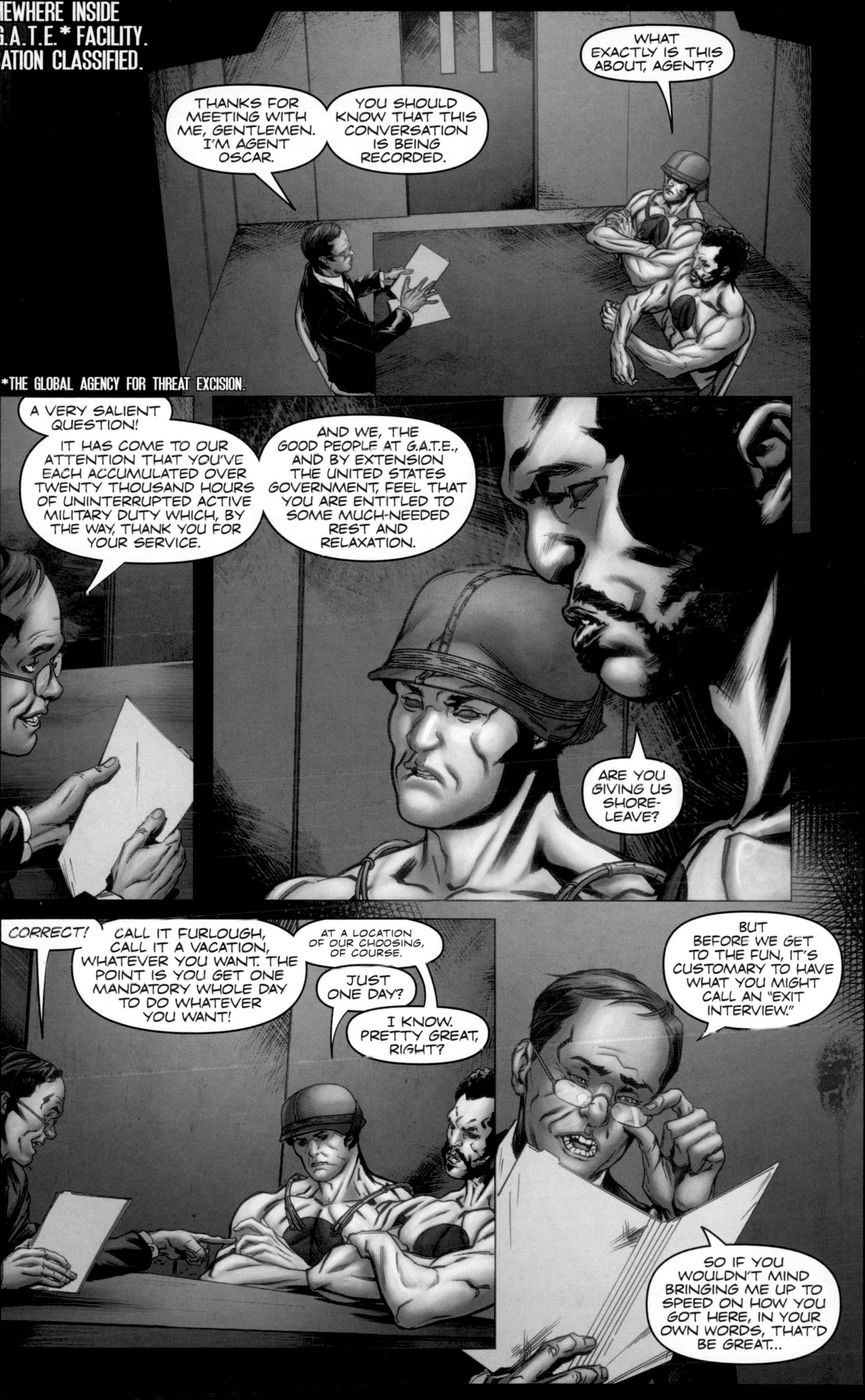

EWHERE INSIDE G.A.T.E.* FACILITY. ATION CLASSIFIED.
THANKS FOR MEETING WITH ME, GENTLEMEN. I'M AGENT OSCAR.
YOU SHOULD KNOW THAT THIS CONVERSATION IS BEING RECORDED.
WHAT EXACTLY IS THIS ABOUT, AGENT?
*THE GLOBAL AGENCY FOR THREAT EXCISION.
A VERY SALIENT QUESTION!
IT HAS COME TO OUR ATTENTION THAT YOU'VE EACH ACCUMULATED OVER TWENTY THOUSAND HOURS OF UNINTERRUPTED ACTIVE MILITARY DUTY WHICH, BY THE WAY, THANK YOU FOR YOUR SERVICE.
AND WE, THE GOOD PEOPLE AT G.A.T.E., AND BY EXTENSION THE UNITED STATES GOVERNMENT, FEEL THAT YOU ARE ENTITLED TO SOME MUCH-NEEDED REST AND RELAXATION.
ARE YOU GIVING US SHORE-LEAVE?
CORRECT!
CALL IT FURLOUGH, CALL IT A VACATION, WHATEVER YOU WANT. THE POINT IS YOU GET ONE MANDATORY WHOLE DAY TO DO WHATEVER YOU WANT!
AT A LOCATION OF OUR CHOOSING, OF COURSE.
JUST ONE DAY?
I KNOW. PRETTY GREAT, RIGHT?
BUT BEFORE WE GET TO THE FUN, IT'S CUSTOMARY TO HAVE WHAT YOU MIGHT CALL AN "EXIT INTERVIEW."
SO IF YOU WOULDN'T MIND BRINGING ME UP TO SPEED ON HOW YOU GOT HERE, IN YOUR OWN WORDS, THAT'D BE GREAT...

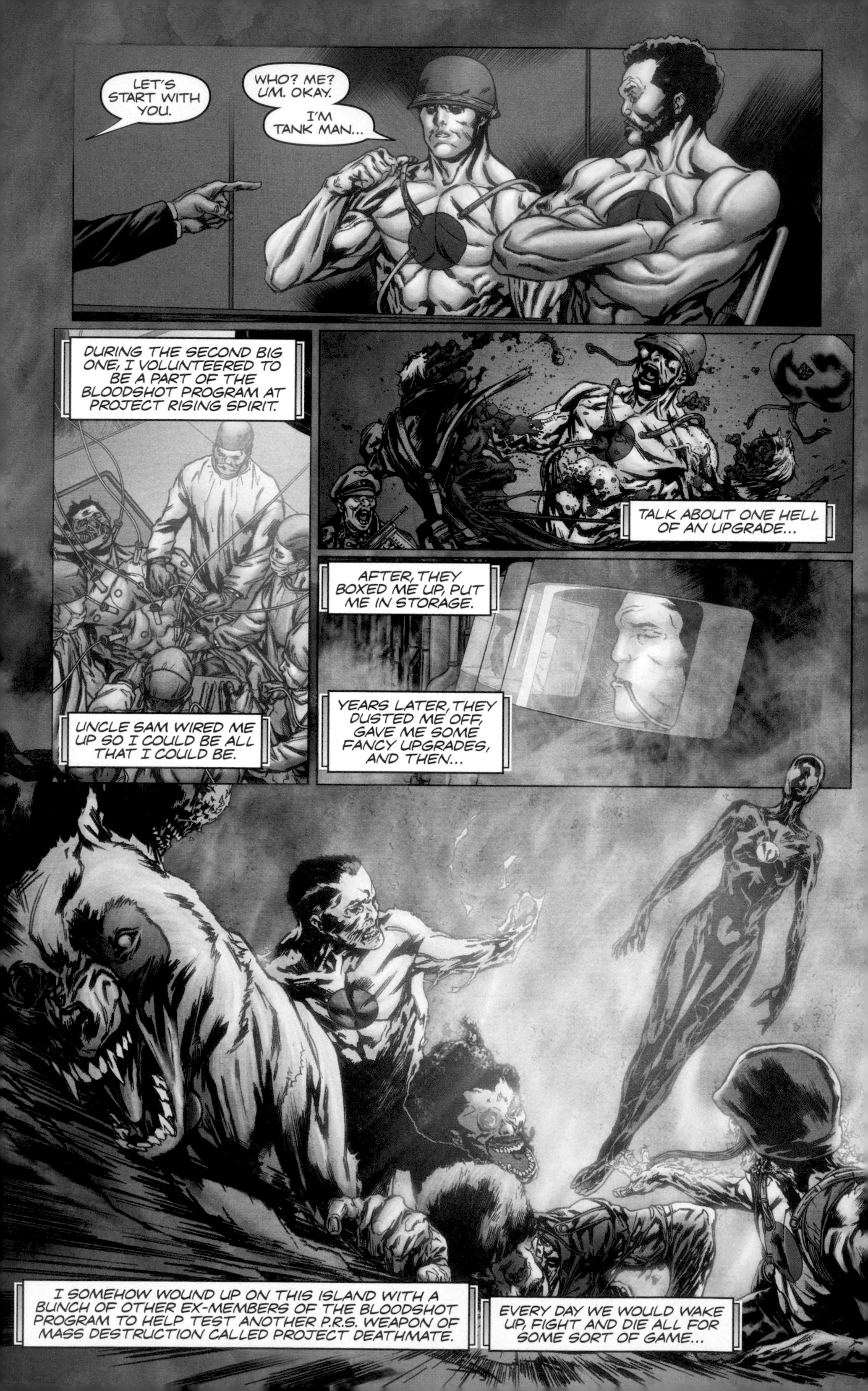
LET'S START WITH YOU.
WHO? ME? UM. OKAY.
I'M TANK MAN...
DURING THE SECOND BIG ONE, I VOLUNTEERED TO BE A PART OF THE BLOODSHOT PROGRAM AT PROJECT RISING SPIRIT.
UNCLE SAM WIRED ME UP SO I COULD BE ALL THAT I COULD BE.
TALK ABOUT ONE HELL OF AN UPGRADE...
AFTER, THEY BOXED ME UP, PUT ME IN STORAGE.
YEARS LATER, THEY DUSTED ME OFF, GAVE ME SOME FANCY UPGRADES, AND THEN...
I SOMEHOW WOUND UP ON THIS ISLAND WITH A BUNCH OF OTHER EX-MEMBERS OF THE BLOODSHOT PROGRAM TO HELP TEST ANOTHER P.R.S. WEAPON OF MASS DESTRUCTION CALLED PROJECT DEATHMATE.
EVERY DAY WE WOULD WAKE UP, FIGHT AND DIE ALL FOR SOME SORT OF GAME...

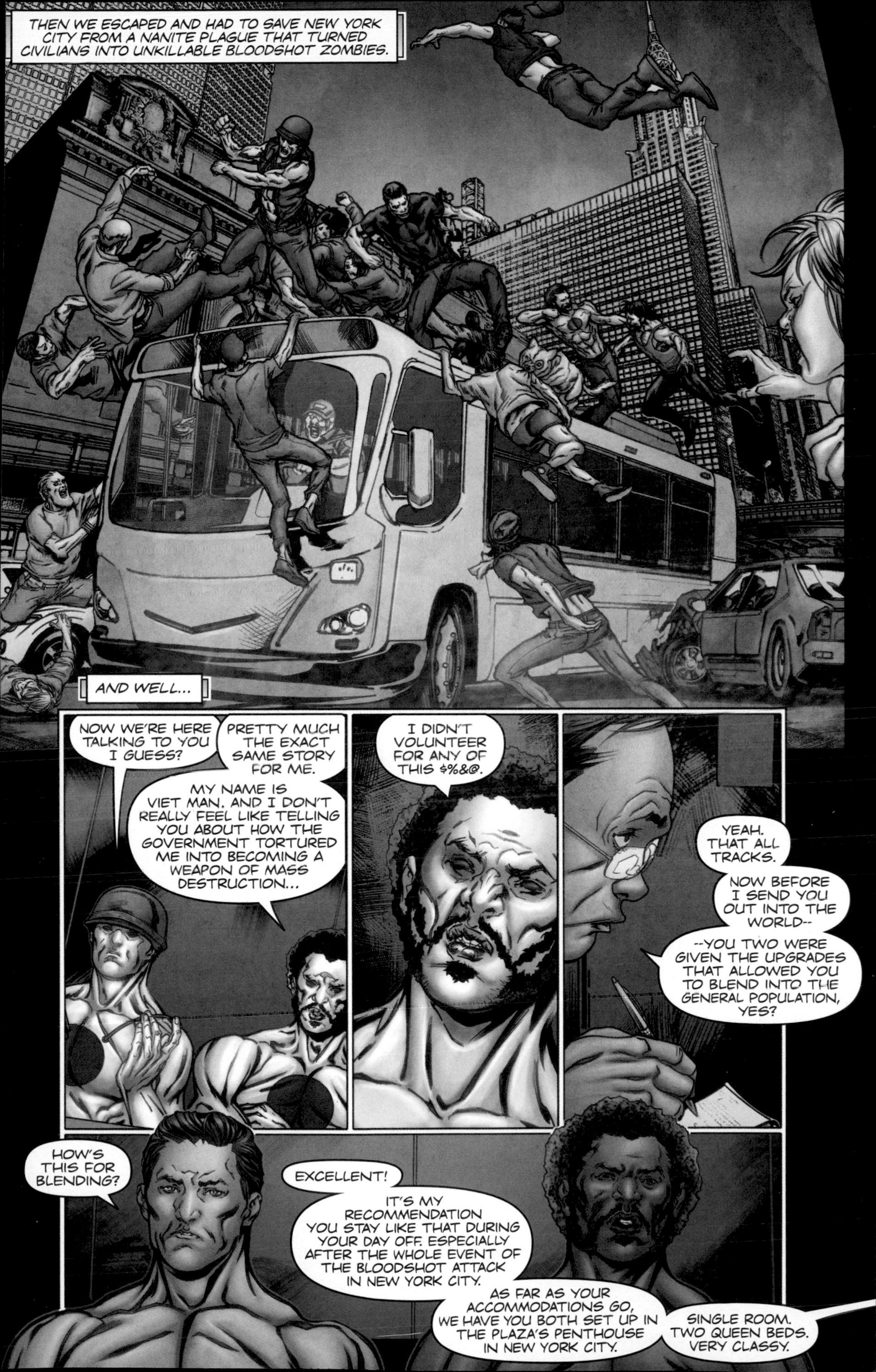
THEN WE ESCAPED AND HAD TO SAVE NEW YORK CITY FROM A NANITE PLAGUE THAT TURNED CIVILIANS INTO UNKILLABLE BLOODSHOT ZOMBIES.
AND WELL...
NOW WE'RE HERE TALKING TO YOU I GUESS?
PRETTY MUCH THE EXACT SAME STORY FOR ME.
MY NAME IS VIET MAN. AND I DON'T REALLY FEEL LIKE TELLING YOU ABOUT HOW THE GOVERNMENT TORTURED ME INTO BECOMING A WEAPON OF MASS DESTRUCTION...
I DIDN'T VOLUNTEER FOR ANY OF THIS $%&@.
YEAH. THAT ALL TRACKS.
NOW BEFORE I SEND YOU OUT INTO THE WORLD--
--YOU TWO WERE GIVEN THE UPGRADES THAT ALLOWED YOU TO BLEND INTO THE GENERAL POPULATION, YES?
HOW'S THIS FOR BLENDING?
EXCELLENT!
IT'S MY RECOMMENDATION YOU STAY LIKE THAT DURING YOUR DAY OFF. ESPECIALLY AFTER THE WHOLE EVENT OF THE BLOODSHOT ATTACK IN NEW YORK CITY.
AS FAR AS YOUR ACCOMMODATIONS GO, WE HAVE YOU BOTH SET UP IN THE PLAZA'S PENTHOUSE IN NEW YORK CITY.
SINGLE ROOM. TWO QUEEN BEDS. VERY CLASSY.

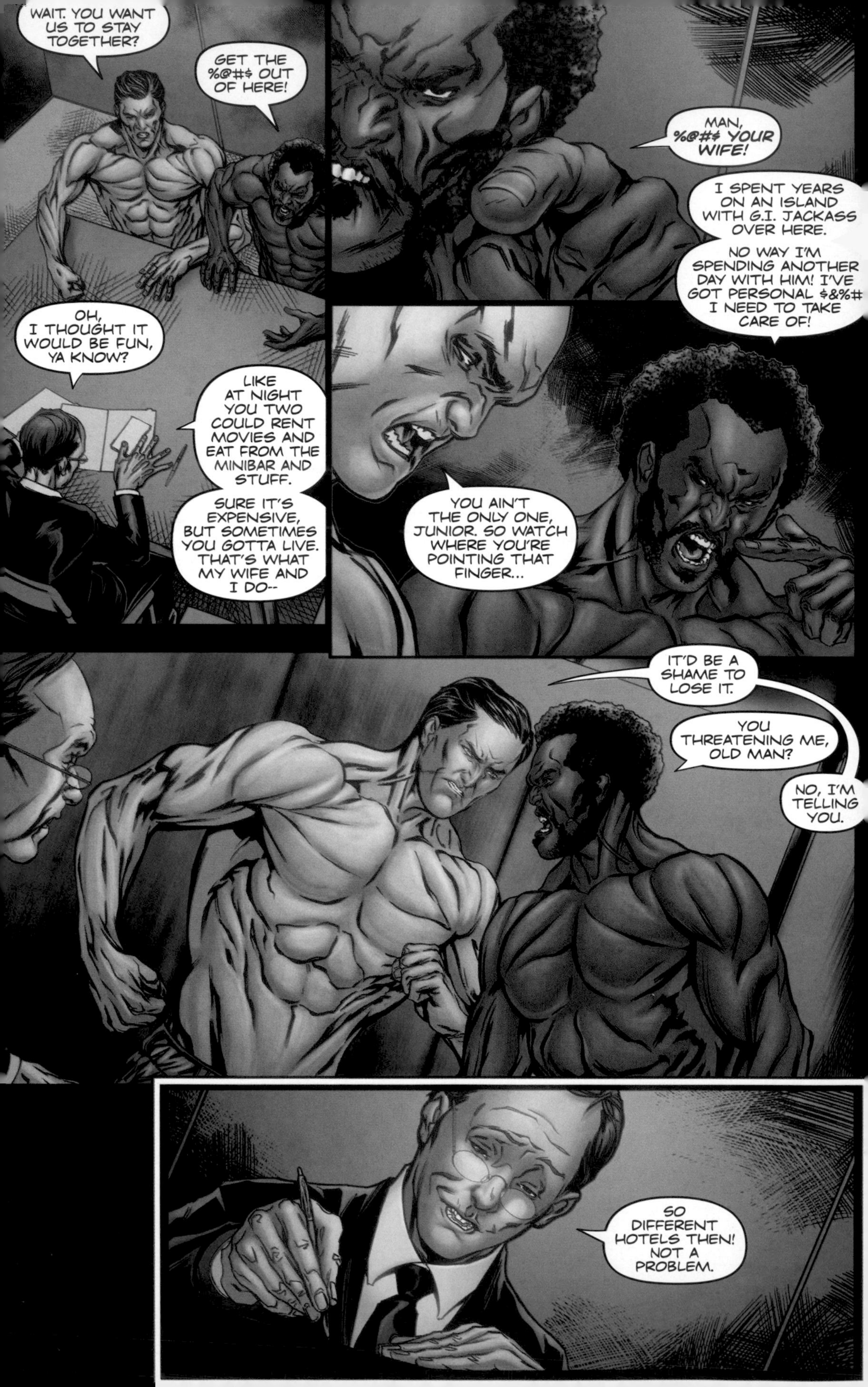
WAIT. YOU WANT US TO STAY TOGETHER?
GET THE %@#$ OUT OF HERE!
MAN, %@#$ YOUR WIFE!
I SPENT YEARS ON AN ISLAND WITH G.I. JACKASS OVER HERE.
NO WAY I'M SPENDING ANOTHER DAY WITH HIM! I'VE GOT PERSONAL $&%# I NEED TO TAKE CARE OF!
OH, I THOUGHT IT WOULD BE FUN, YA KNOW?
LIKE AT NIGHT YOU TWO COULD RENT MOVIES AND EAT FROM THE MINIBAR AND STUFF.
SURE IT'S EXPENSIVE, BUT SOMETIMES YOU GOTTA LIVE. THAT'S WHAT MY WIFE AND I DO--
YOU AIN'T THE ONLY ONE, JUNIOR. SO WATCH WHERE YOU'RE POINTING THAT FINGER...
IT'D BE A SHAME TO LOSE IT.
YOU THREATENING ME, OLD MAN?
NO, I'M TELLING YOU.
SO DIFFERENT HOTELS THEN! NOT A PROBLEM.

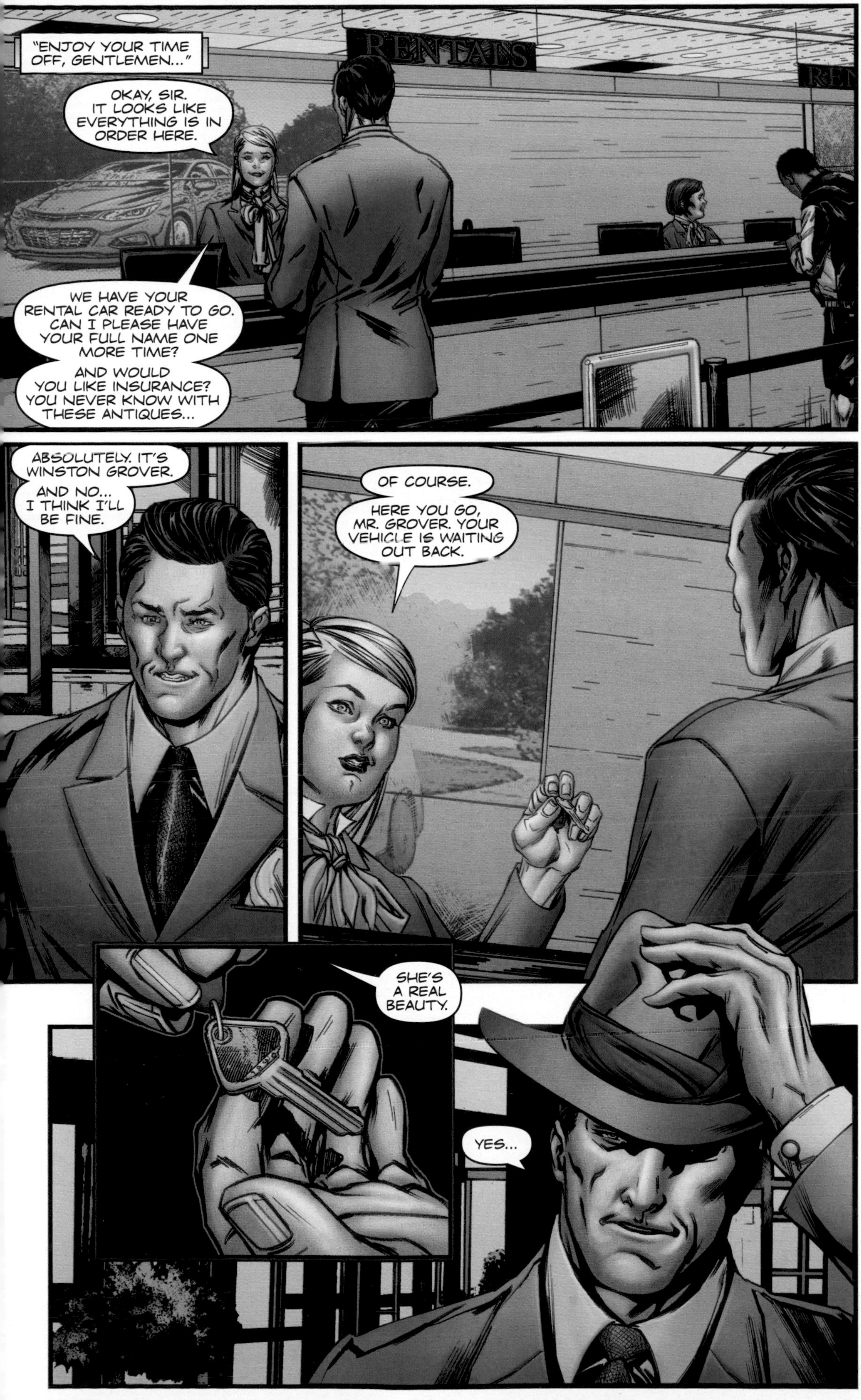
"ENJOY YOUR TIME OFF, GENTLEMEN..."
RENTALS
OKAY, SIR. IT LOOKS LIKE EVERYTHING IS IN ORDER HERE.
WE HAVE YOUR RENTAL CAR READY TO GO. CAN I PLEASE HAVE YOUR FULL NAME ONE MORE TIME?
AND WOULD YOU LIKE INSURANCE? YOU NEVER KNOW WITH THESE ANTIQUES...
ABSOLUTELY. IT'S WINSTON GROVER.
AND NO... I THINK I'LL BE FINE.
OF COURSE.
HERE YOU GO, MR. GROVER. YOUR VEHICLE IS WAITING OUT BACK.
SHE'S A REAL BEAUTY.
YES...

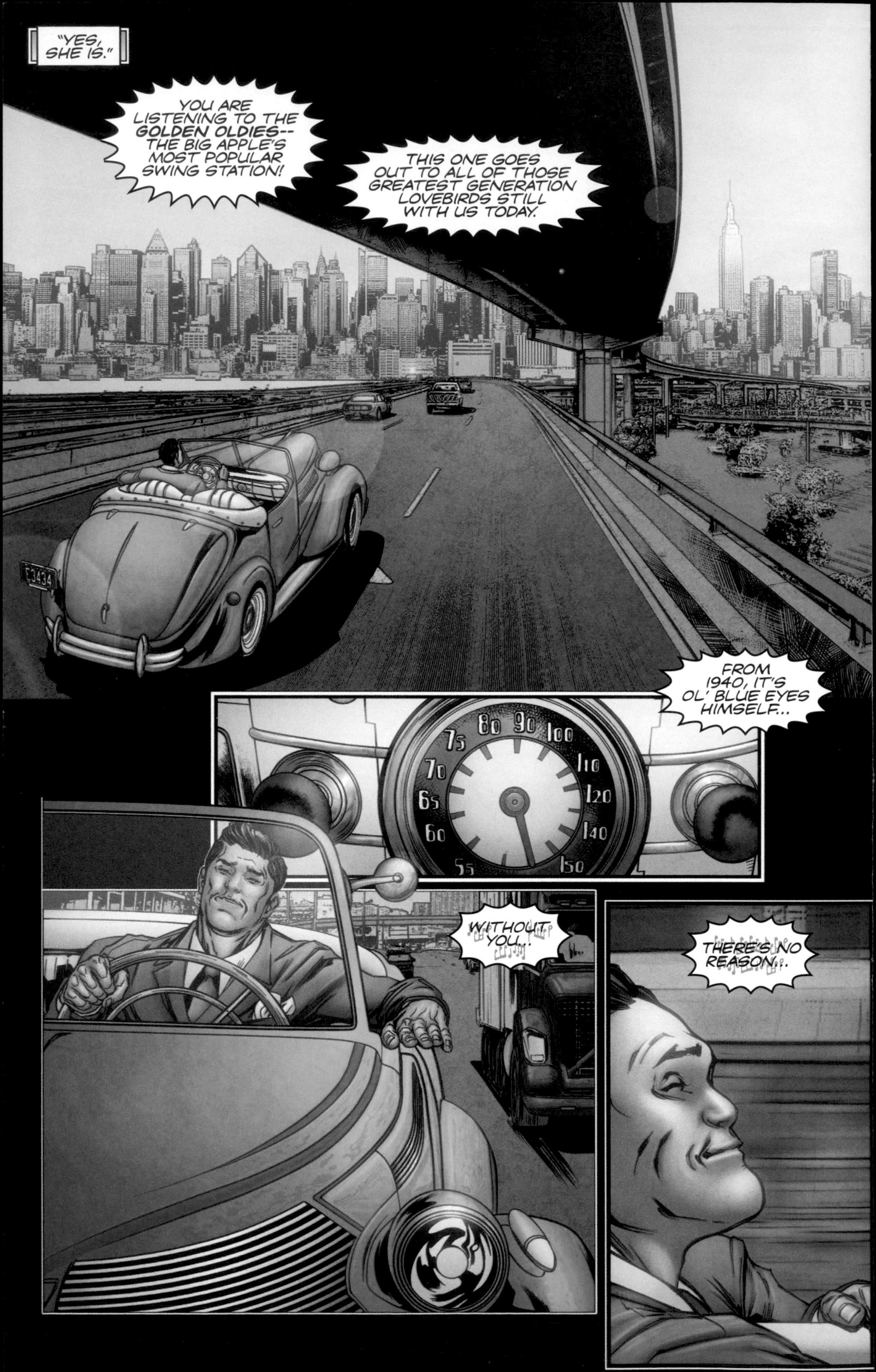
"YES, SHE IS."
YOU ARE LISTENING TO THE GOLDEN OLDIES-- THE BIG APPLE'S MOST POPULAR SWING STATION!
THIS ONE GOES OUT TO ALL OF THOSE GREATEST GENERATION LOVEBIRDS STILL WITH US TODAY.
FROM 1940, IT'S OL' BLUE EYES HIMSELF...
WITHOUT YOU...
THERE'S NO REASON...

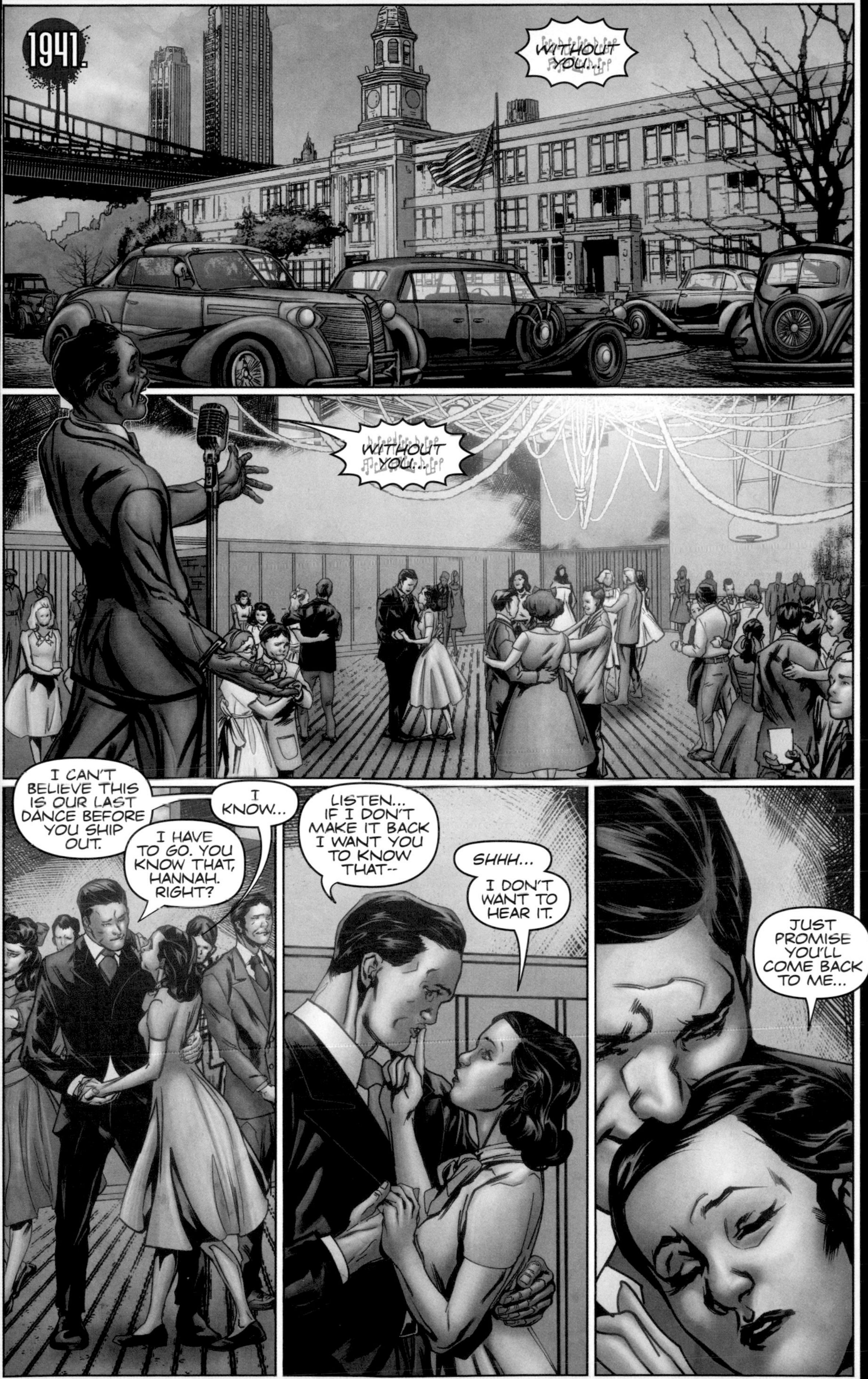
1941.
WITHOUT YOU...
WITHOUT YOU...
I CAN'T BELIEVE THIS IS OUR LAST DANCE BEFORE YOU SHIP OUT.
I KNOW...
I HAVE TO GO. YOU KNOW THAT, HANNAH. RIGHT?
LISTEN... IF I DON'T MAKE IT BACK I WANT YOU TO KNOW THAT--
SHHH...
I DON'T WANT TO HEAR IT.
JUST PROMISE YOU'LL COME BACK TO ME...

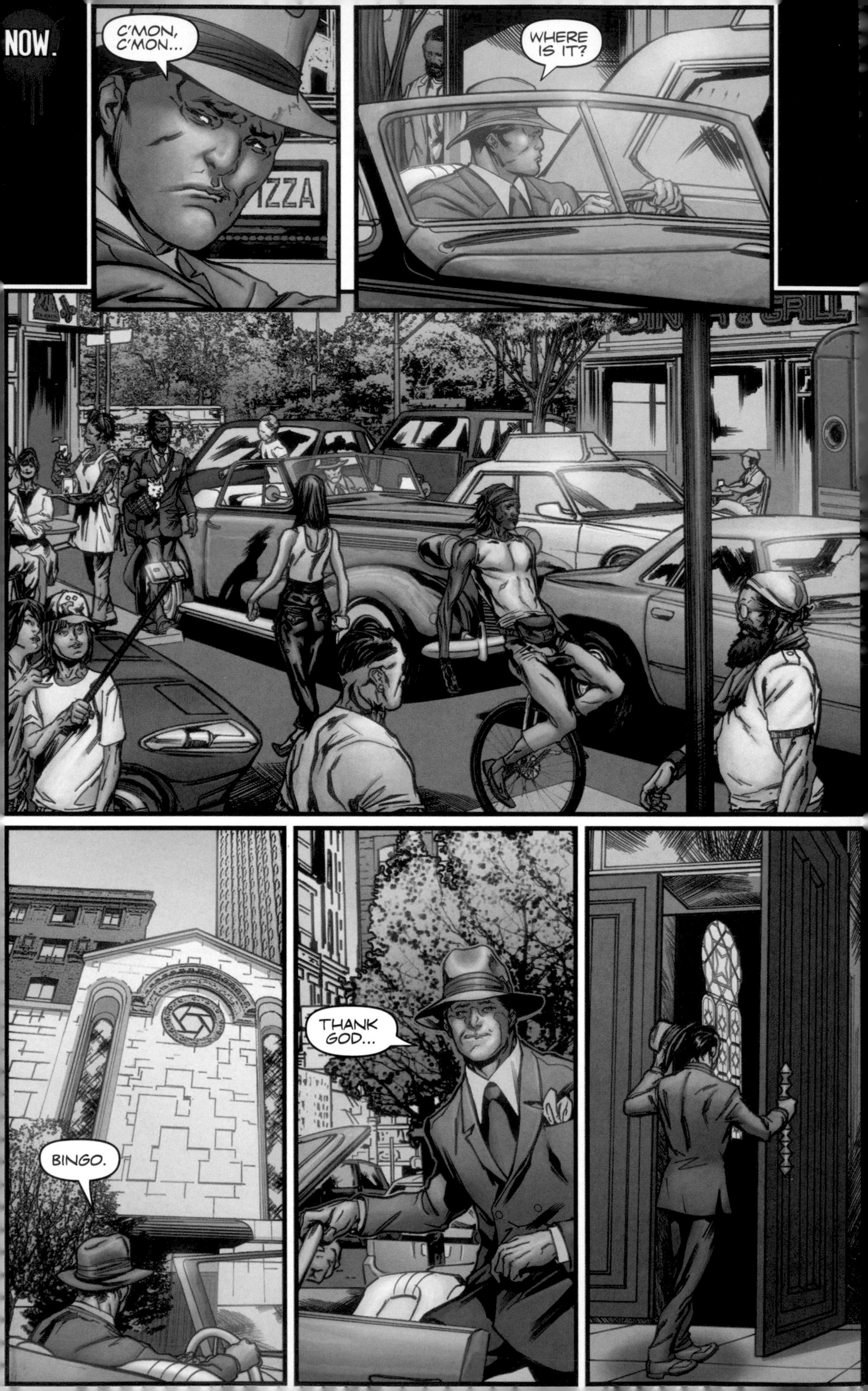
NOW.
C'MON, C'MON...
WHERE IS IT?
BINGO.
THANK GOD...

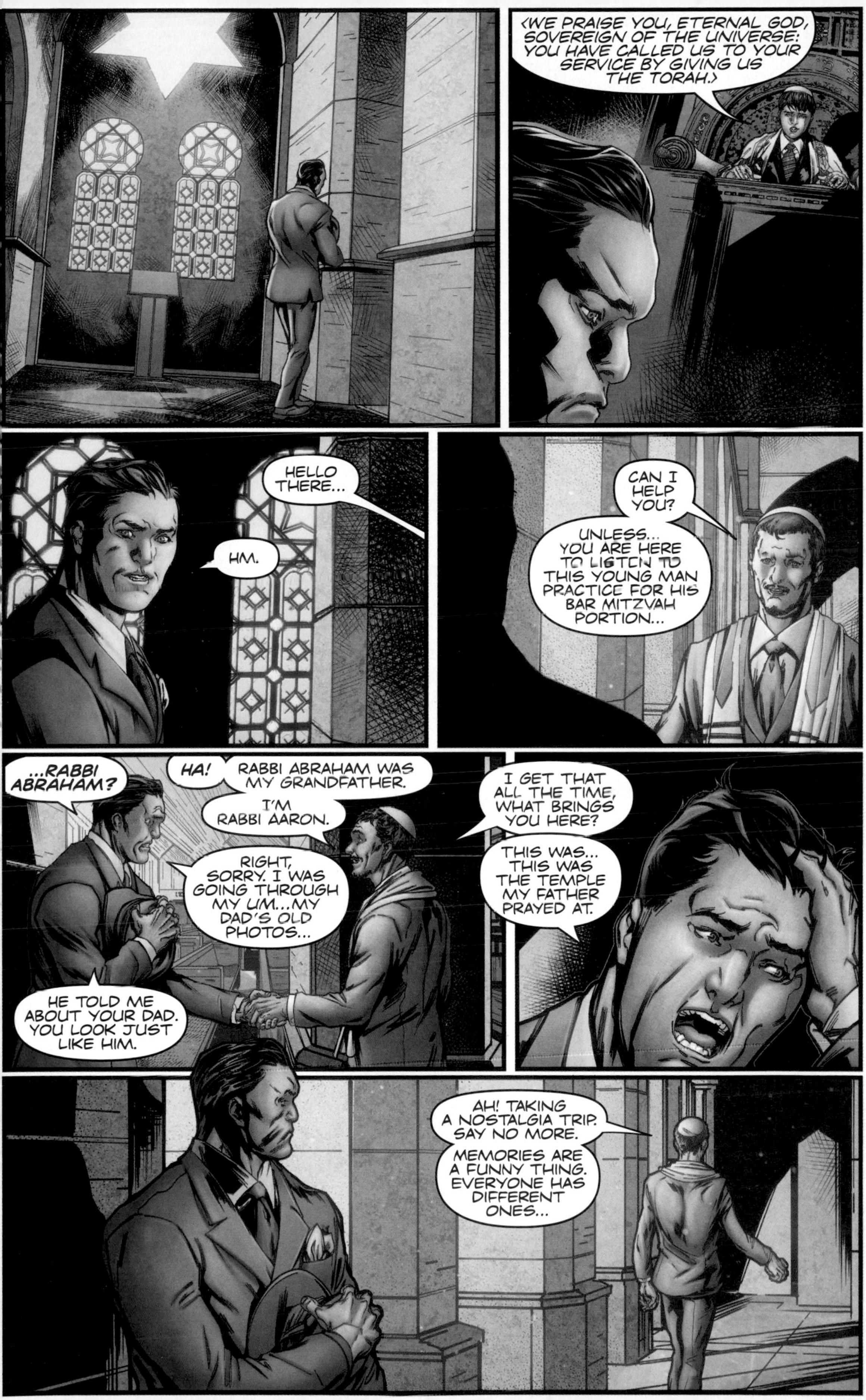

‹WE PRAISE YOU, ETERNAL GOD, SOVEREIGN OF THE UNIVERSE: YOU HAVE CALLED US TO YOUR SERVICE BY GIVING US THE TORAH.›
HELLO THERE...
HM.
CAN I HELP YOU?
UNLESS... YOU ARE HERE TO LISTEN TO THIS YOUNG MAN PRACTICE FOR HIS BAR MITZVAH PORTION...
...RABBI ABRAHAM?
HA!
RABBI ABRAHAM WAS MY GRANDFATHER.
I'M RABBI AARON.
RIGHT, SORRY. I WAS GOING THROUGH MY UM...MY DAD'S OLD PHOTOS...
HE TOLD ME ABOUT YOUR DAD. YOU LOOK JUST LIKE HIM.
I GET THAT ALL THE TIME, WHAT BRINGS YOU HERE?
THIS WAS... THIS WAS THE TEMPLE MY FATHER PRAYED AT.
AH! TAKING A NOSTALGIA TRIP. SAY NO MORE.
MEMORIES ARE A FUNNY THING. EVERYONE HAS DIFFERENT ONES...

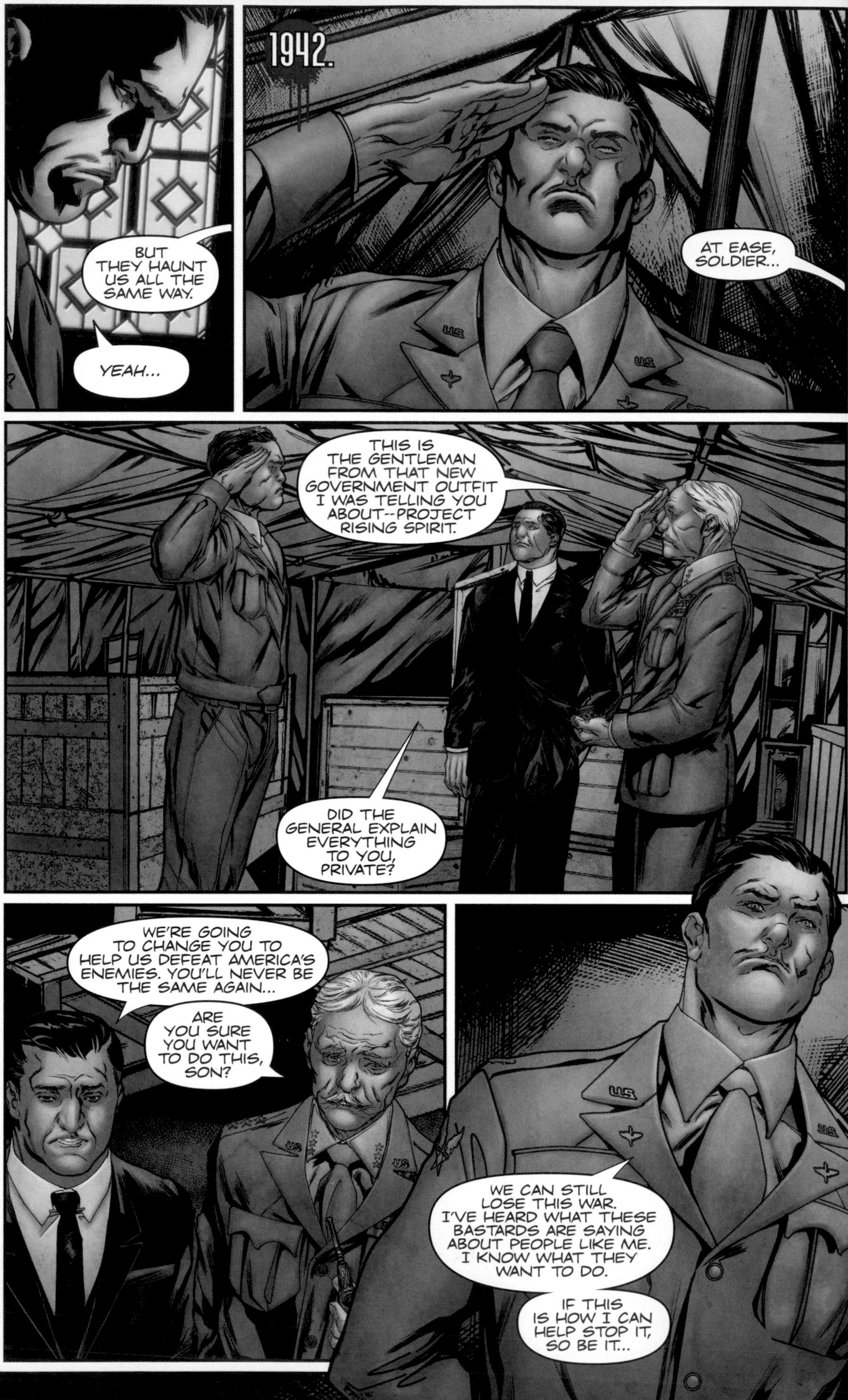
BUT THEY HAUNT US ALL THE SAME WAY.
YEAH...
1942.
AT EASE, SOLDIER...
THIS IS THE GENTLEMAN FROM THAT NEW GOVERNMENT OUTFIT I WAS TELLING YOU ABOUT--PROJECT RISING SPIRIT.
DID THE GENERAL EXPLAIN EVERYTHING TO YOU, PRIVATE?
WE'RE GOING TO CHANGE YOU TO HELP US DEFEAT AMERICA'S ENEMIES. YOU'LL NEVER BE THE SAME AGAIN...
ARE YOU SURE YOU WANT TO DO THIS, SON?
WE CAN STILL LOSE THIS WAR. I'VE HEARD WHAT THESE BASTARDS ARE SAYING ABOUT PEOPLE LIKE ME. I KNOW WHAT THEY WANT TO DO.
IF THIS IS HOW I CAN HELP STOP IT, SO BE IT...

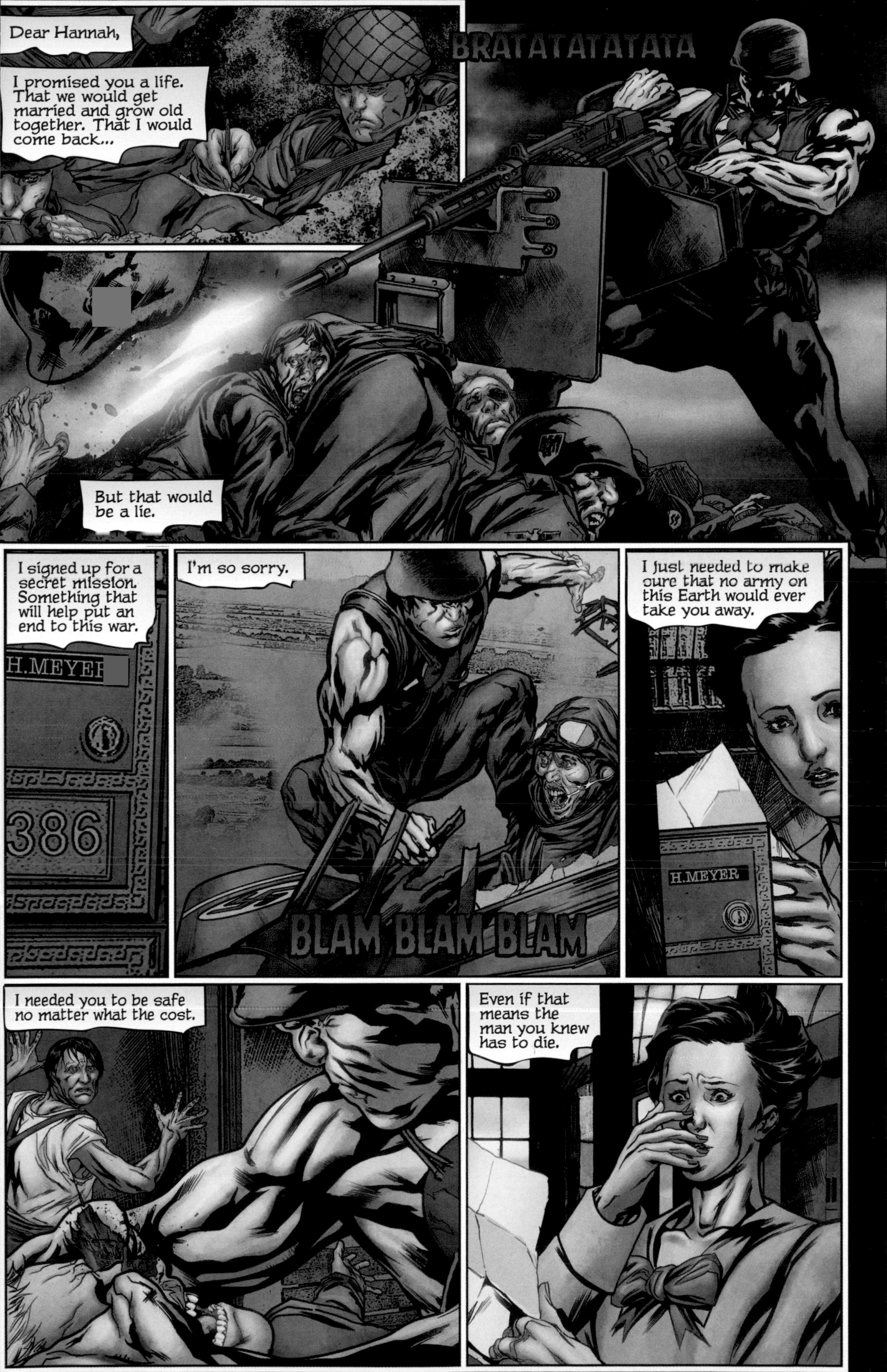

Dear Hannah,
I promised you a life. That we would get married and grow old together. That I would come back...
BRATATATATATA
But that would be a lie.
I signed up for a secret mission. Something that will help put an end to this war.
386
I'm so sorry.
BLAM BLAM BLAM
I just needed to make sure that no army on this Earth would ever take you away.
H.MEYER
I needed you to be safe no matter what the cost.
Even if that means the man you knew has to die.

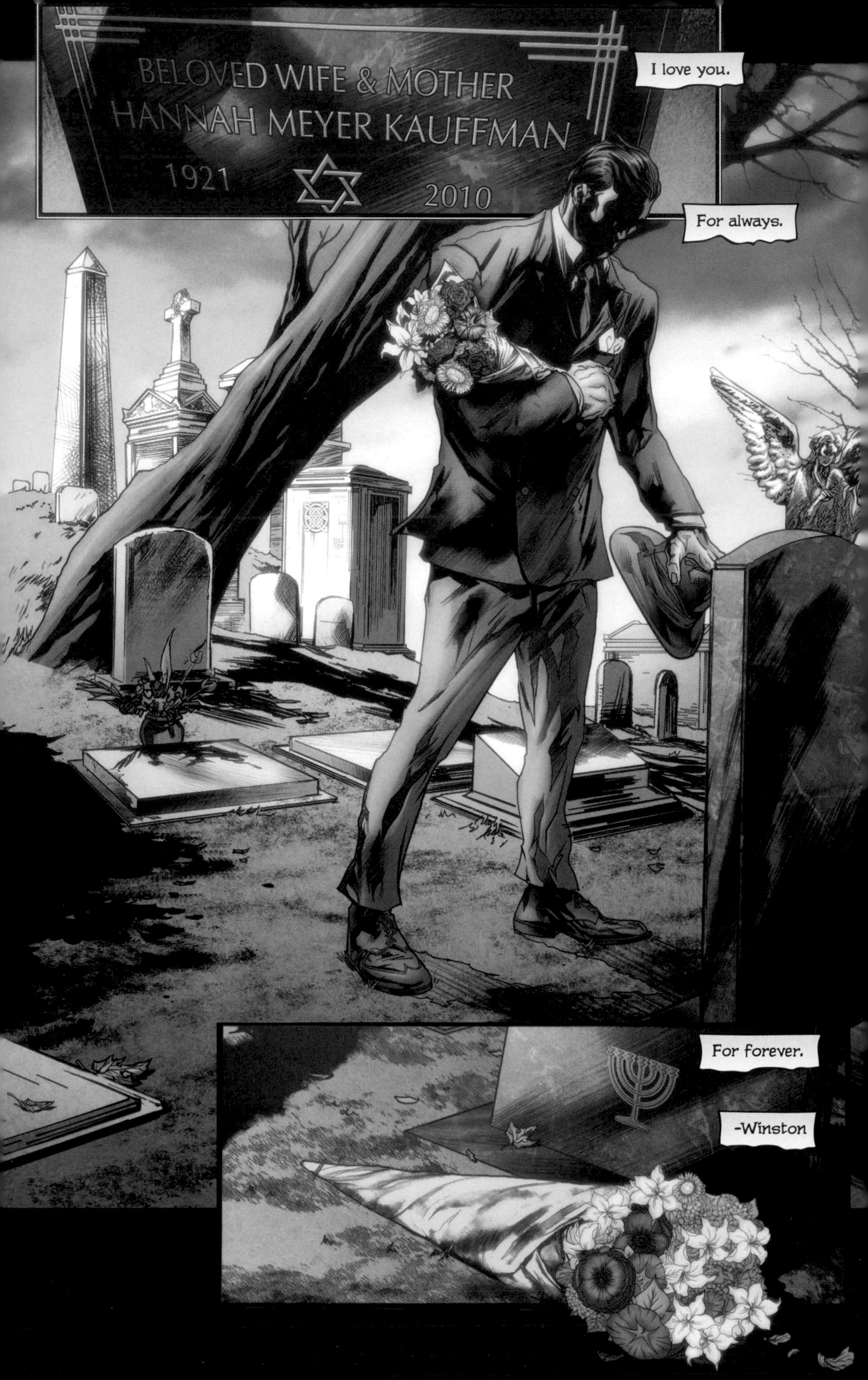
BELOVED WIFE & MOTHER
HANNAH MEYER KAUFFMAN
1921
2010
I love you.
For always.
For forever.
-Winston

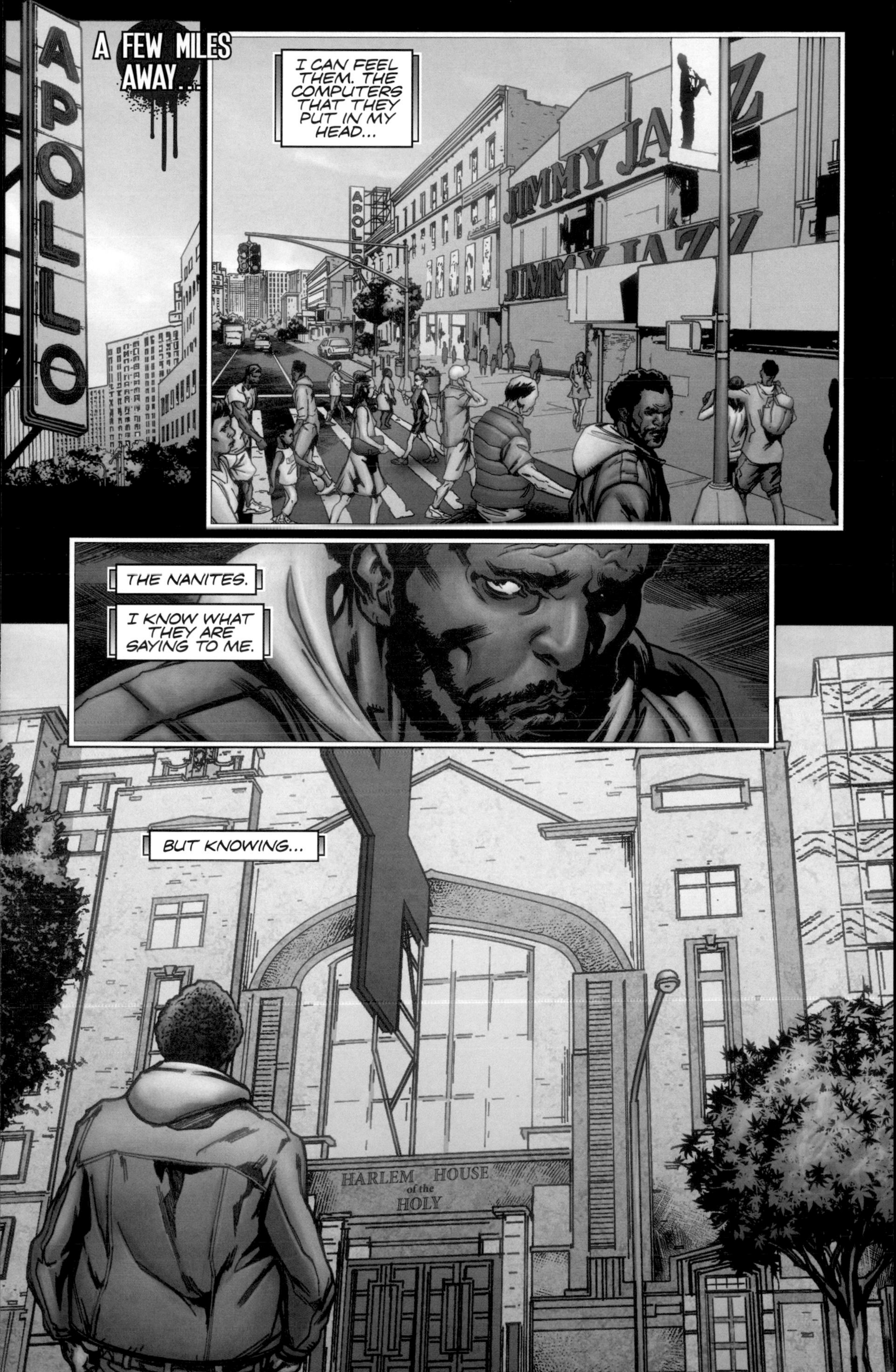
A FEW MILES AWAY...
APOLLO
I CAN FEEL THEM. THE COMPUTERS THAT THEY PUT IN MY HEAD...
JIMMY JAZZ
THE NANITES.
I KNOW WHAT THEY ARE SAYING TO ME.
BUT KNOWING...
HARLEM HOUSE of the HOLY

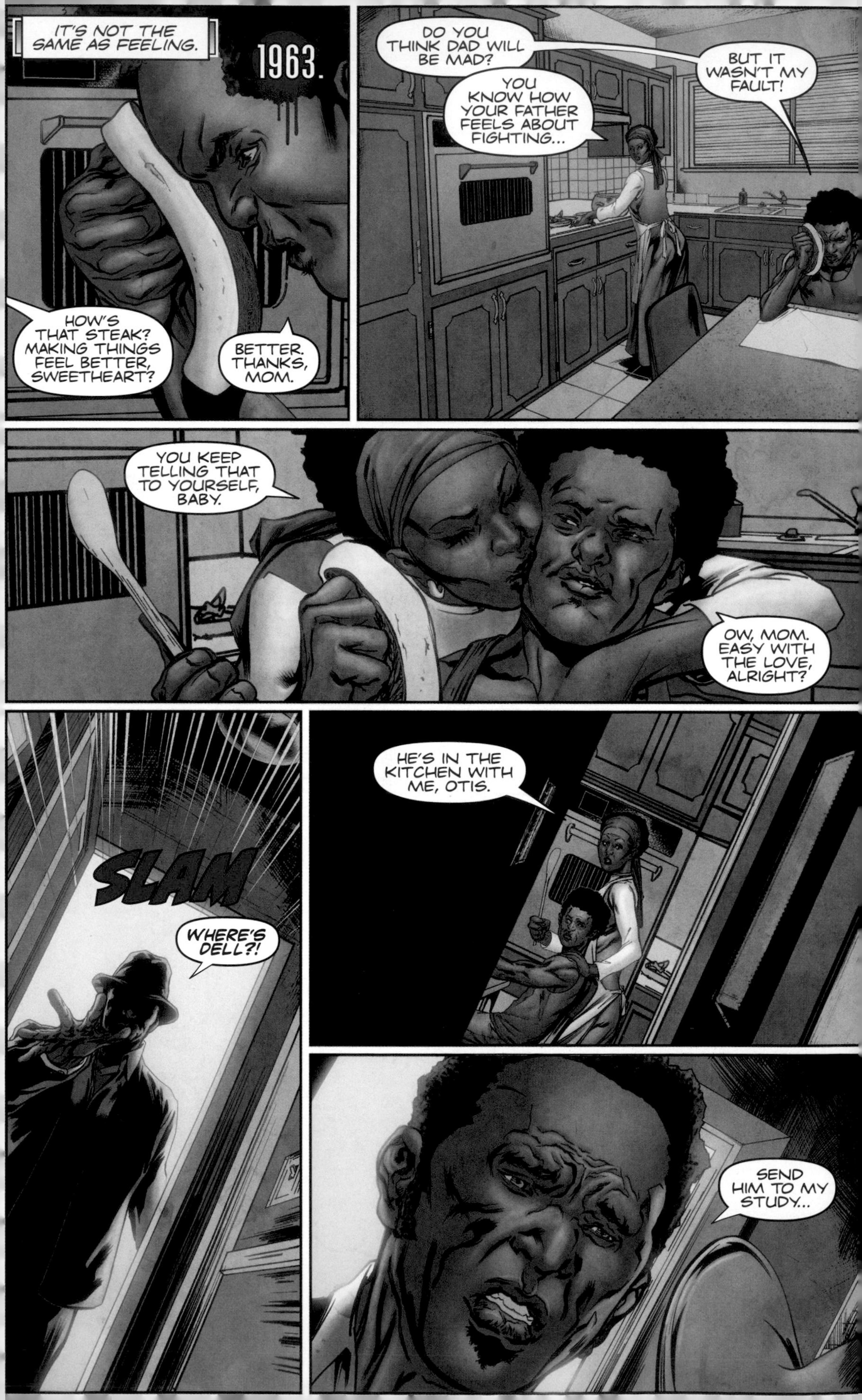
IT'S NOT THE SAME AS FEELING.
1963.
HOW'S THAT STEAK? MAKING THINGS FEEL BETTER, SWEETHEART?
BETTER. THANKS, MOM.
DO YOU THINK DAD WILL BE MAD?
YOU KNOW HOW YOUR FATHER FEELS ABOUT FIGHTING...
BUT IT WASN'T MY FAULT!
YOU KEEP TELLING THAT TO YOURSELF, BABY.
OW, MOM. EASY WITH THE LOVE, ALRIGHT?
SLAM
WHERE'S DELL?!
HE'S IN THE KITCHEN WITH ME, OTIS.
SEND HIM TO MY STUDY...

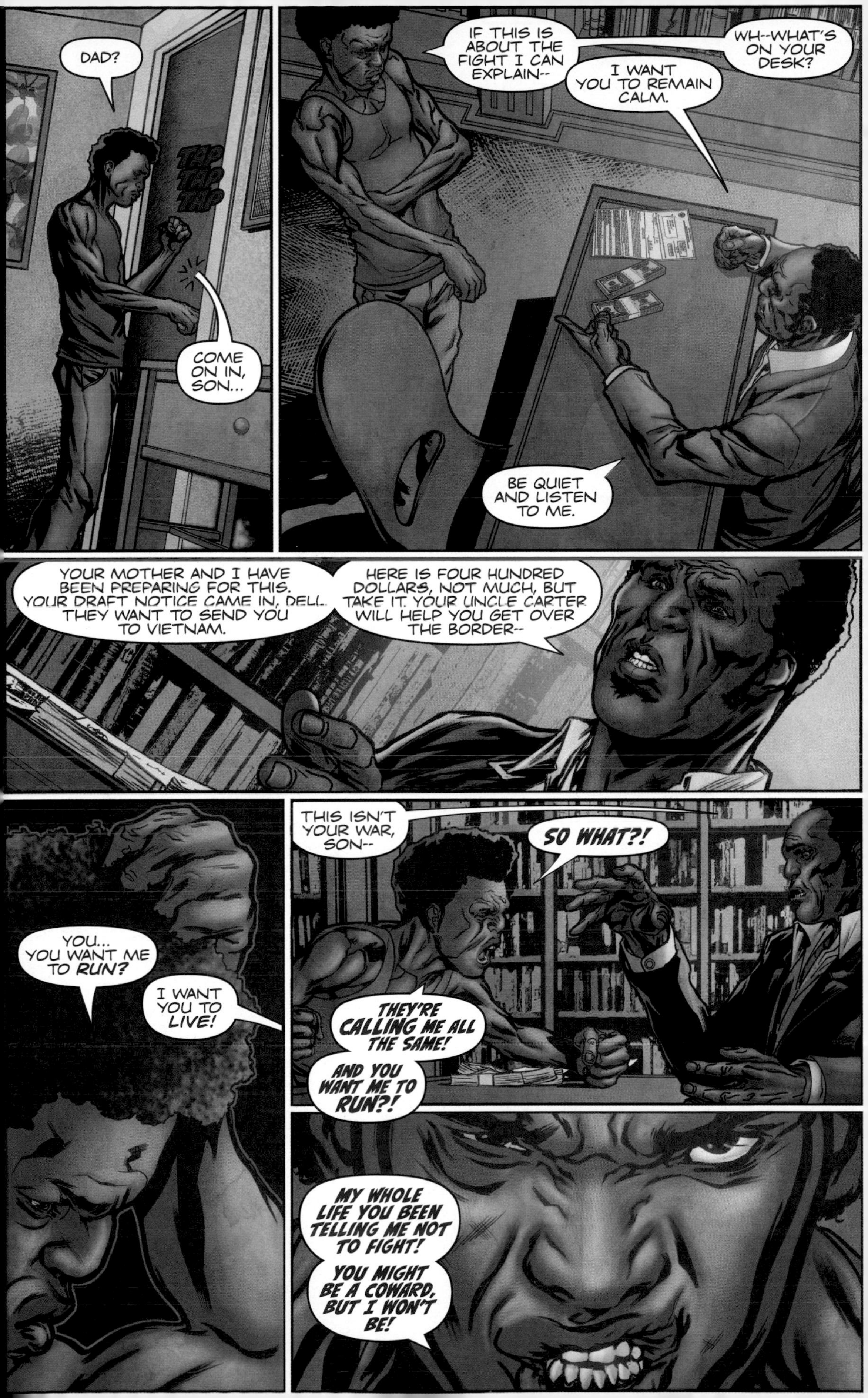
DAD?
TAP TAP TAP
COME ON IN, SON...
IF THIS IS ABOUT THE FIGHT I CAN EXPLAIN--
I WANT YOU TO REMAIN CALM.
WH--WHAT'S ON YOUR DESK?
BE QUIET AND LISTEN TO ME.
YOUR MOTHER AND I HAVE BEEN PREPARING FOR THIS. YOUR DRAFT NOTICE CAME IN, DELL. THEY WANT TO SEND YOU TO VIETNAM.
HERE IS FOUR HUNDRED DOLLARS, NOT MUCH, BUT TAKE IT. YOUR UNCLE CARTER WILL HELP YOU GET OVER THE BORDER--
YOU... YOU WANT ME TO RUN?
I WANT YOU TO LIVE!
THIS ISN'T YOUR WAR, SON--
SO WHAT?!
THEY'RE CALLING ME ALL THE SAME!
AND YOU WANT ME TO RUN?!
MY WHOLE LIFE YOU BEEN TELLING ME NOT TO FIGHT!
YOU MIGHT BE A COWARD, BUT I WON'T BE!

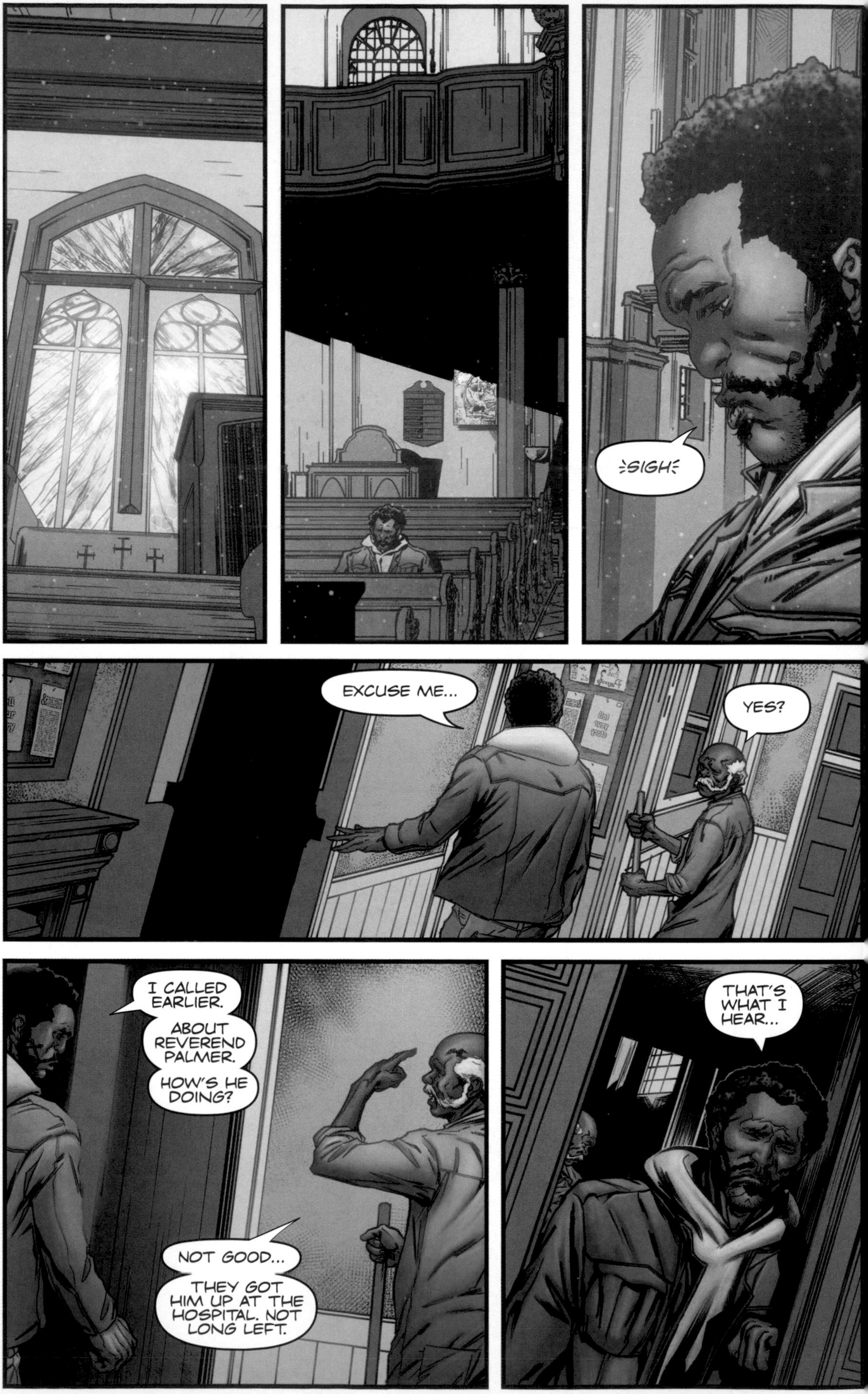

SIGH
EXCUSE ME...
YES?
I CALLED EARLIER.
ABOUT REVEREND PALMER.
HOW'S HE DOING?
NOT GOOD...
THEY GOT HIM UP AT THE HOSPITAL. NOT LONG LEFT.
THAT'S WHAT I HEAR...

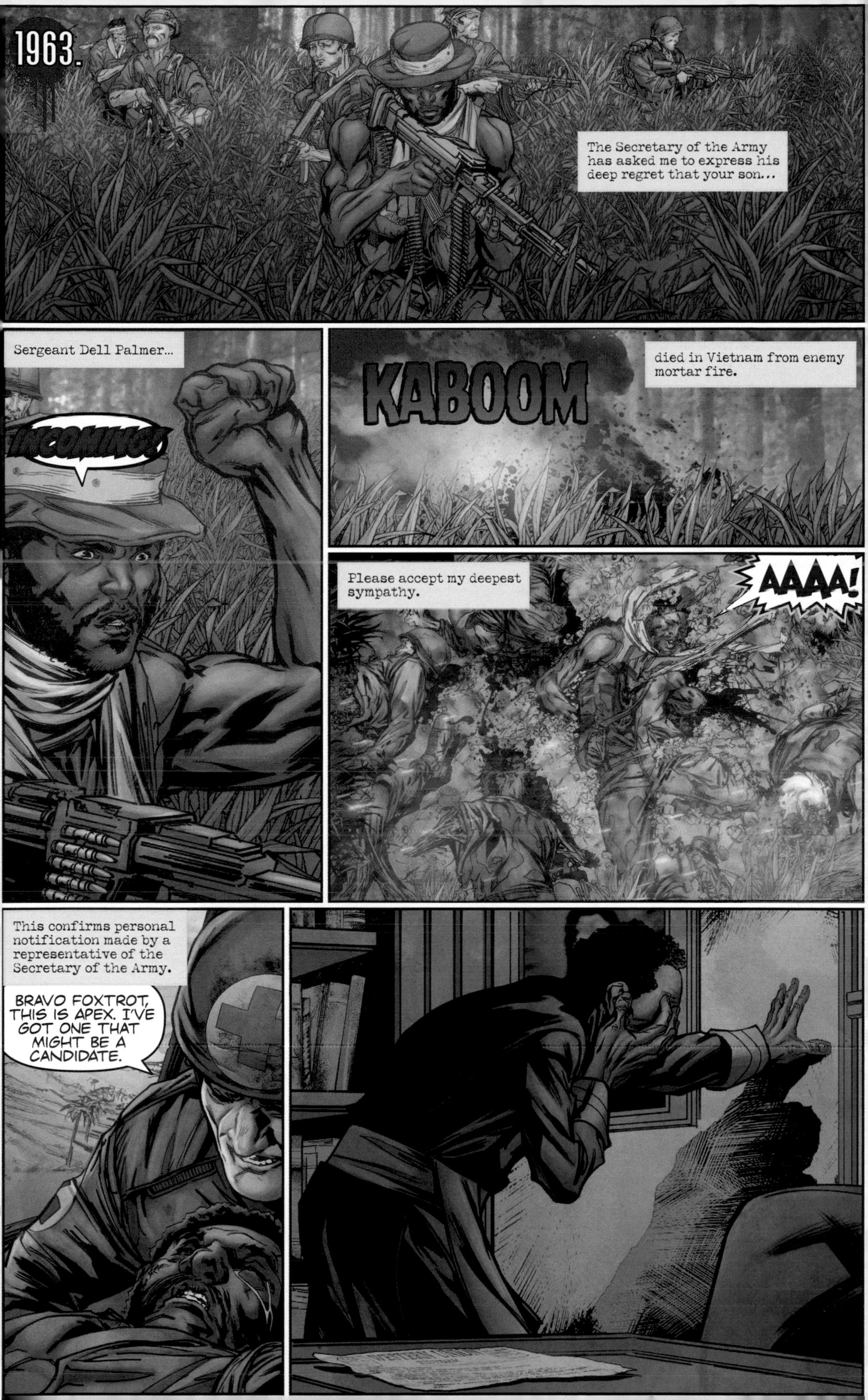
1963.
The Secretary of the Army has asked me to express his deep regret that your son...
Sergeant Dell Palmer...
INCOMING!
KABOOM
died in Vietnam from enemy mortar fire.
Please accept my deepest sympathy.
AAAA!
This confirms personal notification made by a representative of the Secretary of the Army.
BRAVO FOXTROT, THIS IS APEX. I'VE GOT ONE THAT MIGHT BE A CANDIDATE.

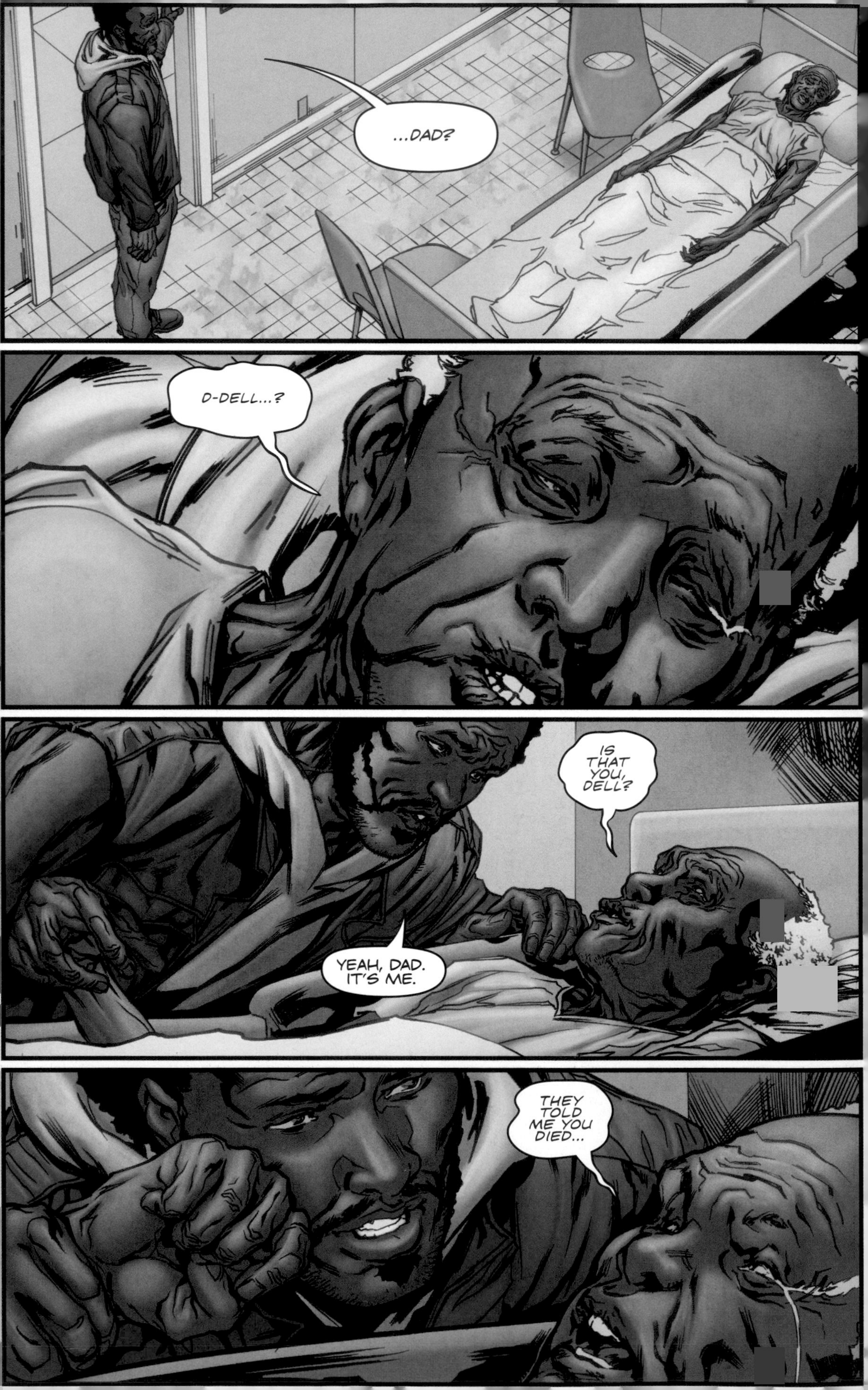
...DAD?
D-DELL...?
IS THAT YOU, DELL?
YEAH, DAD. IT'S ME.
THEY TOLD ME YOU DIED...

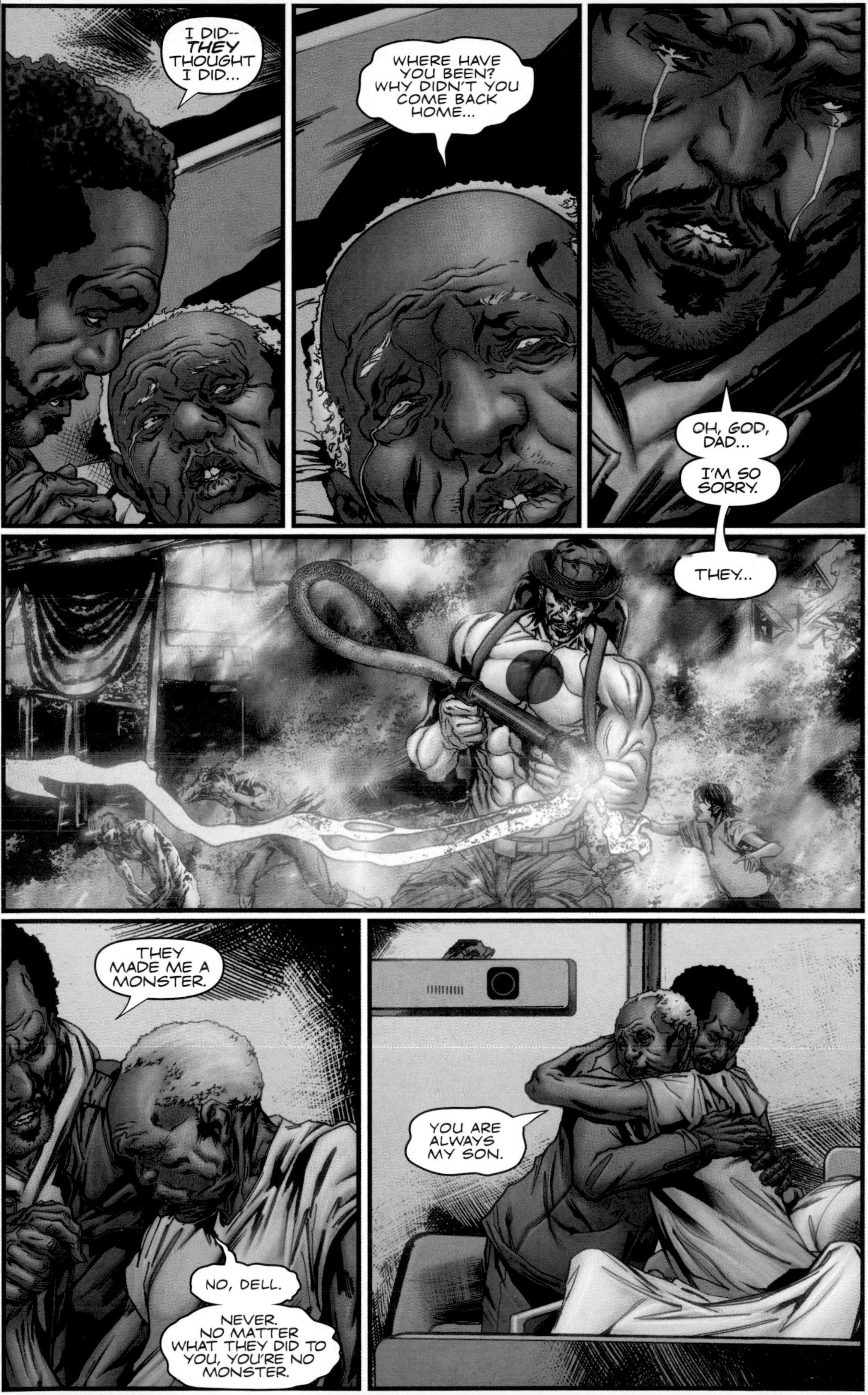

I DID-- THEY THOUGHT I DID...
WHERE HAVE YOU BEEN? WHY DIDN'T YOU COME BACK HOME...
OH, GOD, DAD...
I'M SO SORRY.
THEY...
THEY MADE ME A MONSTER.
NO, DELL.
NEVER. NO MATTER WHAT THEY DID TO YOU, YOU'RE NO MONSTER.
YOU ARE ALWAYS MY SON.

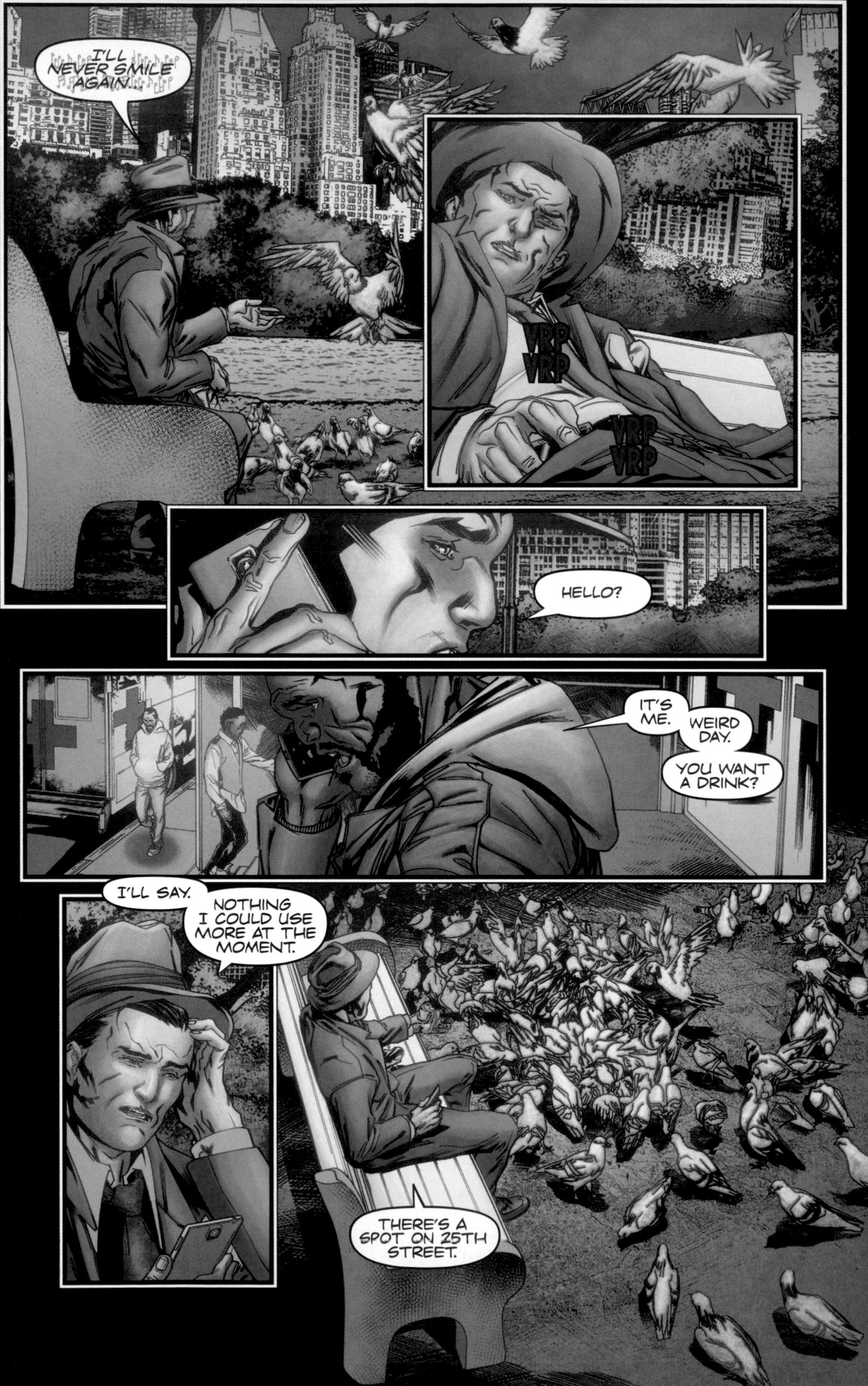
I'LL NEVER SMILE AGAIN...
VRP VRP
VRP VRP
HELLO?
IT'S ME.
WEIRD DAY.
YOU WANT A DRINK?
I'LL SAY.
NOTHING I COULD USE MORE AT THE MOMENT.
THERE'S A SPOT ON 25TH STREET.

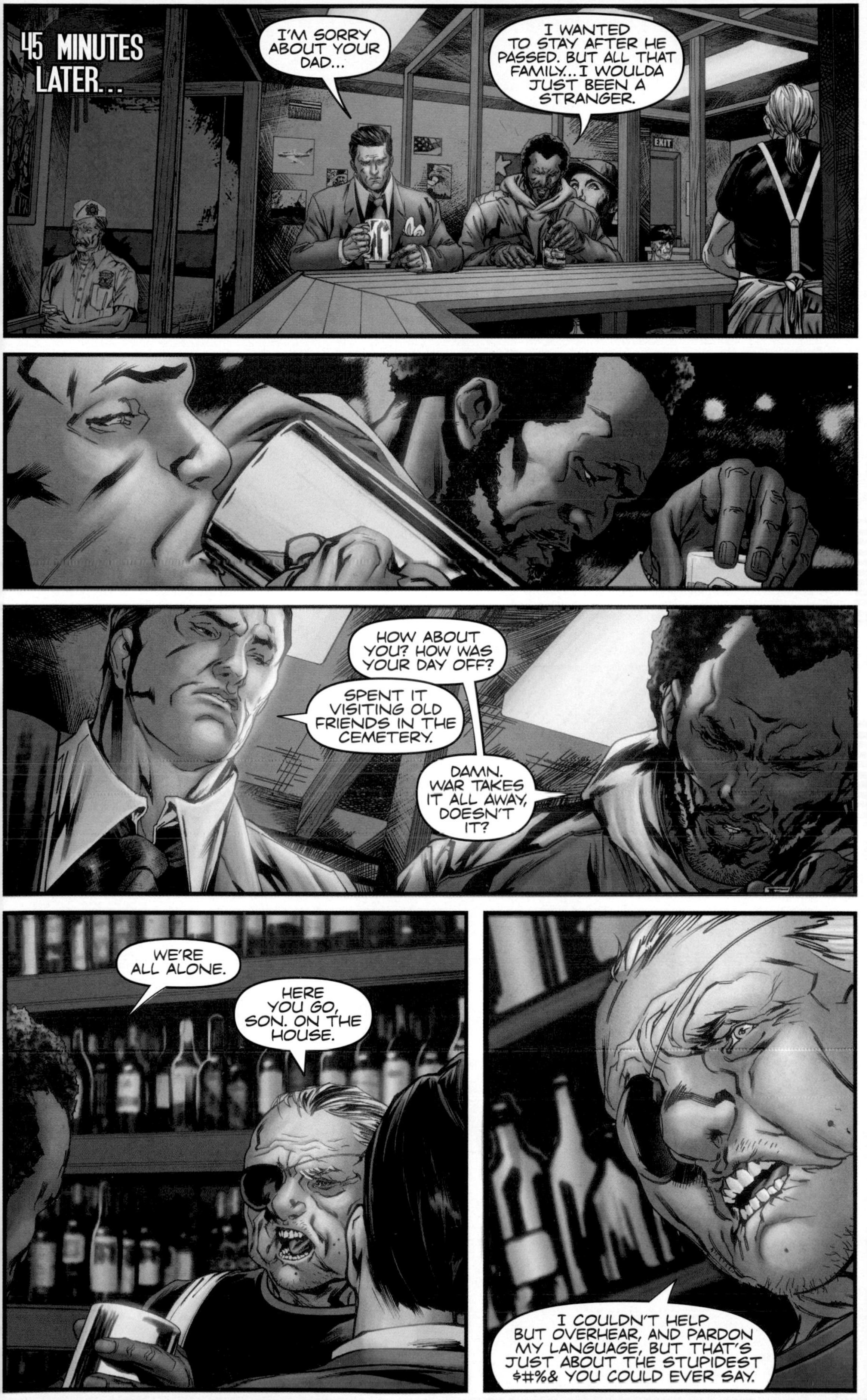
45 MINUTES LATER...
I'M SORRY ABOUT YOUR DAD...
I WANTED TO STAY AFTER HE PASSED. BUT ALL THAT FAMILY... I WOULDA JUST BEEN A STRANGER.
EXIT
HOW ABOUT YOU? HOW WAS YOUR DAY OFF?
SPENT IT VISITING OLD FRIENDS IN THE CEMETERY.
DAMN. WAR TAKES IT ALL AWAY, DOESN'T IT?
WE'RE ALL ALONE.
HERE YOU GO, SON. ON THE HOUSE.
I COULDN'T HELP BUT OVERHEAR, AND PARDON MY LANGUAGE, BUT THAT'S JUST ABOUT THE STUPIDEST $#%& YOU COULD EVER SAY.

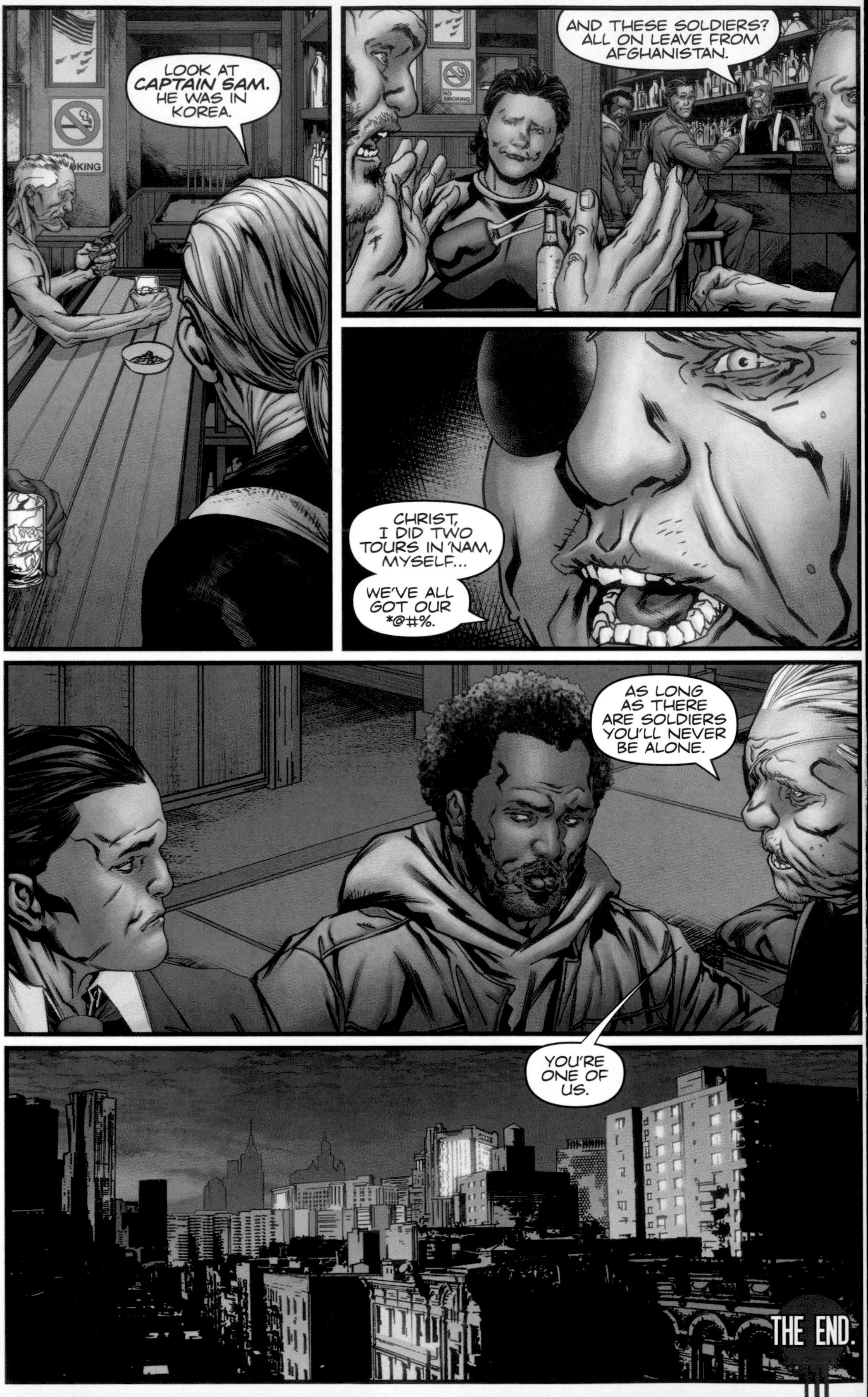
LOOK AT CAPTAIN SAM. HE WAS IN KOREA.
NO SMOKING
AND THESE SOLDIERS? ALL ON LEAVE FROM AFGHANISTAN.
NO SMOKING
CHRIST, I DID TWO TOURS IN 'NAM, MYSELF...
WE'VE ALL GOT OUR *@#%.
AS LONG AS THERE ARE SOLDIERS YOU'LL NEVER BE ALONE.
YOU'RE ONE OF US.
THE END.

GALLERY

BLOODSHOT #6 COVER B
Art by FRITZ CASAS with CANDICE HAN

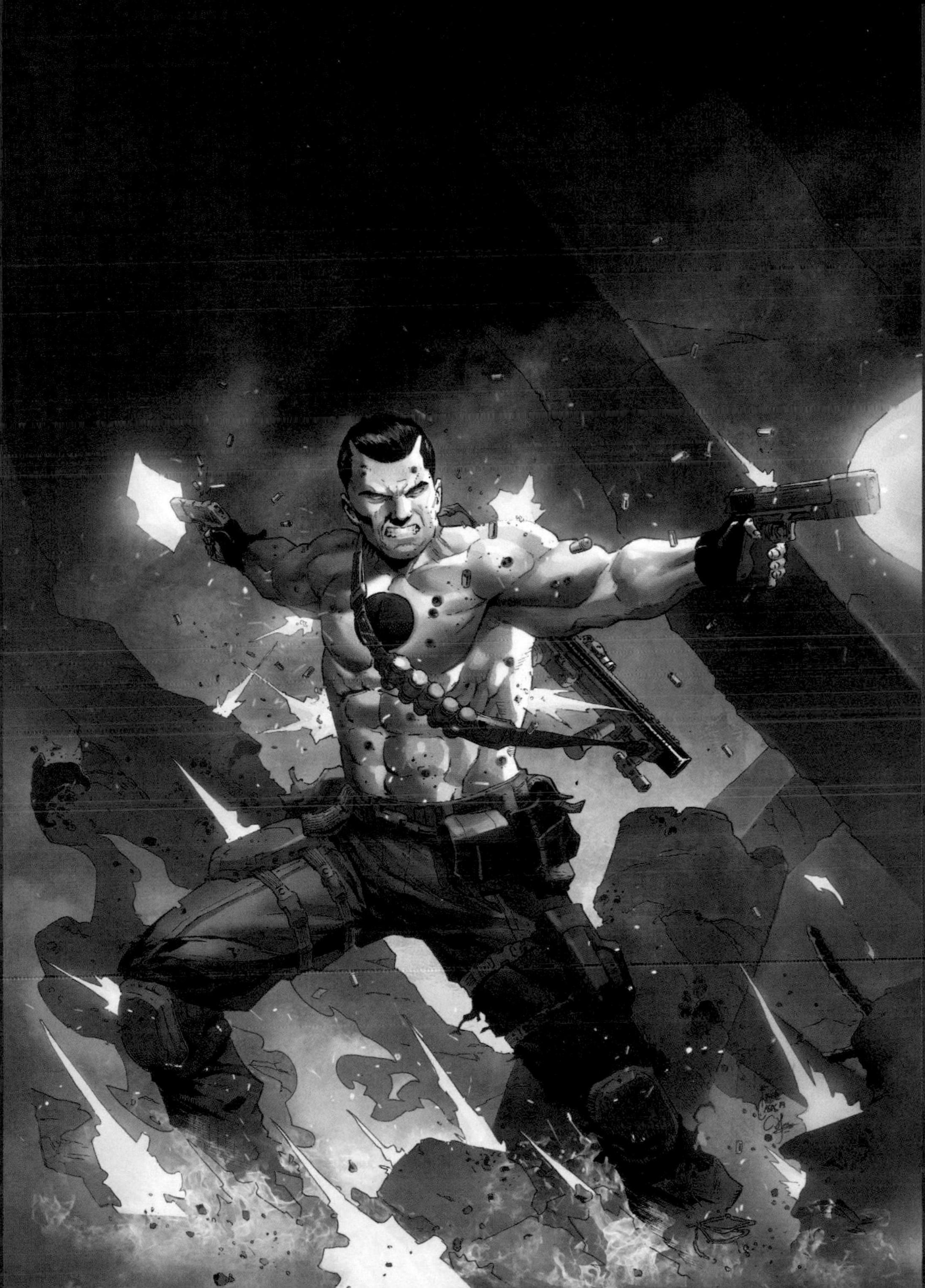

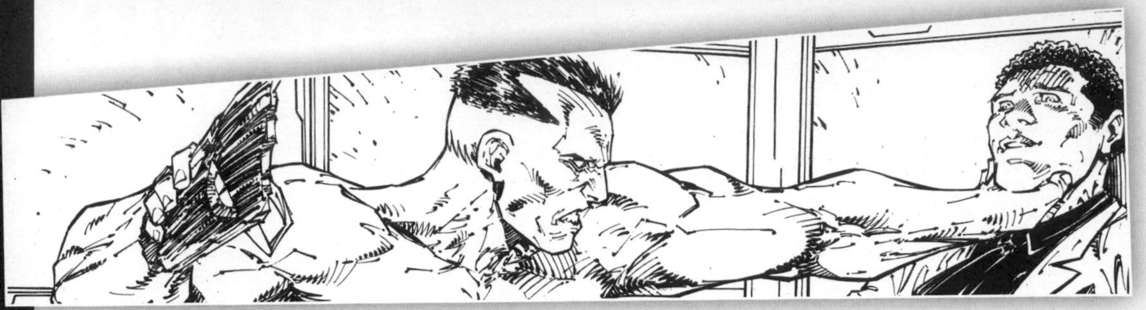

MASKED RAGE:
In profile. An annoyed, angry Bloodshot holding Nix against the wall, one fist pulled back with the BURNED mask he was offered by Nix. It looks like Bloodshot might hit Nix with the mask. Nix is uncomfortable, but trying to keep his humor.

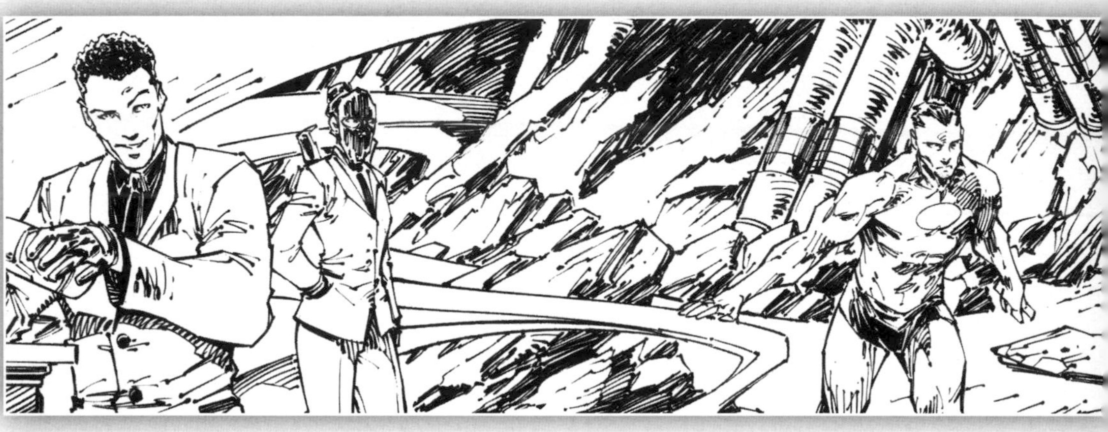

BARSPY:
Bloodshot looks around, standing, as Nix pours a glass of wine for Agent Cant from a nearby table.
There's a variety of stuff on it, including bottles of whisky and drink mix.

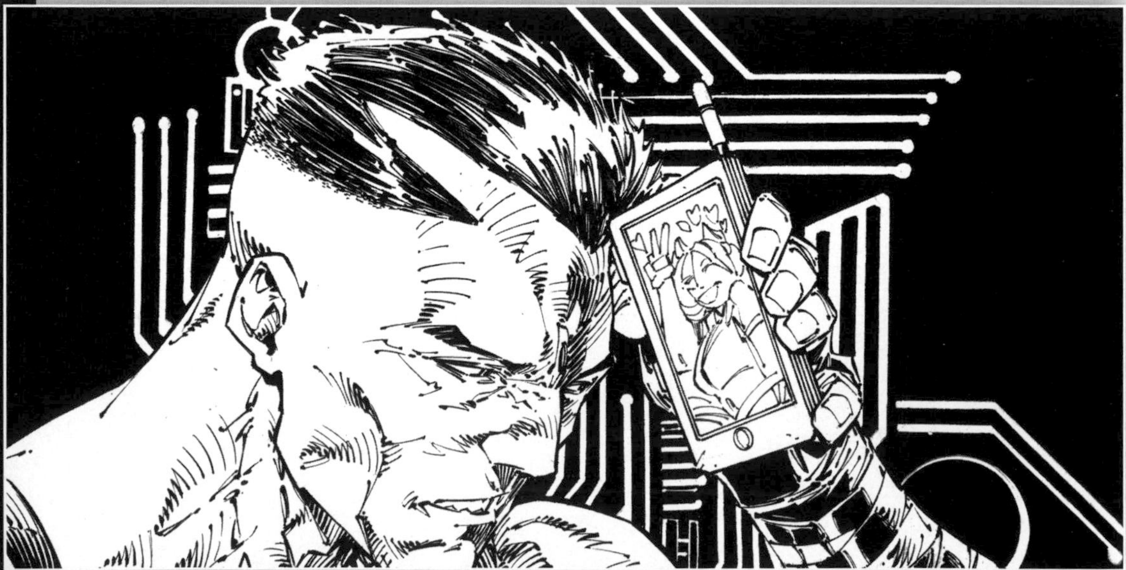

SPYWARE:
Bloodshot holds the device up to his forehead, and we get the tech readout montage/images behind him as he accesses the information contained there.

BY **TIM SEELEY**, ART BY **BRETT BOOTH** WITH **ADELSO CORONA**

BODYGUARD 101:
Big shot! Bloodshot jumps in front of Nix and Cant, pushing both towards the floor, as a torrent of bullets tears through the wall and door! He takes all the shots with his body.

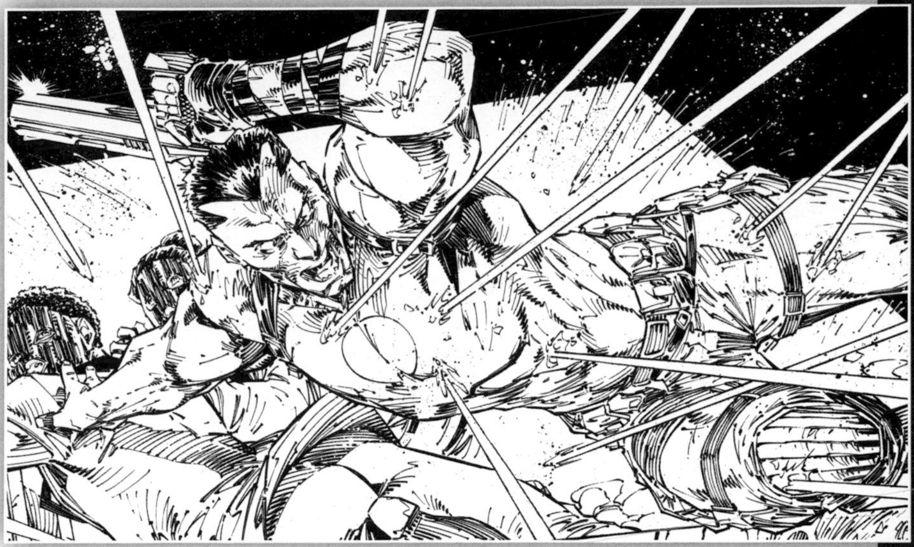

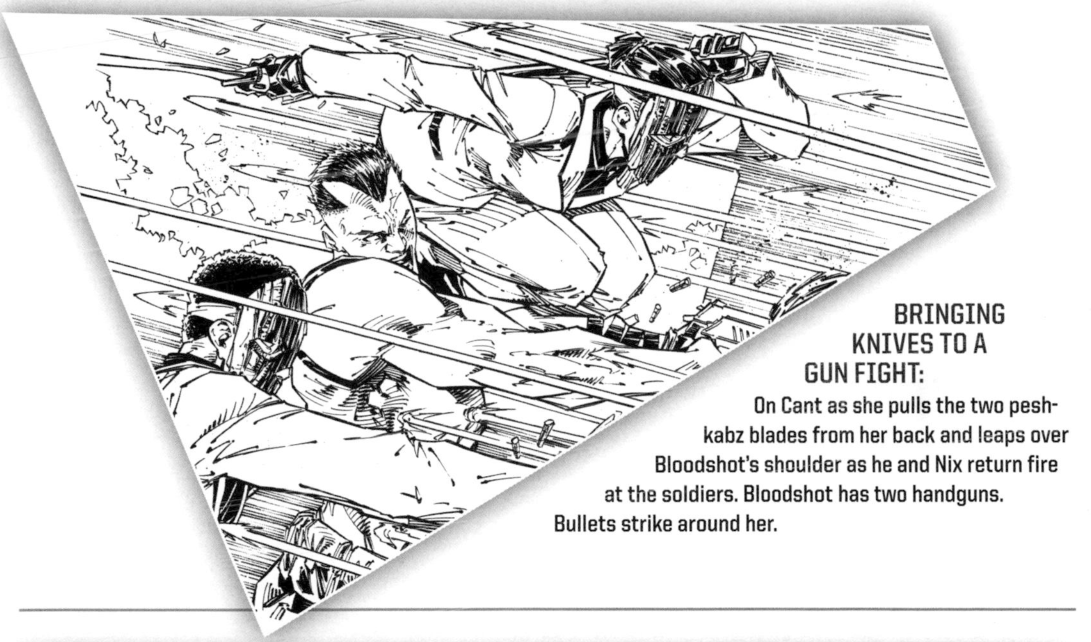

BRINGING KNIVES TO A GUN FIGHT:
On Cant as she pulls the two pesh-kabz blades from her back and leaps over Bloodshot's shoulder as he and Nix return fire at the soldiers. Bloodshot has two handguns. Bullets strike around her.

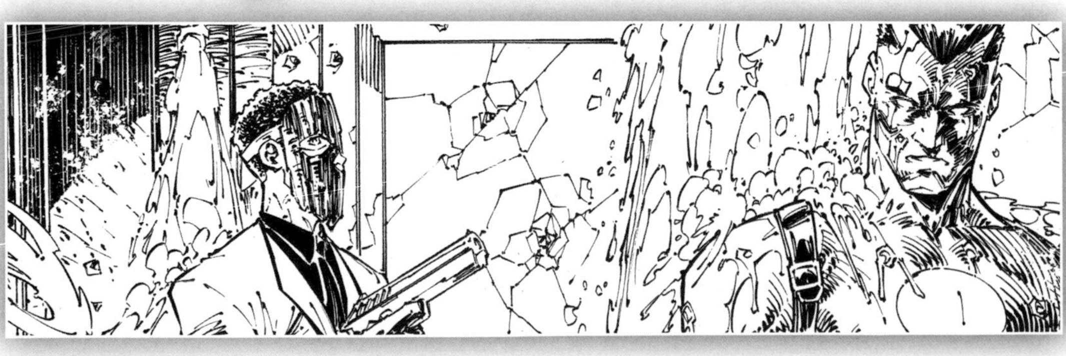

SHOWER POWER:
Bloodshot, with Nix. Bloodshot is full of bloody holes. Water rains down around them from the burst pipes.

BLOOD SHOTS: EXCERPTS FROM BLOODSHOT #5 SCRIPT

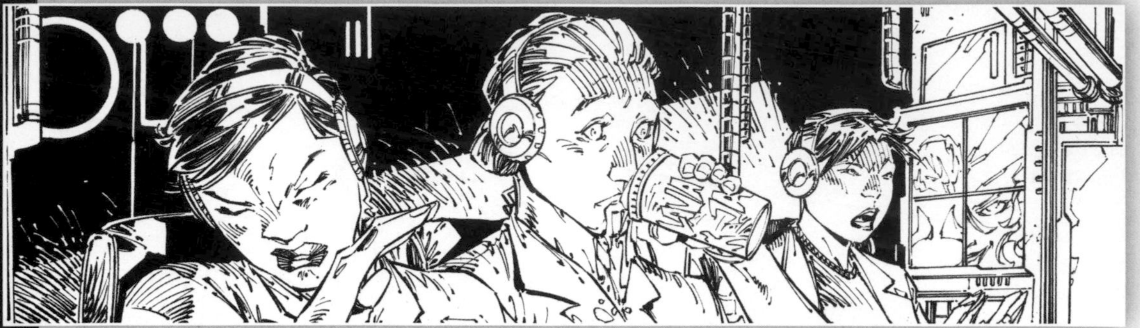

EYEFUL TOWER:

And we cut the command center where Eidolon is observed 24 hours a day. We see this office is all women in military uniforms, wearing headsets, observing rows of monitors. Perhaps two or three women observing Eidolon. And they all wince, having just seen something they did NOT want to see.

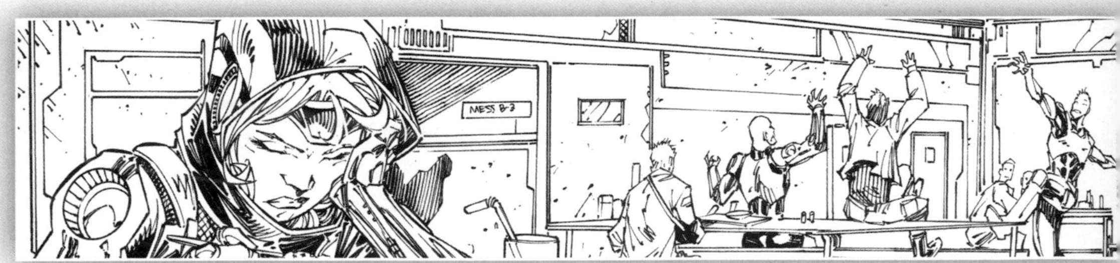

BLACK BAR SNACK BAR:

We cut to the Black Bar base mess hall. Various Black Bar field agents congregating and eating breakfast together. (Maybe we see some of the guys from issue 2, bandaged up and limping after their fight with Bloodshot.)
But Eidolon is eating her breakfast all by herself. She wears the rest of her costume, but the mouth-mask is down so she can chomp of a breakfast of chocolate chip laden oatmeal.

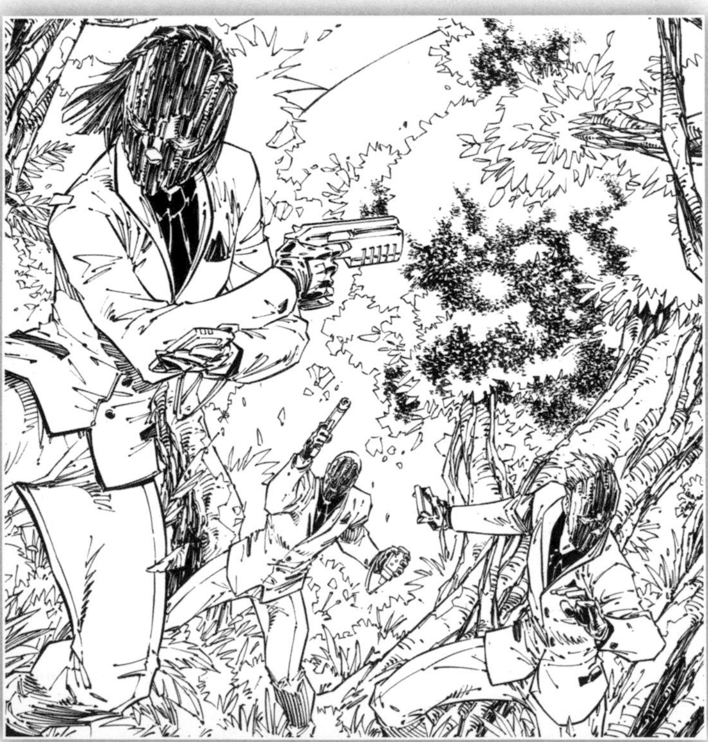

GARDEN TOOLS:

We're inside a dark jungle like area within the house. A green house.
We see three Burned agents (Agent Brink, Agent Yore, Agent Zilch).
Brink and Yore armed with guns and carrying small hand held tracking devices. Zilch is unarmed, but will rely on his taser glove. They all wear their full uniforms and masks.

BY **TIM SEELEY**, ART BY **BRETT BOOTH** WITH **ADELSO CORONA**

A SHOCKING BETRAYAL:

In the background, Bloodshot helps up Brink. She rubs her head.
In the foreground, Zilch activates his taser glove,
letting it spark with electricity.

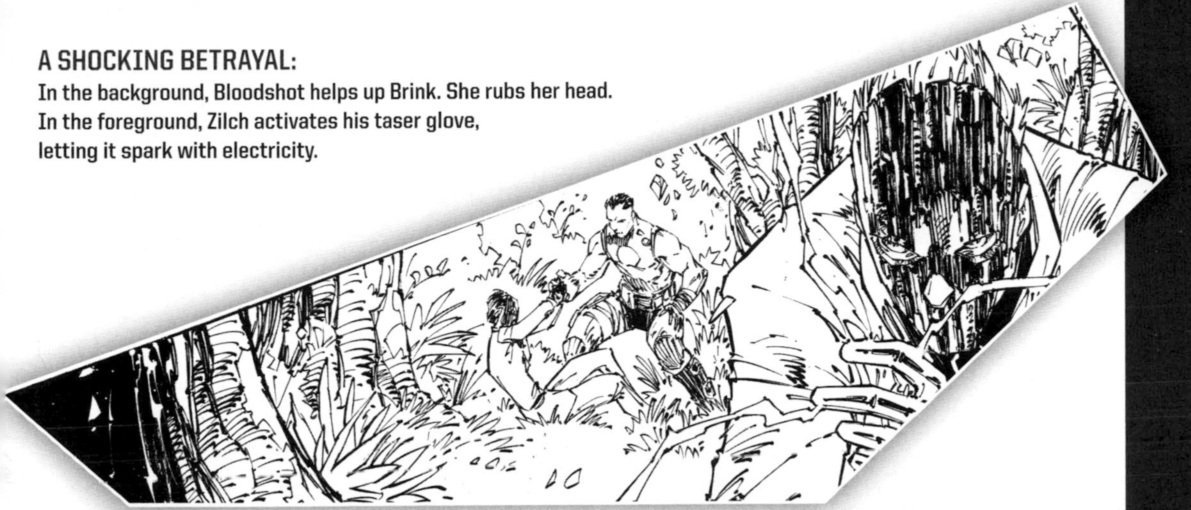

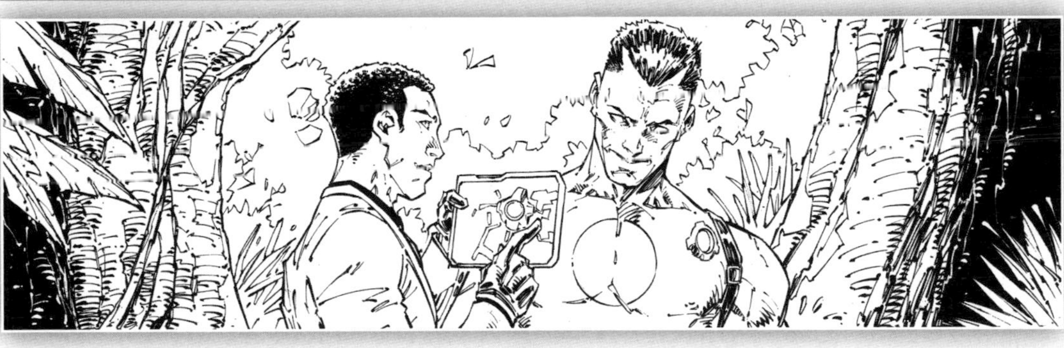

SCAN OF WHOOP-ASS:

Nix has the scanner in front of the ports on Bloodshot's chest, and we get some kind of cool X-ray 3-D scan thing. Whatever is cool. We see the implants in his skin.

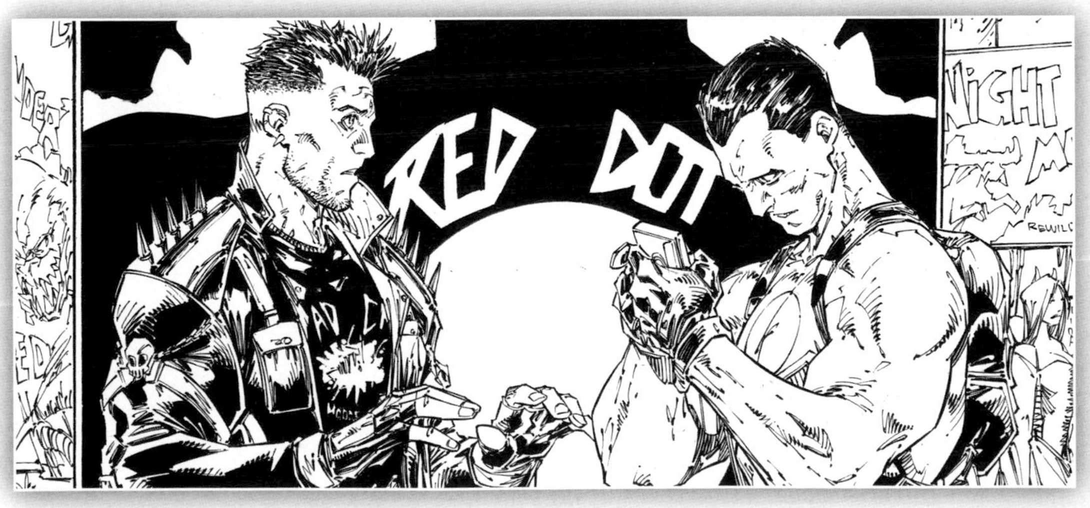
RED DOT
NIGHT

DOUBLE SHOT:

Bloodshot is face to face with another Bloodshot. Or rather, a guy dressed as him. A pretty good cosplay, which I would imagine would be based off his look from BLOODSHOT USA, since that's where he'd have seen him. Real Bloodshot has a pretty shocked expression on his face, unsure what to say or do.

Originally presented in ***BLOODSHOT PRE-ORDER EDITION #5***

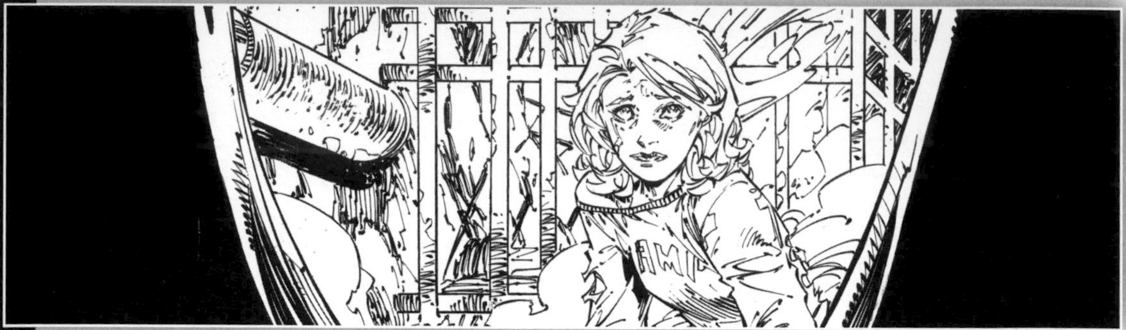

CAPTIVE AUDIENCE:
And we see who is looking up at them. It's young Mina, tears in her eyes. She's dressed just as she was when we saw her in the flashback of issue 3. Her 'cage' is directly behind her (the one Bloodshot got her out of in issue 3).

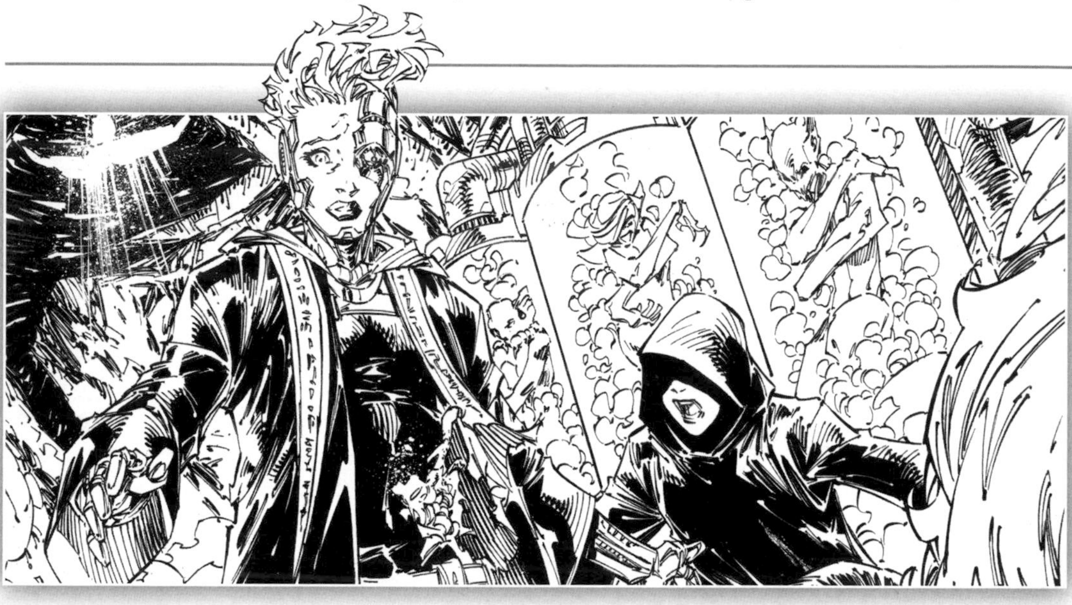

BULLET POINTS:
Past Mina, her face bloodied. And standing there, shocked and horrified is Friday...a bullet has passed through her body from the back and blown out her stomach. We see a small pinpoint of sunlight in the ceiling above her where the bullet went through. One of the scientists beside her looks shocked.

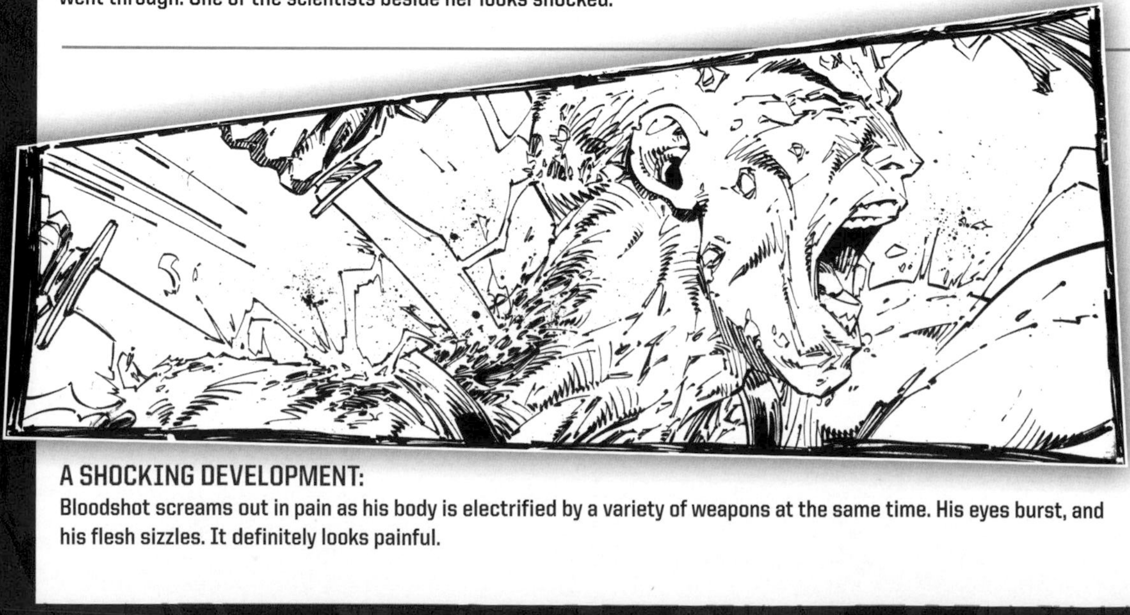

A SHOCKING DEVELOPMENT:
Bloodshot screams out in pain as his body is electrified by a variety of weapons at the same time. His eyes burst, and his flesh sizzles. It definitely looks painful.

BY **TIM SEELEY**, ART BY **BRETT BOOTH** WITH **ADELSO CORONA**

DON'T LEAVE ME HANGING:

Meanwhile, we see a bloodied and seared Bloodshot's hand as it reaches out from where he's being mobbed by attacking Last Sons.

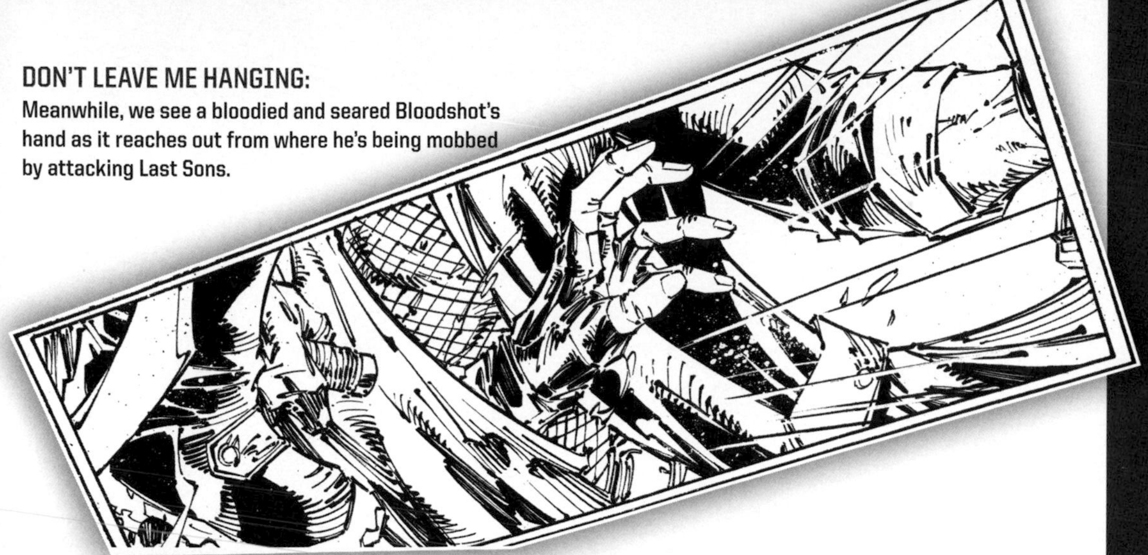

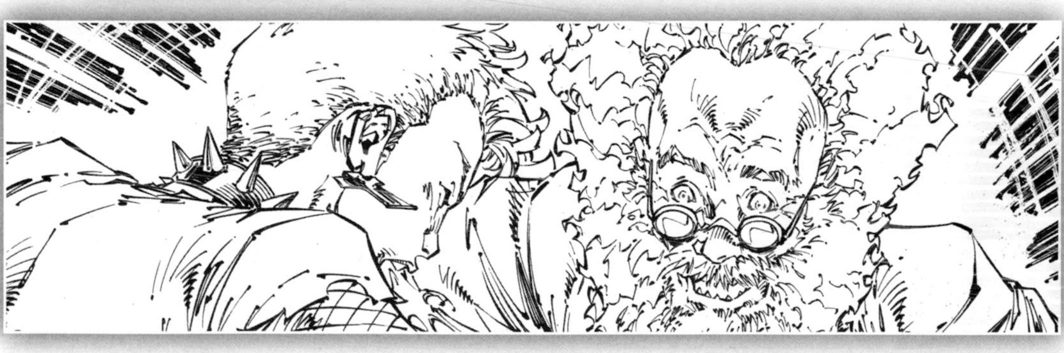

BARF ASSOCIATION:

And she leans over and throws up on the ticket taker (we don't have to see the barf...just her fighting through this and leaning on this unsuspecting guy).

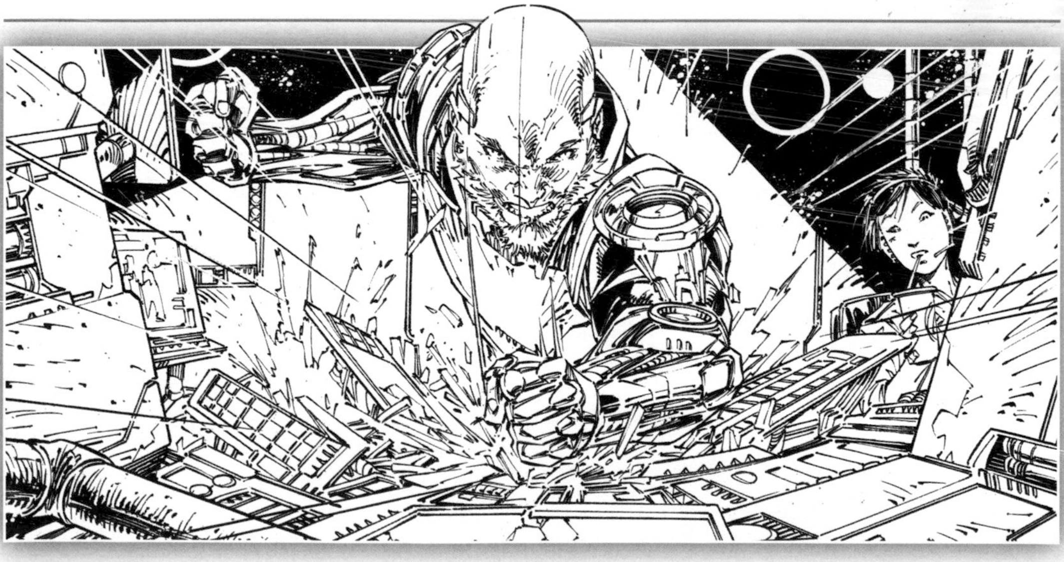

HOLY GRAYLE:

Cut to the Black Bar central command hub...Grayle leaning over a large communications station beside a communications agent, angrily slamming his fist on the console.

BLOODSHOT PRE-ORDER EDITION #4 COVER
Art by SIMON BISLEY

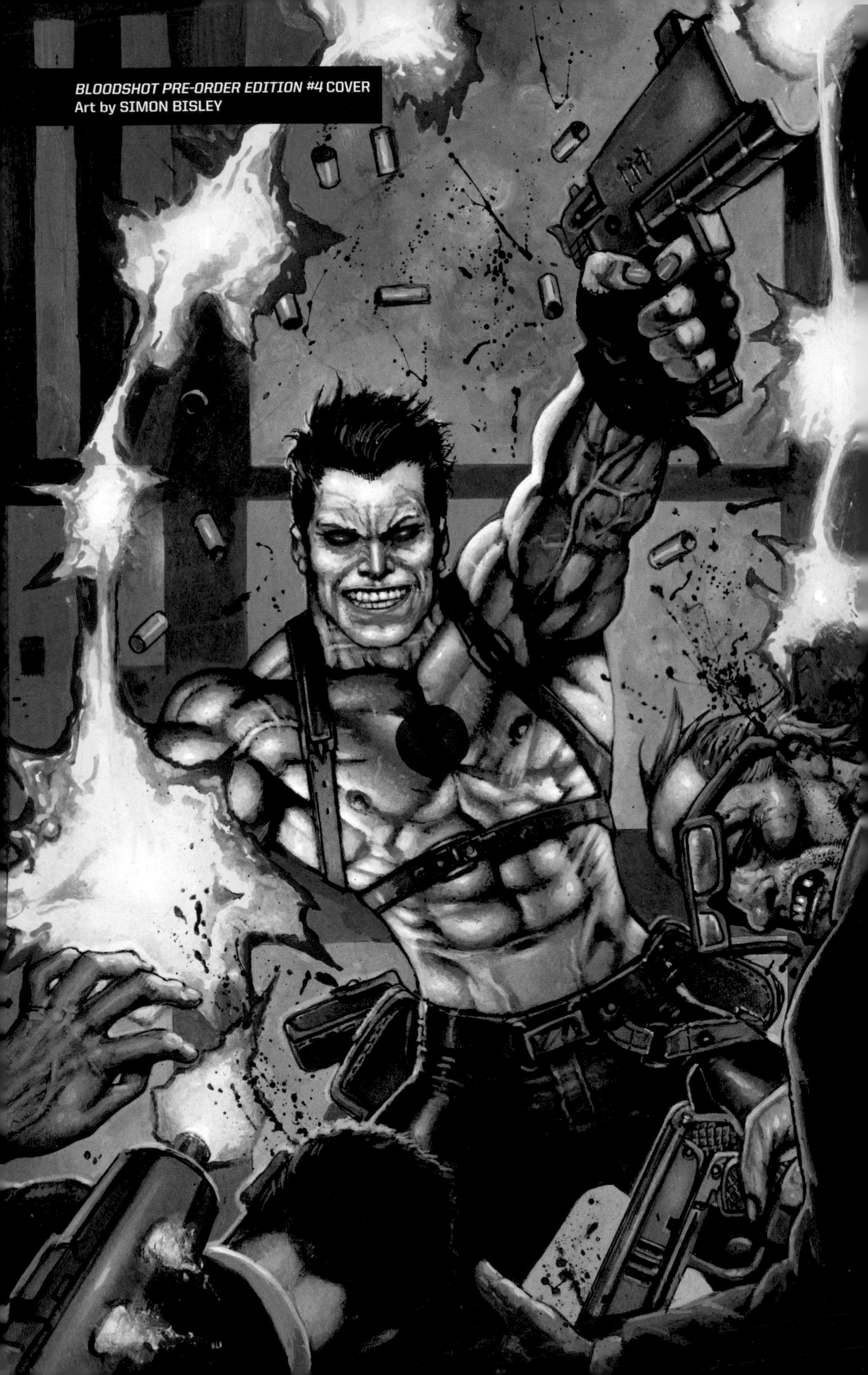

BLOODSHOT #4 COVER B
Art by MIKE MCKONE with GABE ELTAEB

BLOODSHOT #5 COVER B
Art by BILLY TUCCI with WES HARTMAN

BLOODSHOT #5 COVER C
Art by LEO COLAPIETRO

BLOODSHOT PRE-ORDER EDITION #5 COVER
Art by DAVE JOHNSON

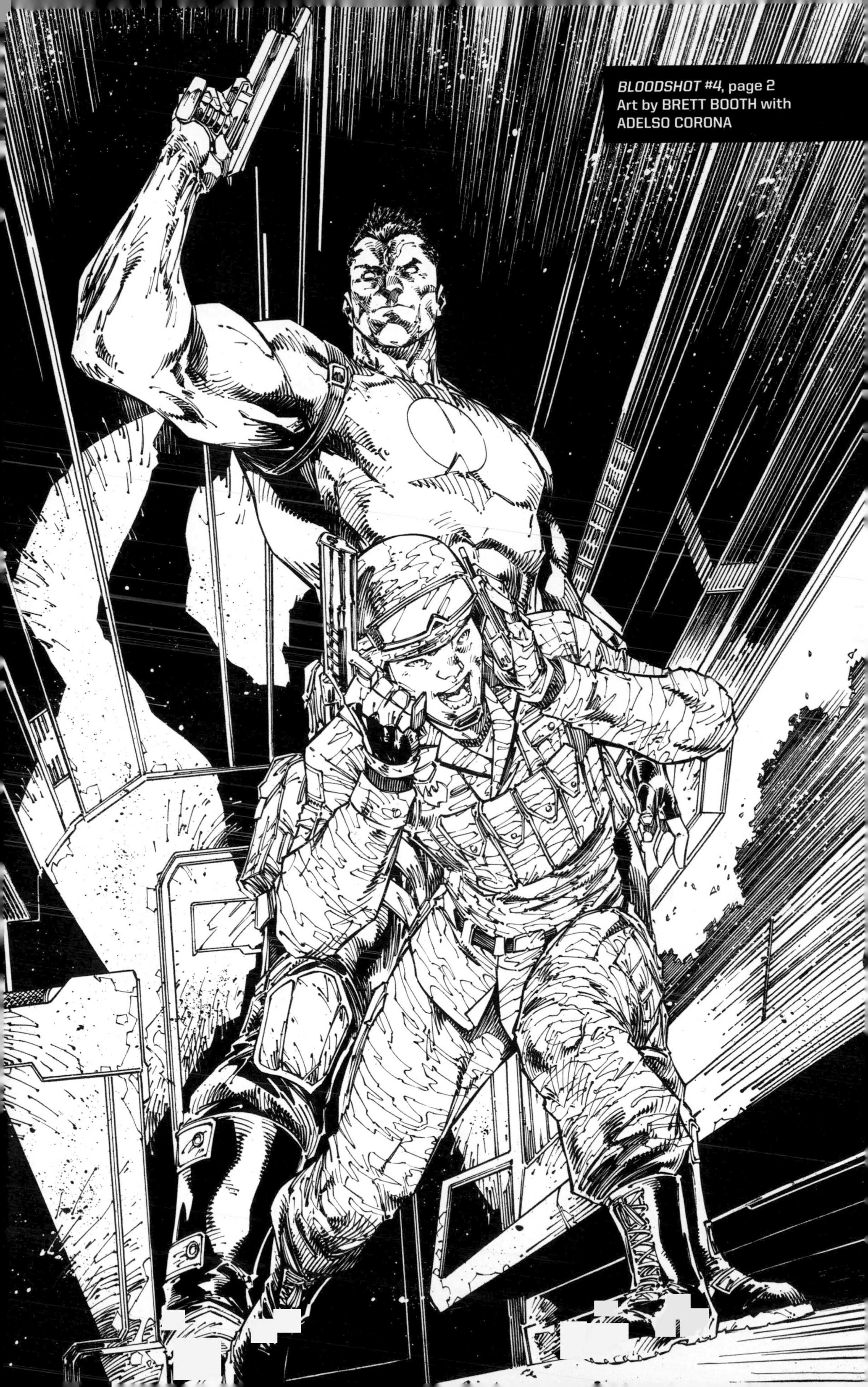

BLOODSHOT #4, page 2
Art by BRETT BOOTH with
ADELSO CORONA

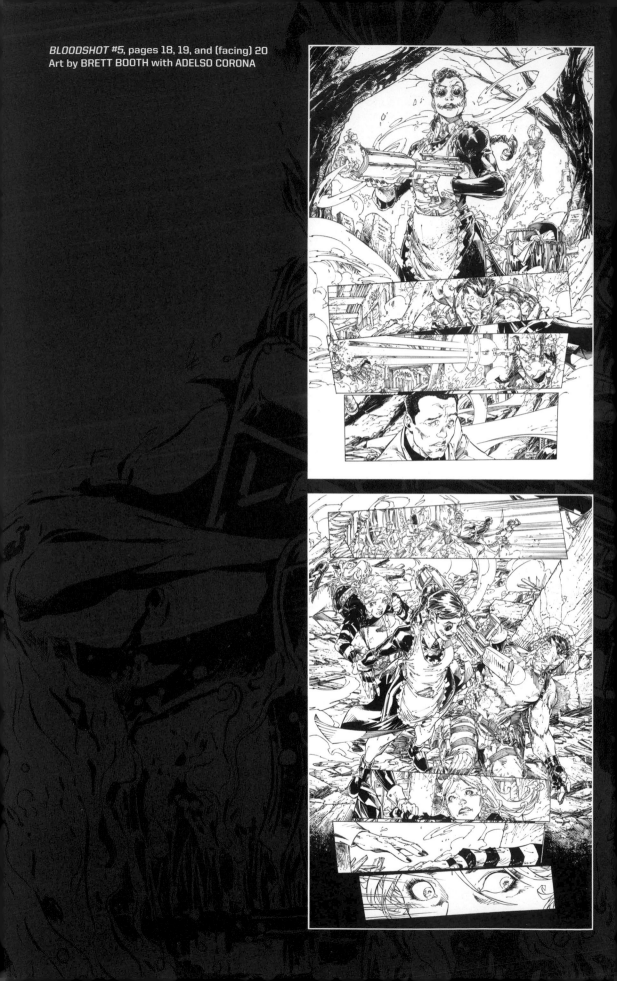

BLOODSHOT #5, pages 18, 19, and (facing) 20
Art by BRETT BOOTH with ADELSO CORONA

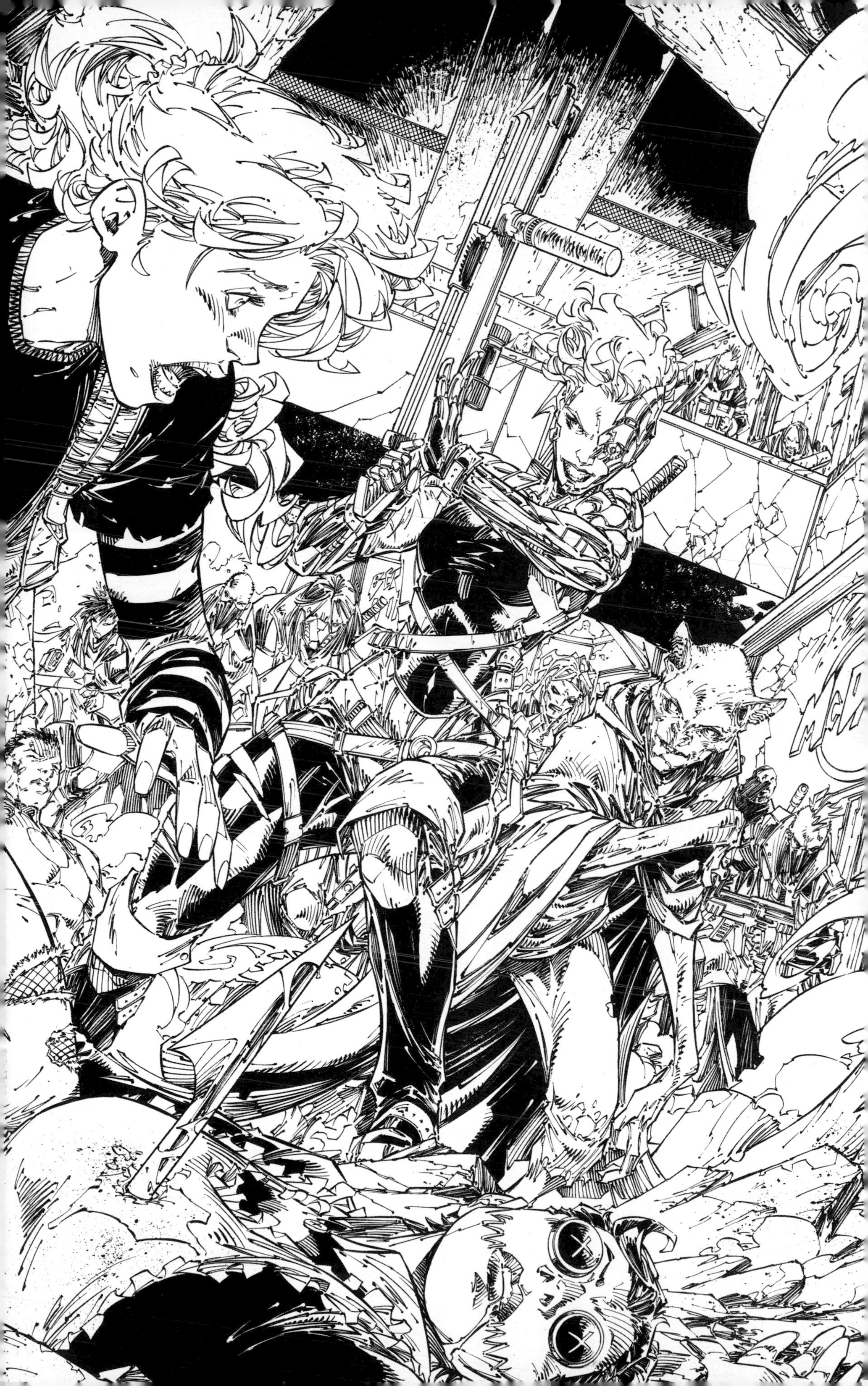

BLOODSHOT #6, pages 14, 15, and (facing) 18
Art by BRETT BOOTH with ADELSO CORONA

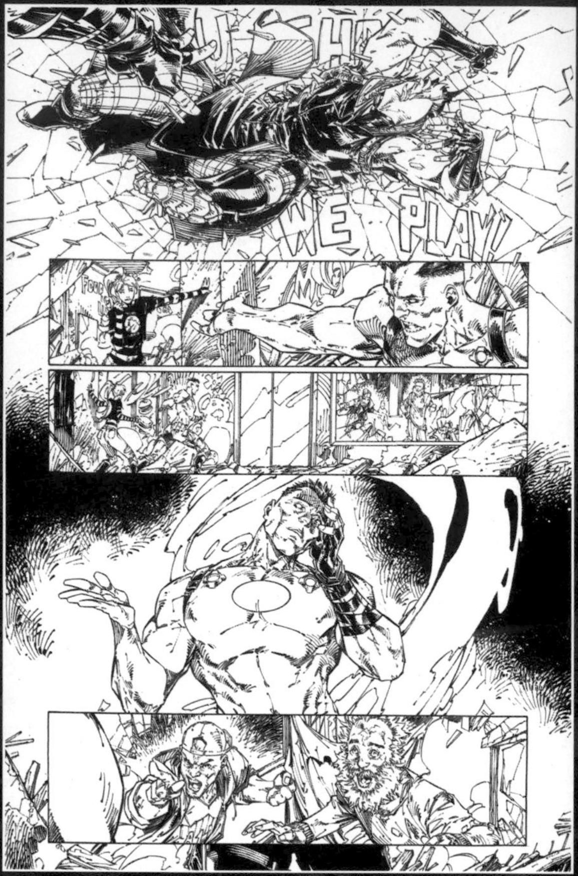
WE PLAY!

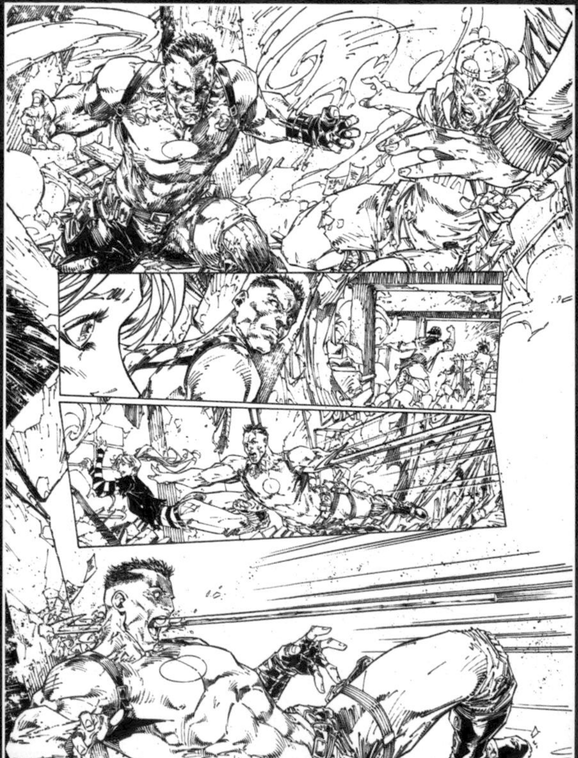

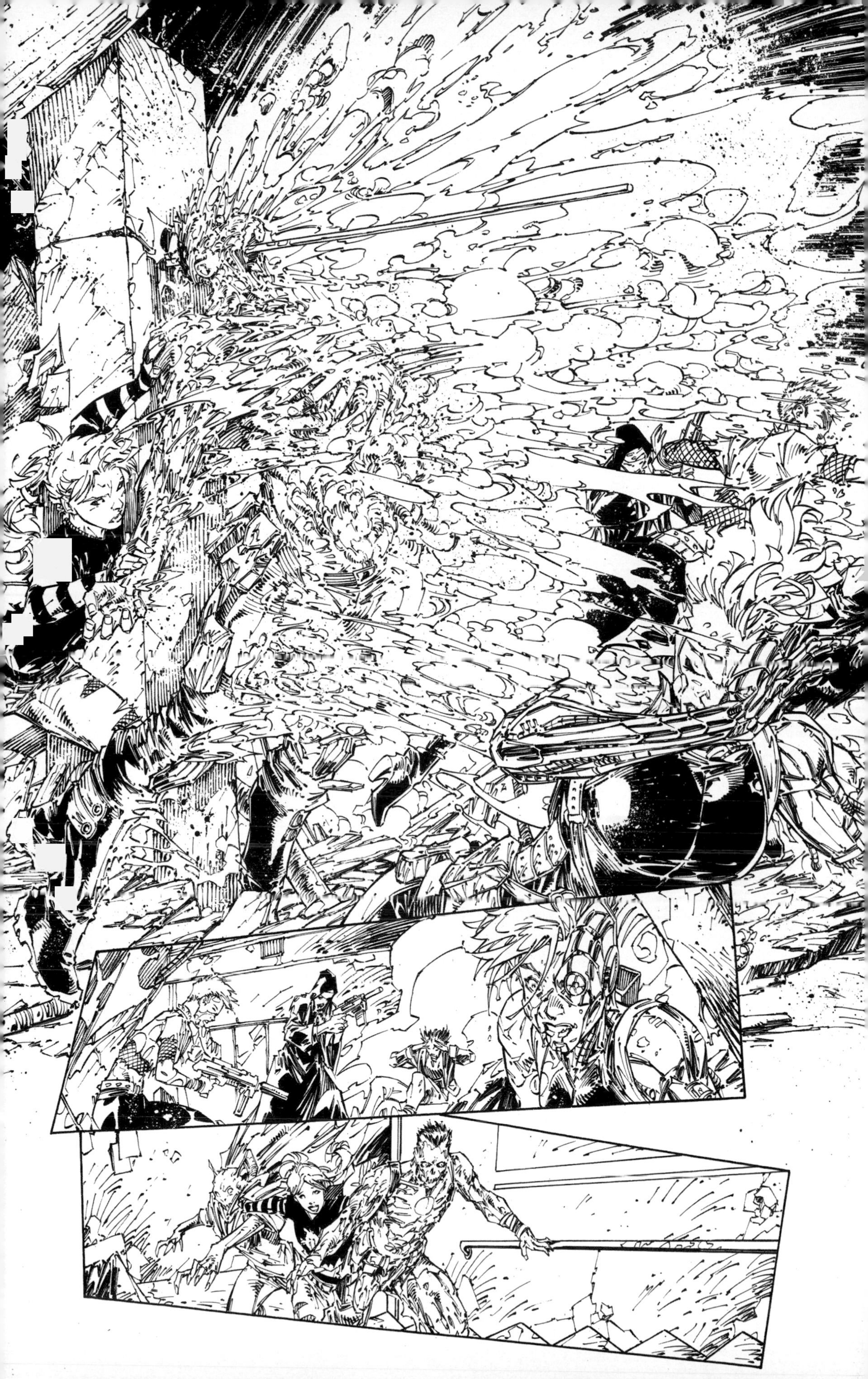

EXPLORE THE VALIANT U

ACTION & ADVENTURE

BLOCKBUSTER ADVENTURE

COMEDY

BLOODSHOT BOOK ONE
ISBN: 978-1-68215-255-3
NINJA-K VOL. 1: THE NINJA FILES
ISBN: 978-1-68215-259-1
SAVAGE
ISBN: 978-1-68215-189-1
WRATH OF THE ETERNAL WARRIOR VOL. 1: RISEN
ISBN: 978-1-68215-123-5
X-O MANOWAR (2017) VOL. 1: SOLDIER
ISBN: 978-1-68215-205-8

4001 A.D.
ISBN: 978-1-68215-143-3
ARMOR HUNTERS
ISBN: 978-1-939346-45-2
BOOK OF DEATH
ISBN: 978-1-939346-97-1
FALLEN WORLD
ISBN: 978-1-68215-331-4
HARBINGER WARS
ISBN: 978-1-939346-09-4
HARBINGER WARS 2
ISBN: 978-1-68215-289-8
INCURSION
ISBN: 978-1-68215-303-1
THE VALIANT
ISBN: 978-1-939346-60-5

A&A: THE ADVENTURES OF ARCHER & ARMSTRONG VOL. 1: IN THE BAG
ISBN: 978-1-68215-149-5
THE DELINQUENTS
ISBN: 978-1-939346-51-3
QUANTUM AND WOODY! (2017) VOL. 1: KISS KISS, KLANG KLANG
ISBN: 978-1-68215-269-0

VERSE STARTING AT $9.99

HORROR & MYSTERY

SCIENCE FICTION & FANTASY

TEEN ADVENTURE

TANNIA
N: 978-1-68215-185-3

OCTOR MIRAGE
BN: 978-1-68215-346-8

UNK MAMBO
SBN: 978-1-68215-330-7

RAPTURE
ISBN: 978-1-68215-225-6

SHADOWMAN (2018) VOL. 1:
FEAR OF THE DARK
ISBN: 978-1-68215-239-3

DIVINITY
ISBN: 978-1-939346-76-6

THE FORGOTTEN QUEEN
ISBN: 978-1-68215-324-6

IMPERIUM VOL. 1: COLLECTING MONSTERS
ISBN: 978-1-939346-75-9

IVAR, TIMEWALKER VOL. 1: MAKING HISTORY
ISBN: 978-1-939346-63-6

RAI VOL. 1: WELCOME TO NEW JAPAN
ISBN: 978-1-939346-41-4

WAR MOTHER
ISBN: 978-1-68215-237-9

FAITH VOL. 1: HOLLYWOOD AND VINE
ISBN: 978-1-68215-121-1

GENERATION ZERO VOL. 1:
WE ARE THE FUTURE
ISBN: 978-1-68215-175-4

HARBINGER RENEGADE VOL. 1:
THE JUDGMENT OF SOLOMON
ISBN: 978-1-68215-169-3

LIVEWIRE VOL. 1: FUGITIVE
ISBN: 978-1-68215-301-7

SECRET WEAPONS
ISBN: 978-1-68215-229-4

Discover the entire Valiant Universe of titles at VALIANTENTERTAINMENT.COM/ALL-SERIES/

VALIANT

BLOODSHOT

BOOK THREE

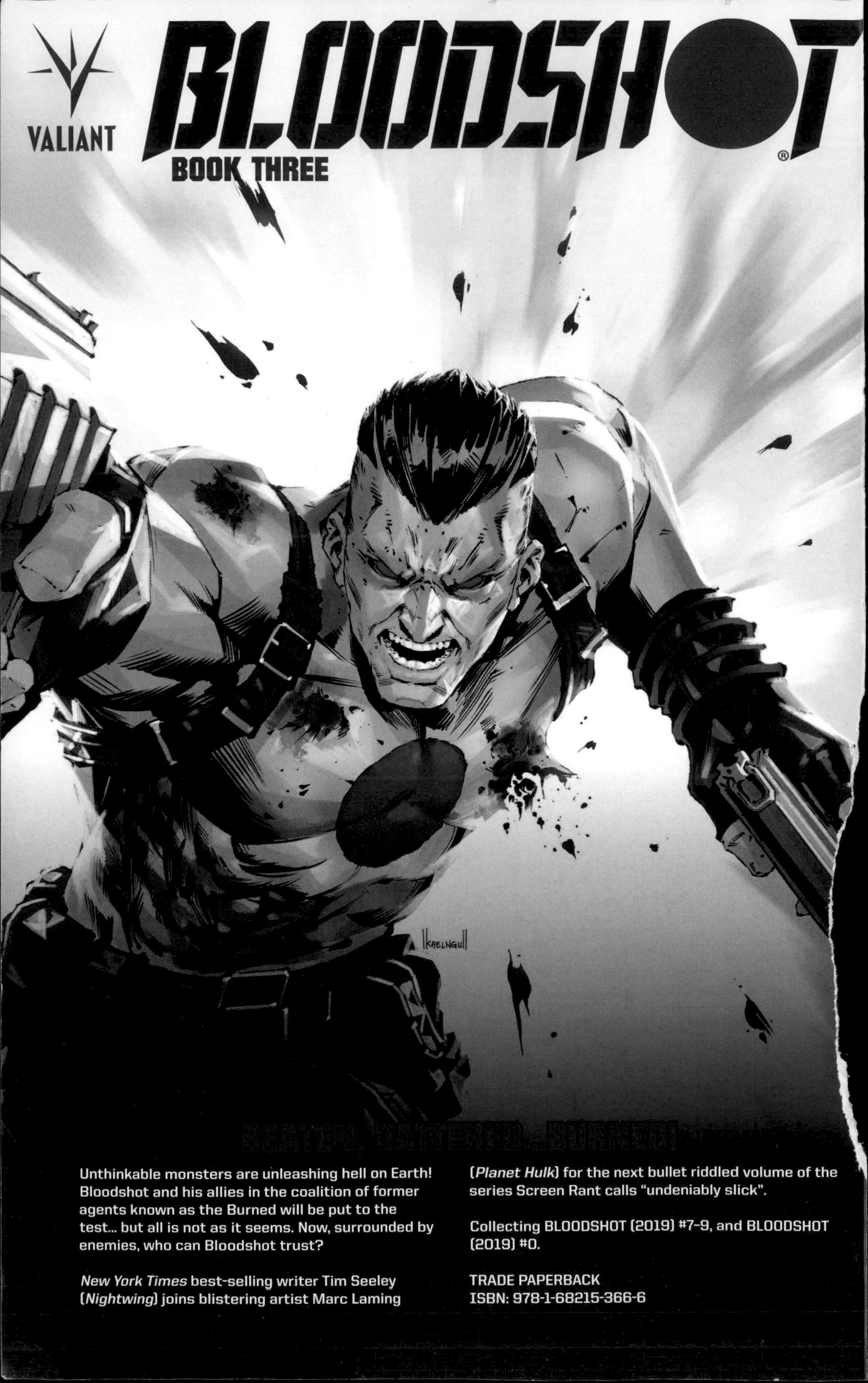

BEATEN, BATTERED...BURNED!

Unthinkable monsters are unleashing hell on Earth! Bloodshot and his allies in the coalition of former agents known as the Burned will be put to the test... but all is not as it seems. Now, surrounded by enemies, who can Bloodshot trust?

New York Times best-selling writer Tim Seeley (*Nightwing*) joins blistering artist Marc Laming (*Planet Hulk*) for the next bullet riddled volume of the series Screen Rant calls "undeniably slick".

Collecting BLOODSHOT (2019) #7-9, and BLOODSHOT (2019) #0.

TRADE PAPERBACK
ISBN: 978-1-68215-366-6